LEGAL

THE NEW REAL BOOK

Jazz Classics
Choice Standards
Pop-Fusion Classics

Created By Musicians - For Musicians

Chuck Sher - Publisher and Editor   Bob Bauer - Musical Editor
From the Publisher of "The World's Greatest Fake Book" and "The Improviser's Bass Method"

Copyright 1988, SHER MUSIC CO., P.O.Box 445, Petaluma, CA 94953
All Rights Reserved. International Copyright Secured. Made in the U.S.A. No part of this book may be reproduced in any form without written permission from the publisher.
ISBN 978-188321725-9

CATEGORICAL INDEX

JAZZ CLASSICS Exactly As Recorded By:

MILES DAVIS	Four	JOHN COLTRANE	Lush Life
	E.S.P.		Theme For Ernie
	Nefertiti	CHARLIE PARKER &	
	Solar	DIZZY GILLESPIE	Anthropology
	Eighty One		Shaw 'Nuff
	Tune Up		
	Fall	BUD POWELL	Bouncin' With Bud
	Joshua		Hallucinations
	Lady Bird	DUKE ELLINGTON	Chelsea Bridge
	If I Were A Bell		Come Sunday
	Dig	WOODY HERMAN	Early Autumn
BILL EVANS	Waltz For Debby		Four Brothers
	Very Early	QUINCY JONES	Quintessence
	Gloria's Step		The Midnight Sun Will Never Set
	Re: Person I Knew		
	Laurie	ORNETTE COLEMAN	Bird Food
	Funkallero		Blues Connotation
THELONIOUS MONK	Well, You Needn't	GERRY MULLIGAN	Line For Lyons
	Ruby, My Dear		Bernie's Tune
	I Mean You	JIM HALL	Waltz New
	Monk's Mood		Simple Samba
	Off Minor	JOHN ABERCROMBIE	Madagascar
	In Walked Bud		Nightlake
WAYNE SHORTER	Footprints	DENNY ZEITLIN	Promenade
	Speak No Evil		Time Remembers One Time Once
	Wildflower	LAMBERT, HENDRICKS	
	Yes And No	AND ROSS	Twisted
	Ana Maria		Farmer's Market
	The Three Marias	MOSE ALLISON	Your Mind Is On Vacation
	Endangered Species		Foolkiller
FREDDIE HUBBARD	Little Sunflower	DAVE FRISHBERG	Blizzard Of Lies
	Up Jumped Spring		My Attorney Bernie
	First Light	IRENE KRAL	Small Day Tomorrow
	Mr. Clean		Love Came On Stealthy Fingers
SONNY ROLLINS	St. Thomas	CLIFFORD BROWN	Sandu
	Oleo	RICHIE BEIRACH	Elm
	Airegin	RON CARTER	Little Waltz
	Pent Up House	OSCAR PETERSON	Nigerian Marketplace
JOE HENDERSON	Blue Bossa	LES McCANN	Compared To What
	Black Narcissus	BENNY GOODMAN	Jersey Bounce
	No Me Esqueca	JAMES MOODY	Last Train From Overbrook
	Fire	HAROLD LAND	Rapture
CANNONBALL ADDERLEY	Mercy, Mercy, Mercy	ILLINOIS JACQUET	Robbin's Nest
	Gemini	MAKOTO OZONE	Crystal Love
	Save Your Love For Me	GARY PEACOCK	Last First
	Blue Daniel	MIKE NOCK	Doors
McCOY TYNER	Search For Peace	SPHERE	Spiral
	Blues On The Corner	BOBBY SHEW	Breakfast Wine
	La Vida Feliz	PETER ERSKINE	Change Of Mind
CHARLES MINGUS	Reincarnation Of A Lovebird		
	Remember Rockefeller At Attica		
	Self Portrait In Three Colors		
WES MONTGOMERY	West Coast Blues		
	Four On Six		
	Unit Seven		
STAN GETZ	Voyage		

LATIN & BRAZILIAN CLASSICS As Written Or Recorded By:

ANTONIO CARLOS JOBIM	Wave	AIRTO	Partido Alto
	Desafinado		Creek
	Triste	IVAN LINS	The Island
	Once I Loved		Velas
	Dindi		Love Dance
	Chega De Saudade		
	Favela	CLARE FISCHER	Gaviota
	If You Never Come To Me		
CAL TJADER	Soul Sauce (Wachi Wara)	RICHIE COLE	I Love Lucy
SARAH VAUGHN	A Little Tear	RAY BRYANT	Cubano Chant

CHOICE STANDARDS With Chords Transcribed From The Best Jazz Versions

All Of Me
All Or Nothing At All*
Angel Eyes
Autumn Leaves
Beautiful Love
Basin St. Blues
But Beautiful
Darn That Dream
Do Nothing Til You Hear From Me*
Don't Get Around Much Anymore*
Don't Go To Strangers
Everything Happens To Me
Gee Baby, Ain't I Good To You
Gone With The Wind
Good Morning Heartache*
Here's That Rainy Day

I Should Care
I Thought About You
If I Were A Bell
I'll Take Romance
I'm All Smiles
Imagination
Like Someone In Love
The Midnight Sun
Misty*
Moonlight In Vermont
My Shining Hour
Polkadots And Moonbeams
Nature Boy
One For My Baby
Out Of This World
Satin Doll

Skylark
Someday My Prince Will Come
A Sleepin' Bee
Speak Low*
Stormy Weather*
Take The 'A' Train
Tenderly
There Will Never Be Another You
These Foolish Things
A Weaver Of Dreams
We'll Be Together Again
What's New?
Where Is Love?
Who Can I Turn To?
Willow Weep For Me
Witchcraft

* = STANDARDS SUPPLEMENT - U.S.A. Only

POP-FUSION CLASSICS Exactly As Recorded By:

AL JARREAU .... Boogie Down
Breakin' Away
Mornin'
Sticky Wicket
Easy
Never Givin' Up

GEORGE BENSON .... This Masquerade
Turn Your Love Around
Affirmation

THE CRUSADERS .... Street Life
Put It Where You Want It
Never Make Your Move Too Soon
Keep That Same Old Feeling
It Happens Everyday
Young Rabbits

THE YELLOWJACKETS .... Matinee Idol
Rush Hour
Goin' Home
Sonja's Sanfona
One Family

WEATHER REPORT .... Mr. Gone
Havona
River People
Plaza Real

SPYRO GYRA .... Morning Dance
Shaker Song
Song For Lorraine

JEFF LORBER .... Always There
Black Ice
Delevans

VICTOR FELDMAN .... Let's Go Dancin'
Rio
Haunted Ballroom

DAVE GRUSIN .... Modadji
Friends And Strangers

JACO PASTORIUS .... Portrait Of Tracy
Three Views Of A Secret

STEPS AHEAD .... Safari
Both Sides Of The Coin

MICHAEL BRECKER .... Nothing Personal
BRECKER BROS. .... Not Ethiopia

ARETHA FRANKLIN .... Baby, I Love You
Chain Of Fools

ROBERTA FLACK .... Feel Like Makin' Love
Killing Me Softly With His Song

MICHAEL JACKSON .... P.Y.T. (Pretty Young Thing)

DAVE SANBORN .... Hideaway

ANGELA BOFILL .... Let Me Be The One

BOB JAMES .... Sunrunner

GROVER WASHINGTON JR. .... Make Me A Memory (Sad Samba)

TOM SCOTT .... Desire

DONALD FAGEN .... The Goodbye Look

RANDY BRECKER &
ELAINE ELIAS .... Guaruja

LEE RITENOUR .... Waterwings

BOB MINTZER .... Papa Lips

MITCHELL FOREMAN .... Monkey's Uncle

NEIL LARSEN .... Sudden Samba

ANDY NARELL .... Oz
La Samba

ALPHABETICAL INDEX

COMPOSITION	AS PLAYED BY	PAGE
AFFIRMATION	George Benson	1
AIREGIN	Sonny Rollins	2
ALL OF ME		4
ALWAYS THERE	Jeff Lorber	5
ANA MARIA	Wayne Shorter	7
ANGEL EYES		9
ANTHROPOLOGY	Charlie Parker	11
AUTUMN LEAVES		12
BABY, I LOVE YOU	Aretha Franklin	13
BASIN STREET BLUES		15
BEAUTIFUL LOVE	Bill Evans	16
BERNIE'S TUNE	Gerry Mulligan	17
BIRD FOOD	Ornette Coleman	18
BLACK ICE	Jeff Lorber	19
BLACK NARCISSUS	Joe Henderson	22
BLIZZARD OF LIES	Dave Frishberg	23
BLUE BOSSA	Joe Henderson	25
BLUE DANIEL	Cannonball Adderley	26
BLUES CONNOTATION	Ornette Coleman	27
BLUES ON THE CORNER	McCoy Tyner	28
BOOGIE DOWN	Al Jarreau	29
BOTH SIDES OF THE COIN	Steps Ahead	33
BOUNCIN' WITH BUD	Bud Powell	35
BREAKFAST WINE	Bobby Shew	37
BREAKIN' AWAY	Al Jarreau	39
BUT BEAUTIFUL		42
CHAIN OF FOOLS	Aretha Franklin	43
CHANGE OF MIND	Peter Erskine	45
CHEGA DE SAUDADE	Antonio Carlos Jobim	47
CHELSEA BRIDGE	Duke Ellington	49
COME SUNDAY	Duke Ellington	50
COMPARED TO WHAT	Les McCann	51
CREEK	Airto	54
CRYSTAL LOVE	Makoto Ozone	55
CUBANO CHANT	Ray Bryant	57
DARN THAT DREAM		60
DELEVANS	Jeff Lorber	61
DESAFINADO	Antonio Carlos Jobim	63
DESIRE	Tom Scott	65
DIG	Miles Davis	66
DINDI	Antonio Carlos Jobim	67
DON'T GO TO STRANGERS		69
DOORS	Mike Nock	70
EARLY AUTUMN	Woody Herman	72
EASY	Al Jarreau	73
EIGHTY ONE	Miles Davis	76
ELM	Richie Beirach	77
ENDANGERED SPECIES	Wayne Shorter	79
E.S.P.	Miles Davis	82
EVERYTHING HAPPENS TO ME		83
FALL	Miles Davis	85
FARMER'S MARKET	Lambert, Hendricks & Ross	86
FAVELA	Antonio Carlos Jobim	87
FEEL LIKE MAKIN' LOVE	Roberta Flack	88
FIRE	Joe Henderson	89

COMPOSITION	AS PLAYED BY	PAGE
FIRST LIGHT	Freddie Hubbard	90
FOOLKILLER	Mose Allison	91
FOOTPRINTS	Wayne Shorter/Miles Davis	92
FOUR	Miles Davis/Lambert, Hendricks & Ross	93
FOUR BROTHERS	Woody Herman	95
FOUR ON SIX	Wes Montgomery	96
FRIENDS AND STRANGERS	Dave Grusin	97
FUNKALLERO	Bill Evans	100
GAVIOTA	Clare Fischer	101
GEE BABY, AIN'T I GOOD TO YOU		104
GEMINI	Cannonball Adderley	105
GLORIA'S STEP	Bill Evans	108
GOIN' HOME	The Yellowjackets	109
GONE WITH THE WIND		112
THE GOODBYE LOOK	Donald Fagen	113
GUARUJA	Randy Brecker & Elaine Elias	117
HALLUCINATIONS	Bud Powell	119
HAUNTED BALLROOM	Victor Feldman	122
HAVONA	Weather Report	123
HERE'S THAT RAINY DAY		124
HIDEAWAY	Dave Sanborn	125
I LOVE LUCY	Richie Cole	126
I MEAN YOU	Thelonious Monk	127
I SHOULD CARE		129
I THOUGHT ABOUT YOU		130
IF I WERE A BELL	Miles Davis	131
IF YOU NEVER COME TO ME	Antonio Carlos Jobim	134
I'LL TAKE ROMANCE		135
I'M ALL SMILES		137
IMAGINATION		139
IN WALKED BUD	Thelonious Monk	140
THE ISLAND	Mark Murphy/Ivan Lins	141
IT HAPPENS EVERY DAY	The Crusaders	143
JERSEY BOUNCE	Benny Goodman	146
JOSHUA	Miles Davis	147
KEEP THAT SAME OLD FEELING	The Crusaders	149
KILLING ME SOFTLY WITH HIS SONG	Roberta Flack	152
LA SAMBA	Andy Narell	153
LA VIDA FELIZ	McCoy Tyner	155
LADY BIRD	Miles Davis/Tadd Dameron	157
LAST FIRST	Gary Peacock	159
LAST TRAIN FROM OVERBROOK	James Moody	161
LAURIE	Bill Evans	162
LET ME BE THE ONE	Angela Bofill	163
LET'S GO DANCIN'	Victor Feldman	165
LIKE SOMEONE IN LOVE		166
LINE FOR LYONS	Gerry Mulligan	167
LITTLE SUNFLOWER	Freddie Hubbard	168
A LITTLE TEAR	Sarah Vaughn	170
LITTLE WALTZ	Ron Carter	171
LOVE CAME ON STEALTHY FINGERS	Irene Kral/Bob Dorough	172
LOVE DANCE	Diane Schuur/Ivan Lins	173
LUSH LIFE	John Coltrane	175
MADAGASCAR	John Abercrombie	177
MAKE ME A MEMORY (Sad Samba)	Grover Washington Jr.	178
MATINEE IDOL	The Yellowjackets	179
MERCY, MERCY, MERCY	Cannonball Adderley	180
THE MIDNIGHT SUN		181
THE MIDNIGHT SUN WILL NEVER SET	Quincy Jones	182
MODADJI	Dave Grusin	183
MONKEY'S UNCLE	Mitchell Foreman	185

COMPOSITION	AS PLAYED BY	PAGE
MONK'S MOOD	Thelonious Monk	184
MOONLIGHT IN VERMONT		188
MORNIN'	Al Jarreau	189
MORNING DANCE	Spyro Gyra	191
MR. CLEAN	Freddie Hubbard	194
MR. GONE	Weather Report	195
MY ATTORNEY BERNIE	Dave Frishberg	197
MY SHINING HOUR		199
NATURE BOY		200
NEFERTITI	Miles Davis	202
NEVER GIVIN' UP	Al Jarreau	203
NEVER MAKE YOUR MOVE TOO SOON	The Crusaders	206
NIGERIAN MARKETPLACE	Oscar Peterson	207
NIGHTLAKE	John Abercrombie	208
NO ME ESQUECA	Joe Henderson	209
NOT ETHIOPIA	The Brecker Bros.	211
NOTHING PERSONAL	Michael Brecker	213
OFF MINOR	Thelonious Monk	214
OLEO	Miles Davis	215
ONCE I LOVED	Antonio Carlos Jobim	216
ONE FAMILY	The Yellowjackets	217
ONE FOR MY BABY (And One More For The Road)		219
OUT OF THIS WORLD		221
OZ	Andy Narell	223
PAPA LIPS	Bob Mintzer	225
PARTIDO ALTO	Airto	227
PENT UP HOUSE	Sonny Rollins	230
PLAZA REAL	Weather Report	231
POLKADOTS AND MOONBEAMS		233
PORTRAIT OF TRACY	Jaco Pastorius	236
PROMENADE	Denny Zeitlin	237
PUT IT WHERE YOU WANT IT	The Crusaders	239
P.Y.T. (Pretty Young Thing)	Michael Jackson	240
QUINTESSENCE	Quincy Jones	242
RAPTURE	Harold Land	243
RE: PERSON I KNEW	Bill Evans	244
REINCARNATION OF A LOVEBIRD	Charles Mingus	245
REMEMBER ROCKEFELLER AT ATTICA	Charles Mingus	248
RIO	Victor Feldman	249
RIVER PEOPLE	Weather Report	251
ROBBIN'S NEST	Illinois Jacquet	252
RUBY, MY DEAR	Thelonious Monk	254
RUSH HOUR	The Yellowjackets	255
SAFARI	Steps Ahead	256
SANDU	Clifford Brown	259
SATIN DOLL	Duke Ellington	260
SAVE YOUR LOVE FOR ME	Cannonball Adderley & Nancy Wilson	261
SEARCH FOR PEACE	McCoy Tyner	264
SELF PORTRAIT IN THREE COLORS	Charles Mingus	265
SHAKER SONG	Manhattan Transfer/Spyro Gyra	267
SHAW 'NUFF	Charlie Parker/Dizzy Gillespie	269
SIMPLE SAMBA	Jim Hall	271
SKYLARK		273
A SLEEPIN' BEE		274
SMALL DAY TOMORROW	Irene Kral	275
SOLAR	Miles Davis	277
SOMEDAY MY PRINCE WILL COME		278
SONG FOR LORRAINE	Spyro Gyra	280
SONJA'S SANFONA	The Yellowjackets	281
SOUL SAUCE (Wachi Wara)	Cal Tjader	283

COMPOSITION	AS PLAYED BY	PAGE
SPEAK NO EVIL	Wayne Shorter	284
SPIRAL	Sphere	285
ST. THOMAS	Sonny Rollins	288
STICKY WICKET	Al Jarreau	289
STREET LIFE	The Crusaders	291
SUDDEN SAMBA	Neil Larsen	294
SUNRUNNER	Bob James	295
TAKE THE "A" TRAIN	Duke Ellington	297
TENDERLY		299
THEME FOR ERNIE	John Coltrane	300
THERE WILL NEVER BE ANOTHER YOU		301
THESE FOOLISH THINGS		302
THIS MASQUERADE	George Benson	304
THE THREE MARIAS	Wayne Shorter	305
THREE VIEWS OF A SECRET	Jaco Pastorius	307
TIME REMEMBERS ONE TIME ONCE	Denny Zeitlin	309
TRISTE	Antonio Carlos Jobim	310
TUNE UP	Miles Davis	312
TURN YOUR LOVE AROUND	George Benson	313
TWISTED	Lambert, Hendricks & Ross	315
UNIT SEVEN	Wes Montgomery	317
UP JUMPED SPRING	Art Blakey/Freddie Hubbard	320
VELAS (Velas Icadas)	Quincy Jones/Ivan Lins	321
VERY EARLY	Bill Evans	323
VOYAGE	Stan Getz	324
WALTZ FOR DEBBY	Bill Evans	325
WALTZ NEW	Jim Hall	328
WATERWINGS	Lee Ritenour	329
WAVE	Antonio Carlos Jobim	331
A WEAVER OF DREAMS		333
WE'LL BE TOGETHER AGAIN		334
WELL, YOU NEEDN'T	Thelonious Monk/Miles Davis	335
WEST COAST BLUES	Wes Montgomery	336
WHAT'S NEW?		337
WHERE IS LOVE?	Irene Kral	338
WHO CAN I TURN TO?		339
WILDFLOWER	Wayne Shorter	340
WILLOW WEEP FOR ME		341
WITCHCRAFT		342
YES AND NO	Wayne Shorter	343
YOUNG RABBITS	The Jazz Crusaders	344
YOUR MIND IS ON VACATION	Mose Allison	345

APPENDIX

APPENDIX - Sources		347

STANDARDS SUPPLEMENT (U.S.A. Only)

ALL OR NOTHING AT ALL		357
DO NOTHING 'TIL YOU HEAR FROM ME	Duke Ellington	359
DON'T GET AROUND MUCH ANYMORE	Duke Ellington	360
GOOD MORNING HEARTACHE		361
MISTY		362
SPEAK LOW		363
STORMY WEATHER		365

PUBLISHER'S FOREWORD ("Why A New Real Book?")

We at Sher Music Co. are proud to bring you the second in a series of great, legal anthologies of jazz and jazz-related compositions (the first was "The World's Greatest Fake Book"). We hope that these books bring you years of pleasure and that they make your job of creating beautiful music easier.

It has been almost twenty years since the old Real Book came out and we hope that "The New Real Book" will become the new standard book for aspiring and professional musicians and singers around the world. Like the old Real Book, "The New Real Book" has been designed to be useful for any musical occasion - casual (club date), jazz gig, rehearsal band, jam session, etc. This book, however, has taken the old Real Book's basic format and improved upon it in several important respects:

1) The standard tunes have been throughly researched and often synthesized from as many as eight different classic recordings as well as the original sheet music. This reliance on the weight of history eliminates the arbitrariness of much of the old Real Book. (See Appendix II - Sources, for complete documentation of this).

2) The jazz classics here have been transcribed by one of the world's great musical minds (and ears!), Bob Bauer - often with the input of those composers who are still living. On those tunes that were also in the old Real Book, Bob has corrected many mistakes. This will become apparent if you compare both books with the original recordings.

3) In response to the request "Play something we can dance to!", this book contains many great, danceable pop-fusion tunes recorded after the old Real Book was already out. We hope that their inclusion will allow you to satisfy the needs of your younger audiences without compromising your own integrity.

4) The last twenty years have been fertile ones for jazz composition and "The New Real Book" (in both the Jazz and Fusion sections) contains many tunes written since 1970 that deserve to become part of the standard repetroire of the jazz player. We hope that you will take the time to play and/or listen to the recordings of those tunes unfamiliar to you - you'll be glad you did!

5) Unlike the old, illegal Real book, we obtained the owner's permission to include each tune in the book, in exchange for royalties paid. Besides acknowledging the composers' rights to benefit from their creations, this has given us access to their own lead sheets and/or approval of our charts, whenever the composers were still living.

One of the pleasant surprises of being in business is how many people are willing to go out of their way to help a worthy project. My sincere thanks to the following people who have been instrumental in making this book a reality: Chris James of Bourne Co., Dave Bickman of MPL Communications, Judy Bell of TRO, Maureen Woods, Ilyce Dawes, Chet Zdrowski of The Mac Garden in San Rafael, Mary Kay Landon of Kazan Typeset Services in S.F., Jim Zimmerman, Jim Marshall, Susan Muscarella-Park and all the other Bay Area musicians who helped with proofreading, and, of course, all the composers and musicians who played on the recordings we used to derive the charts.

Special thanks go to my father, Maury Sher, for all his help; Ann and Morse Bettison, for their invaluable assistance; BobParlocha of KJAZ, one of the world's great jazz DJ's, for his friendship and wealth of information; Ernie Mansfield and Ann Krinitsky for the amazing calligraphy work; Bob Bauer, for being a superb person, as well as a genius; and my sweet wife, Sueann for all her love and support (and the hand-weaving on the cover!).

Finally, I would like to dedicate this book to the memories of my uncle, Ben Swartz, who was a friend beyond the call of duty, and my mother, Esther Sher, a real beacon of goodness in this world, who showed me that beauty and meaning in life can always be found if we do our part.

CHUCK SHER - Publisher & Editor

MUSICAL EDITOR'S FOREWORD

As musical editor, my job has been to produce the charts in this book, using a wide variety of resources. This involved transcribing records, consulting printed music and manuscripts, communicating with composers, and comparing and synthesizing different recordings of a given tune. In addition, it has been my responsibility to ensure, through a process of proofreading and playing the charts (carried out by myself and others), that errors and weaknesses be found and corrected, so that each chart might be as clear, complete, and accurate as possible.

All the information necessary for proper use of the charts is contained in the General Rules and the table of Chord Symbols. It is my intention in the foreword to describe in some detail the process of producing the charts, and especially to point out certain choices made, priorities set, and criteria established by the publisher and myself which shaped the process.

SOURCES

The various sources - records, sheet music, manuscripts, etc. - are at the heart of the process, and every effort has been made to acquire all pertinent source materials. (See Appendix II, Sources, for a description of types of sources and a listing of the particular sources used for each tune.) We obtained music from publishers, composers, retail stores, and private collections. For records we had access to extensive collections and also ransacked new and used record stores. The gathering of source materials continued throughout the creation of the book, and we often hunted down specific sources or simply additional sources of any kind in order to clear up uncertainties.

It was then necessary to decide which sources would be most useful in creating the final chart for each tune. For most tunes, the sources on paper (lead sheets, sheet music, etc.) fell into a fixed order of usefulness, based on how reliably they conveyed the intent of the composer: 1) Composer's lead sheet (most reliable), 2) Published sheet music, 3) Publisher's lead sheet, 4) Published transcription, and 5) Legal and illegal fake books.

As for the recordings, the following criteria helped determine their usefulness and ultimate contribution:

Historical Importance And Influence. With the help of other jazz fans and historians (especially Bob Parlocha of KJAZ) we were able to select classic versions of some tunes, versions that have had the greatest influence on how the tune is played (e.g., Bird & Diz's "All The Things You Are" and Miles Davis's "I Thought About You" and "If I Were A Bell"). The final chart is often based largely on this classic version.

Agreement With Other Sources. Except in the case of classic versions, versions which differed greatly from the general consensus, wonderful though they may be, were given less emphasis (e.g., Stan Getz's "Here's That Rainy Day" and Miles Davis's "Nature Boy").

Clarity And Consistency. Especially when no sheet music or composer's lead sheet was available, recordings where melody and chords were clear and consistent were more useful than highly interpretive recordings.

Applicability To Small-Group Setting. We assume that most players using this book will do so in small-group settings. Many big band arrangements are not easily transferred to a small-group setting, being too complex or relying too much on dense, colorful harmonies.

Please note that the presence or absence of a metronome marking tells how closely a chart is based on a single recording. Those charts with metronome markings (that is, almost all of the more recent tunes and most of the jazz classics) are based largely or wholly on a single recording, from which the metronome marking derives. Such elements as intros, endings, chords, and melody are most likely to be taken from this predominant recording. On the other hand, those charts without metronome markings (the standards and certain well-worn swing, bebop and latin tunes) are each a synthesis of two or more recordings where no one recording predominates.

THE STANDARDS

The standards (see list of "Choice Standards" in the Index) were the most consistent group of tunes in the book, not only stylistically but also in terms of what resources were available for them. Every standard had published sheet music available (except one: "Weaver Of Dreams"); none had composer's lead sheets. And every standard had been recorded a number of times.

An early choice was made concerning the standards: that their charts, while conveying the composer's intent, should also reflect modern common practice - how the tune is commonly performed today, as demonstrated in recordings by jazz artists. Many elements of a tune may evolve over the years - melody, chords, arrangement, key, tempo, time feel - and to ignore this evolution would limit any chart's current usefulness. Therefore, any consistent change has been incorporated whenever possible. When there is a concensus (agreement among a number of recordings) the change is included in the body of the chart; changes found in only a small number of recordings appear peripherally - as alternate chords or as comments or suggestions accompanying the chart - or not at all.

The keys of the standards reflect common practice. Ignoring vocal renditions (which are transposed to suit a singer's range), there was usually general agreement concerning the key among various instrumental recordings. When two or fewer instrumental versions were available (e.g., "All Of Me" and "Stormy Weather"), the key of the sheet music was given added emphasis. At other times more than one valid key emerged (e.g., "Someday My Prince Will Come" and "Autumn Leaves"). In these cases we looked to the most well-known recording or used our own best sense of contemporary practice.

After much listening and consideration, we determined that, for the standards, trying to reflect common practice regarding melody would be futile - there is far too little agreement among different interpretations, or even between the first and last chorus of most single recordings. Therefore, the melody that appears has been taken directly from the sheet music. There are three exceptions to this: 1) change of key (simple transposition), 2) change of rhythmic notation due to modern convention (e.g., dotted eighth-sixteenth figures were turned into two eighth notes), and 3) actual changes in melody reflecting a true concensus (see "All Of Me", "What's New", and "Darn That Dream").

There was a greater concensus concerning the chords of the standards. Often it was clear after listening to only two recordings what common practice was. Other times it was necessary to consult several recordings before a concensus began to emerge. On occasion we hunted far and wide to find recordings which contained certain chords we felt were needed (e.g., the alternate changes in "All The Things You Are" and "Willow Weep For Me"). Sheet music was never used as a direct source for chords, but only to confirm common practice. Not wishing to be arbitrary, we have provided many alternate chords in addition to the common practice chords (examples abound; see "I Should Care", "One For My Baby", and "Polkadots And Moonbeams"). Certain alternate chords resulting from the most common chord substitutions have been generally omitted. These substitutions include: 1) iimi7 V7 for V7 or vice versa, 2) iiimi7 for Ima7, 3) bII7 for V7, and 4) secondary dominant substitutions at the tritone: bII7/V for V7/V, bII7/ii for V7/ii, etc.

When naming chords, it was necessary to decide whether or not to include the upper extentions (9, 11, 13) or their alterations (b9, #11, etc.) in the chord name. While this issue arose in most of the tunes to some degree, it was most prevalent in the standards. Extentions are only included in the chord name when present in the melody and are more likely to be included when any of the following are true: 1) the melody note falls on a strong beat, 2) the rhythmic value of the note is a half note or greater, 3) the chord lasts for an entire measure, 4) the melody note does not resolve, 5) the tune has a large number of melodic 'color tones' (upper extentions) throughout, 6) a particular extention is used repeatedly in the melody or one section of the melody, or 7) the chord in question has a dominant function or quality.

OTHER TUNES

Those tunes which are not standards fall into two broad categories: jazz classics and contemporary tunes (including jazz, fusion and pop tunes). Within these stylistic categories, however, a consistent treatment was not possible - the available resources varied too greatly. It is therefore more useful to consider the following categories of tunes which received similar treatment: 1) Tunes for which the composer's lead sheet was available, 2) Tunes for which no chart was available, and 3) Tunes for which published sheet music, a published transcription, or a publisher's lead sheet was available.

Composer's lead sheet available. Some composers were kind enough to provide us with their original lead sheets. Certain elements not present in the composer's lead sheet have been added if they form an important part of the recording(s). These elements include intros, endings, horn parts, bass lines, grace notes, and "diacritical markings" (accents, staccato marks, scoops, etc.) The melody has been taken directly from the composer's lead sheet unless it was necessary to change the octave to correspond to the record. Sometimes the rhythmic notation has been adjusted to conform to the record, without changing where the notes fall. Chord symbols have been changed only to conform to our system of chord naming or for consistency within a tune. The final charts have been sent to the composers for their approval, and even composers who provided no charts originally were later able to give us helpful and much appreciated feedback.

No chart available. When no chart was available, it was necessary to work solely from recordings. Corresponding sections were compared both between different recorded versions and within single versions. In this way it was possible, for the most part, to distinguish composition from interpretation. Some recordings were fairly straightforward melodically, rhythmically, and harmonically, making accurate transcription an easy task (e.g., "Blue Bossa" and "Mercy, Mercy, Mercy"). Others were more complex or more freely interpreted and careful choices and educated reconstruction were necessary (e.g., "Save Your Love For Me", "Theme For Ernie", and "Quintessence"). Certain blues-based tunes have been recorded in such a highly interpretive style that uncovering an "original melody" is neither possible nor desirable (e.g., "Compared To What" and the Mose Allison and Aretha Franklin tunes). These have simply been transcribed directly as performed, with a few rough edges polished.

Published sheet music, publisher's lead sheet or published transcription available. With rare exception, publisher's lead sheets, published transcriptions, and even published sheet music for those tunes other than standards all appear to be someone's transcription of a particular recording of a tune. Though these charts had some use, we did not wish to rely too heavily on the work of others with different priorities and abilities. Therefore, these tunes were all transcribed from scratch, much as if no chart were available.

As with the standards, it has been our intention to provide alternatives. If two valid ways of approaching a tune exist, we have tried to include both in some way.

COMPLETENESS AND CLARITY

One of our highest priorities has been to include everything considered essential to recreating each tune. To this end, the charts will be found to contain intros, endings, solo sections, metronome markings, descriptions of the time feel, indications of instrumentation, kicks, breaks, dynamics, diacritical markings, rehearsal letters, chord rhythms, alternate changes, sample bass lines, sample solos and fills, and plentiful comments and instructions. In addition, many charts have separate bass parts, horn parts, sample drum parts, and lyrics. Indeed, the degree of completeness distinguishes this volume (and *The World's Greatest Fake Book*) from most other fake books or jazz books of any kind, and makes possible a full, musical rendering of the tunes.

Another priority concerns the layout of the charts - how they appear on the page. A number of things have been done to make the charts clear and easy to follow. Major sections of a tune have been arranged to begin at the start of a line and rehearsal letters have been provided. The *segno* (𝄋) has also been placed at the start of a line whenever possible. Page turns have been kept to an absolute minimum, with every two-page chart placed on facing pages. The form of each tune is explicitly stated (or implied in the simplest cases - see 'General Rules') so that the proper progression of a tune from the intro, through the head, solos, last head, to the ending is always clear. Finally, the charts have been copied clearly, cleanly, and beautifully by our calligraphers, Michael Smolens and Ann Krinitsky. Michael's contribution, moreover, extends far beyond his excellent calligraphy. He is chiefly responsible for the system of chord symbols we used (see Chord Symbols in the General Rules section). He has also been consulted on numerous technical matters such as chord naming, enharmonics, stacking of chords and accidentals, stemming, layout, and much more.

THE OLD REAL BOOK

The old *Real Book* has been for some time one of the few printed sources for a number of classic jazz tunes and jazz versions of standards, and its contribution to the jazz community must be acknowledged. Though *The New Real Book* contains more than fifty tunes in common with the old *Real Book*, these tunes have all been transcribed anew from the sources we list - the *Real Book* and other fake books were never used as direct sources.

The present charts contain a wealth of information not found in the old *Real Book*. This includes all of the elements listed above under "completeness" as well as entire new sections (e.g., the intro to "All The Things You Are" and the intro and interlude for "Take he 'A' Train"). The charts also offer more performance alternatives in the form of alternate changes and sample lines. In addition, many elements of the charts differ from the old *Real Book* in their greater faithfulness to common practice as found on recordings. These elements include the keys of tunes (e.g., "Here's That Rainy Day", "Triste", and "Once I Loved") as well as numerous notes, rhythms, and chords (e.g., the turnaround in "Footprints").

Perhaps more importantly, many errors in the old *Real Book* will not be found in the present volume. Every chart has been compared to the old *Real Book* and all areas of difference have been scrupulously checked against our sources, including composer's lead sheets. Some of the major corrections include: a number of chords &/or melody notes in "Wildflower","Speak No Evil", "Self Portrait In Three Colors", "Eighty One", and "Ana Maria", four bars previously missing from the middle of "Desafinado", and the key of "Reincarnation Of A Lovebird". On first hearing, these and other tunes which have been corrected may sound just plain wrong to those who learned them from the old *Real Book* and have become accustomed to hearing them that way, errors and all. Some time may be needed to appreciate these corrections and to come to hear the tunes in a new way.

Even after a long and careful process of eliminating faults, it is inevitable that errors remain in a book of this complexity. I am confident, however, that those errors we failed to discover are few and relatively minor. This aside, no chart can capture a tune absolutely or for all time. Thus, we do not claim that the charts within represent the only proper way to perform these tunes, only that they accurately reflect the current concensus. With these charts as a starting point, an unlimited number of arrangements and interpretations are possible. We encourage you to let your creativity run free.

One of the great pleasures in producing this book was that of working with Chuck Sher. His vision guided this project at every step, and he was always willing to do everything necessary to ensure the highest quality. I also wish to acknowledge Ernie Mansfield and Ann Krinitsky for their consistently fine work. My thanks to Bill Ganz for ongoing support and for help with the Foreword, and to those who helped with proofreading. Finally, I thank the composers and recording artists for their gift of music.

BOB BAUER - Musical Editor

PREFACE TO THE Bb AND Eb VERSIONS

We at Sher Music Co. hope that transposing " The New Real Book" for Bb and Eb instruments makes this landmark publication easier to use and even more valuable to the music community. As in the concert version, Ann Krinitsky has beautifully hand-copied the chord symbols, but the notes themselves in the transposed versions were done on a Macintosh by Ernie Mansfield of Mansfield Music Graphics of Berkeley, CA. We are quite pleased with the resulting legibility and hope that you are too.

We are sorry to report that eleven of the standard tunes present in the first edition of the concert version (mostly Jerome Kern tunes) could not be included in the transposed versions, due to copyright problems that arose after the C version was published. We apologise for any inconvenience this may cause.

Here are a few points that we hope will clear up any possible confusion in using the transposed versions:

1.All pitches and chord names in the Bb and Eb versions are transposed to be read by Bb or Eb horn players respectively (even if guitar, piano, or other instruments that read in a different key are indicated). Instrumental markings (e.g., ten., trp., gtr., pn.) indicate only the instrumentation on the particular recording of the tune that was used to derive the chart.

2.All melodies and horn parts in the concert version have been included in the Bb and Eb versions. Bass parts, most keyboard parts and some intros, endings and piano/guitar voicings have been omitted if they were likely to be of little interest to horn players. The number of bars and the form is unchanged from the concert version.

3. In the Bb version, pitches have generally been transposed up a major second from the concert version, although sometimes up a major ninth to make it easier for both tenor and trumpet to read. Since we cannot know whether a given line will be played on trumpet, tenor, clarinet or soprano, such octave indications as 'ten. 8va b.' and 'loco' do not necessarily apply to the notes on the page. Rather, they apply to the original pitches in the concert version. Use your own best sense in choosing the appropriate octave for your instrument.

In the Eb version, pitches have been transposed to place the melody in the middle range of alto and baritone saxophones.

ENJOY!

GENERAL RULES FOR USING THIS BOOK

FORM
1. Key signatures will be found at the top of page one, and at the top of page three for tunes longer than two pages. Any change of key will be noted not only where it occurs but also at the start of the next line. The key signature holds even if there is a change of clef, and is not restated. A change of key to C Major will appear as a clef followed by the naturals needed to cancel the previous key signature.
2. The Coda sign is to be taken only when ending the tune unless otherwise stated. Some tunes have dual Codas ($\oplus^1$ and $\oplus^2$) to make it possible to fit a complex tune on two pages.
3. All repeats are observed during a 'D.C. al Coda' or 'D.S. al Coda' except in the following cases:
    a) when a Coda sign appears in a repeated section; the Coda is taken before repeating (unless marked 'on repeat').
    b) when an instruction to the contrary appears (e.g. 'D.S. al 2nd ending al Coda').
4. A Coda sign just within repeats is taken before repeating. A Coda sign just outside of repeats is taken after repeating.
5. When no solo form is specified, the whole tune is used for solos (except any Coda).
6. |Till Cue| On Cue signifies dual endings for a section that repeats indefinitely. The 'till cue' ending is played until cue, at which point the 'on cue' ending is played instead.
7. A section marked '4x's' is played four times (repeated three times).
8. A section marked 'ENDING' is played to end a tune; it directly follows the last bar of the head.

CHORDS
9. Chords fall on the beat over which they are placed.
10. Chords carry over to the next bar when no other chords or rests appear.
11. Chords in parentheses are optional except in the following cases:
    a) turn arounds
    b) chords continued from the line before
    c) verbal comment explaining thier use (for solos, for bass but not piano, only at certain times, etc.)
12. Optional chords in parentheses last as long as the chord they are written over or until the closing parenthesis is encountered, whichever is longer.
13. Written-out piano or guitar voicings are meant to be played as written. Chord symbols appearing with such voicings often will not describe the complete voicing; they are meant to aid sight reading and are often used for solos.
14. Multiple voices playing different rhythms are separated by having their stems lie in opposite directions whenever possible.

TERMS
15. An 'altered' dominant chord is one in which neither the fifth nor the ninth appears unaltered. Thus it contains b5 &/or #5, and b9 &/or #9.
16. 'Freely' signifies the absense of a steady tempo.
17. During a 'break......♩' piano, bass and drums all observe the same rests. The last beat played is notated as ♪ or x to the left of the word 'break'.
18. A 'sample bass line', 'sample solo', or 'sample fill' is a transcribed line given as a point of reference.

TRANSPOSITIONS
19. Bass lines are always written to be read by a bass player, i.e. one octave higher than they sound.
20. Tenor sax and guitar lines are often written an octave higher than they sound and flute lines an octave lower to put them in a more readable range. There will be a verbal note to this effect in every case.
21. All horn and harmony parts are written in concert key (not transposed).

ABBREVIATIONS

15ma	two octaves higher	elec. pn.	electric piano	sop.	soprano saxophone
15ma b.	two octaves lower	fl.	flute	stac.	staccato
8va	one octave higher	gliss.	glissando	susp.	suspended
8va b.	one octave lower	gtr.	guitar	synth.	synthesizer
accel.	accelerando	indef	indefinite (till cue)	ten.	tenor saxophone
alt	altered	L.H.	piano left hand	trb.	trombone
bari	baritone saxophone	Med.	Medium	trbs.	trombones
bkgr.	background	N.C.	No Chord	trp.	trumpet
bs.	bass	Orig.	Original	trps.	trumpets
cresc.	crescendo	perc.	percussion	unis.	unison
decres.	decrescendo	pn.	piano	V.S.	Volti Subito (quick page turn)
dr.	drums	rall.	rallentando	w/	with
elec. bs.	electric bass	R.H.	piano right hand	x	time
		rit.	ritardando	x's	times

ORNAMENTS AND SYMBOLS

Slide into the note from a short distance below

Slide into the note from a greater distance below

Fall away from the note a short distance

Fall away from the note a greater distance

Top note of a complete voicing

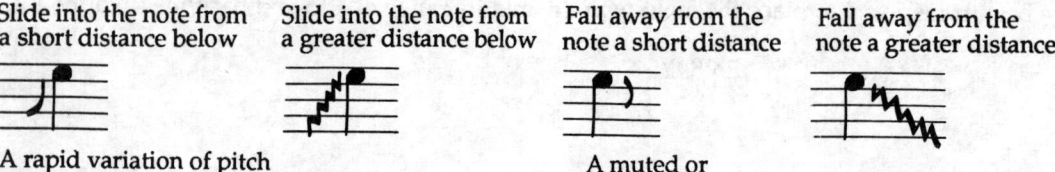

A rapid variation of pitch upward, much like a trill

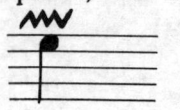

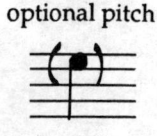

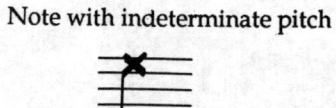

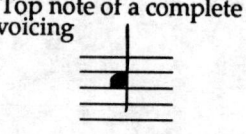

Mordent

A muted or optional pitch

Note with indeterminate pitch

Rhythm played by drums or percussion

CHORD SYMBOLS

The chord symbols used in this book follow (with some exceptions) the system outlined in "Standard Chord Symbol Notation" by Carl Brandt and Clinton Roemer. It is hoped you will find them clear, complete and unambiguous.

Below are two groups of chord spellings:
1) The full range of chords normally encountered, given with a C root, and
2) Some more unusual chords, all of which appear in tunes in this book. (Note: some groups of notes below could be given different names, depending on context. See previous page for a definition of 'altered' chords).

Affirmation

Medium Funk/Rock

♩= 108

Jose Feliciano

(As played by George Benson)

Guitar sounds one octave lower than written. Coda may be used as an interlude between solos (vamp til cue).

Medium-Up Latin
(Head Swings)
♩= 232

Airegin

Sonny Rollins
(As played by Miles Davis)

AL JARREAU

Photo by Tom Copi ©1988

All Of Me

Seymour Simons
Gerald Marks

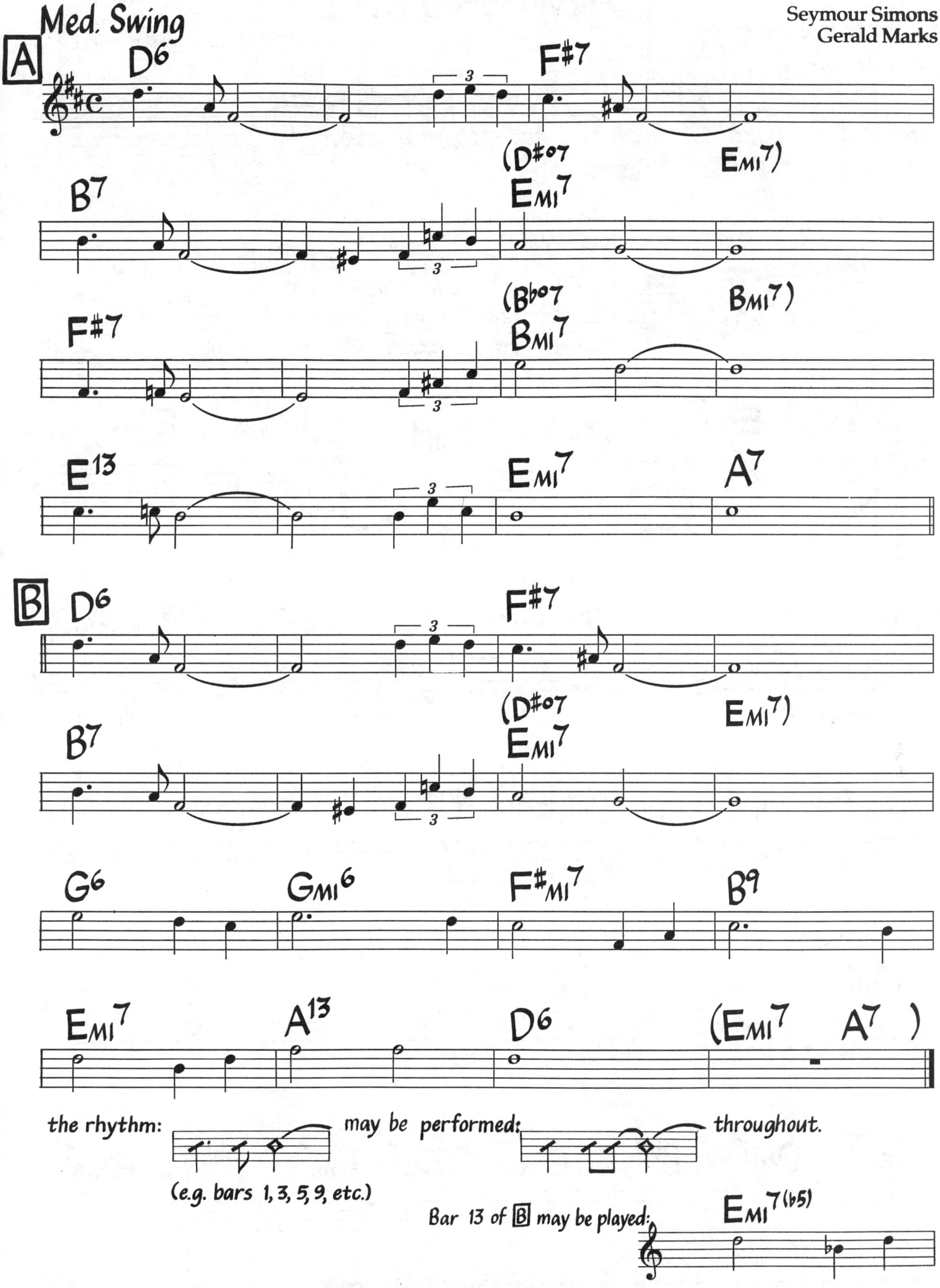

Always There

Ronnie Laws
William Jeffrey
(As played by Jeff Lorber)

B
(Synth. Solo)
Gmi7 Dmi7 Bb9sus EbMA7
(Vamp till cue)
(On Cue)
Gmi7 Dmi7
Bb9sus EbMA7 Gmi7 Dmi7 Bb9sus EbMA7
(Half-Time Rock feel)
C
G#mi7 C#9sus F#MA7 A/B B/Bb F#/A
(ten.)
F#/A DMA7 GMA7 GMA7 DMA7 Emi7
Emi7 A13(b9) Bb6/9/Ab F(add 9)/A D/C G(add 9)/B E/F# Gmi9
cresc.
(synth.)
(Orig. Feel) (Gtr. Solo)
D
Gmi7 Dmi7 Bb9sus EbMA7
f
(Vamp till cue)
On cue, D.S. al Coda
Gmi7 Dmi7 Bb9sus EbMA7 Bb6/9/Ab
(synth. fill)

Ana Maria

Wayne Shorter

Half-time Rock Feel
♩= 124

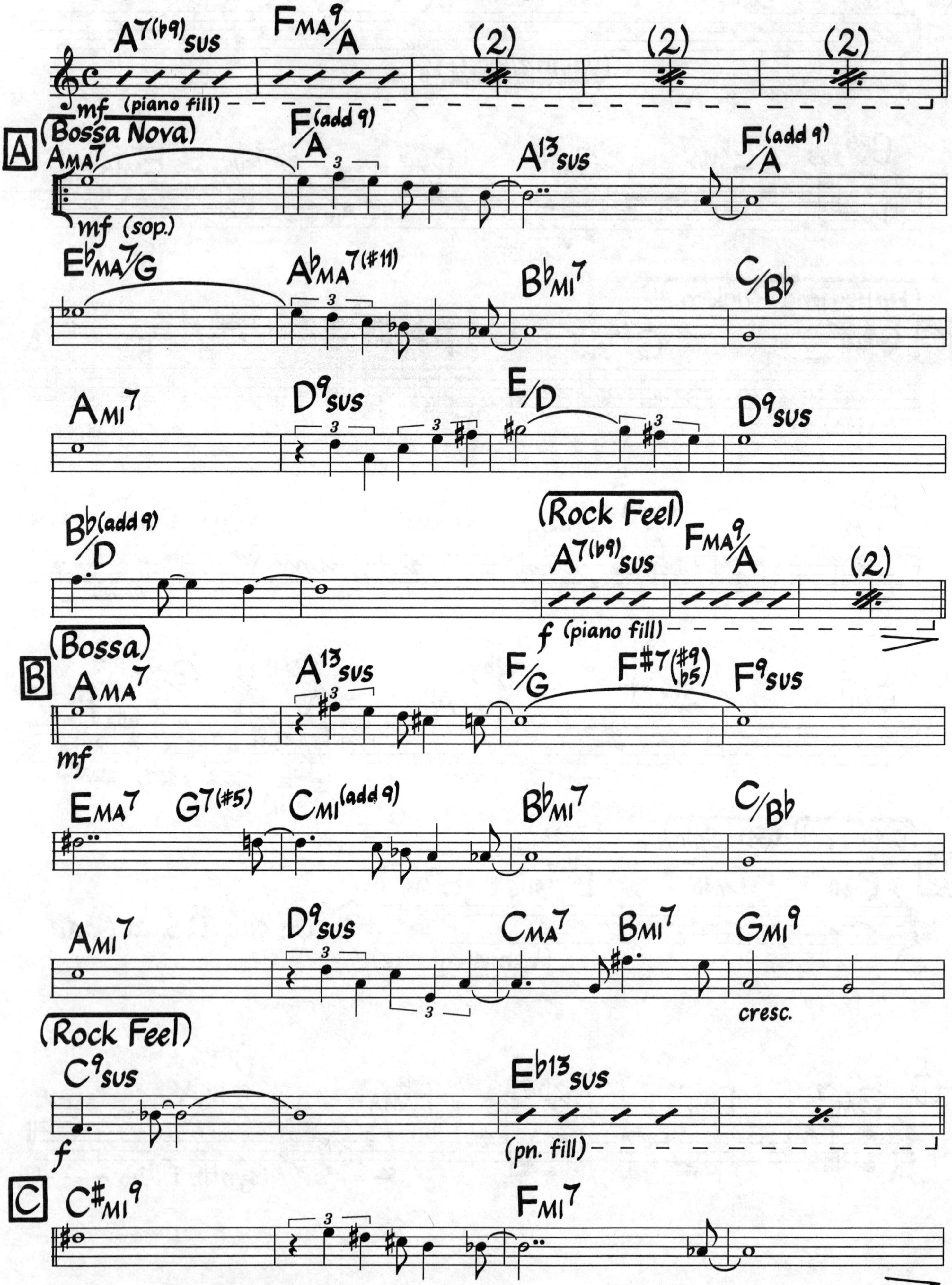

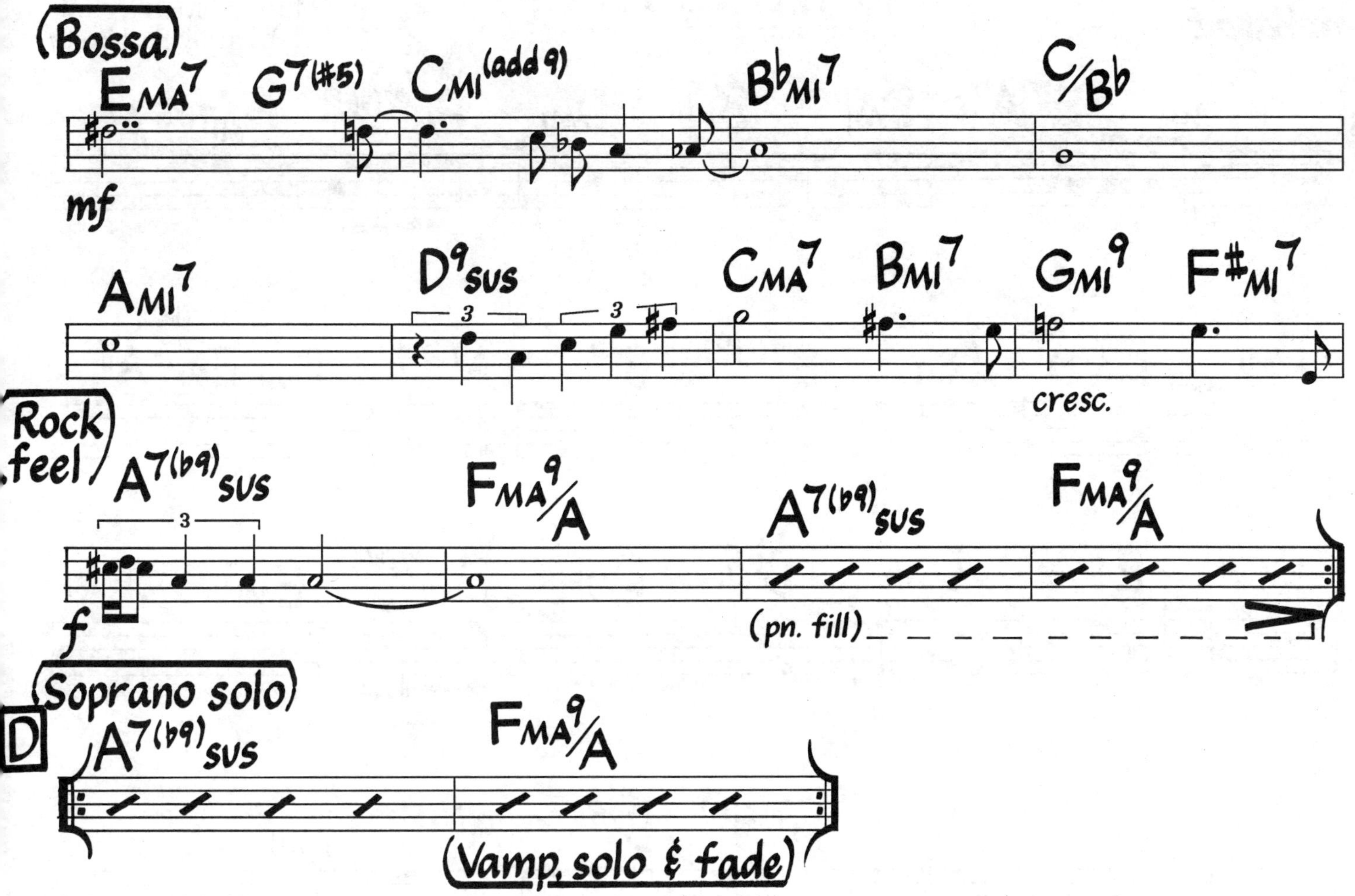

(Bossa)
EMA7
G7(#5)
CMI(add 9)
BbMI7
C/Bb
mf
AMI7
D9sus
CMA7
BMI7
GMI9
F#MI7
cresc.
Rock feel
A7(b9)sus
FMA9/A
A7(b9)sus
FMA9/A
f
(pn. fill)
(Soprano solo)
D
A7(b9)sus
FMA9/A
(Vamp, solo & fade)

Angel Eyes

Music by Matt Dennis
Lyric by Earl Brent

Med. Ballad

(Ending (freely))

Alternate changes for bars 1 & 2, 5 & 6, 9 & 10, 13 & 14, 25 & 26, 29 & 30:

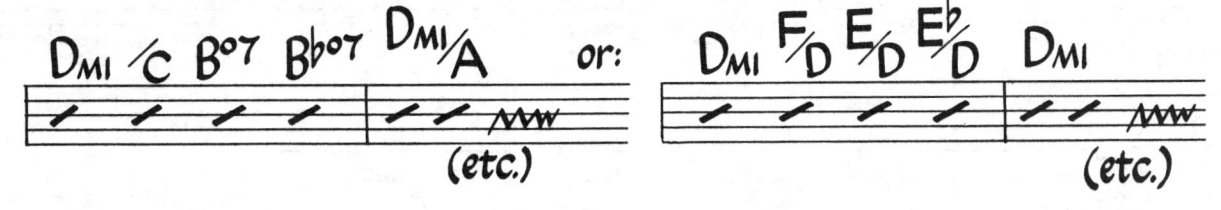

Anthropology

Charlie Parker
Dizzy Gillespie

Fast Bebop

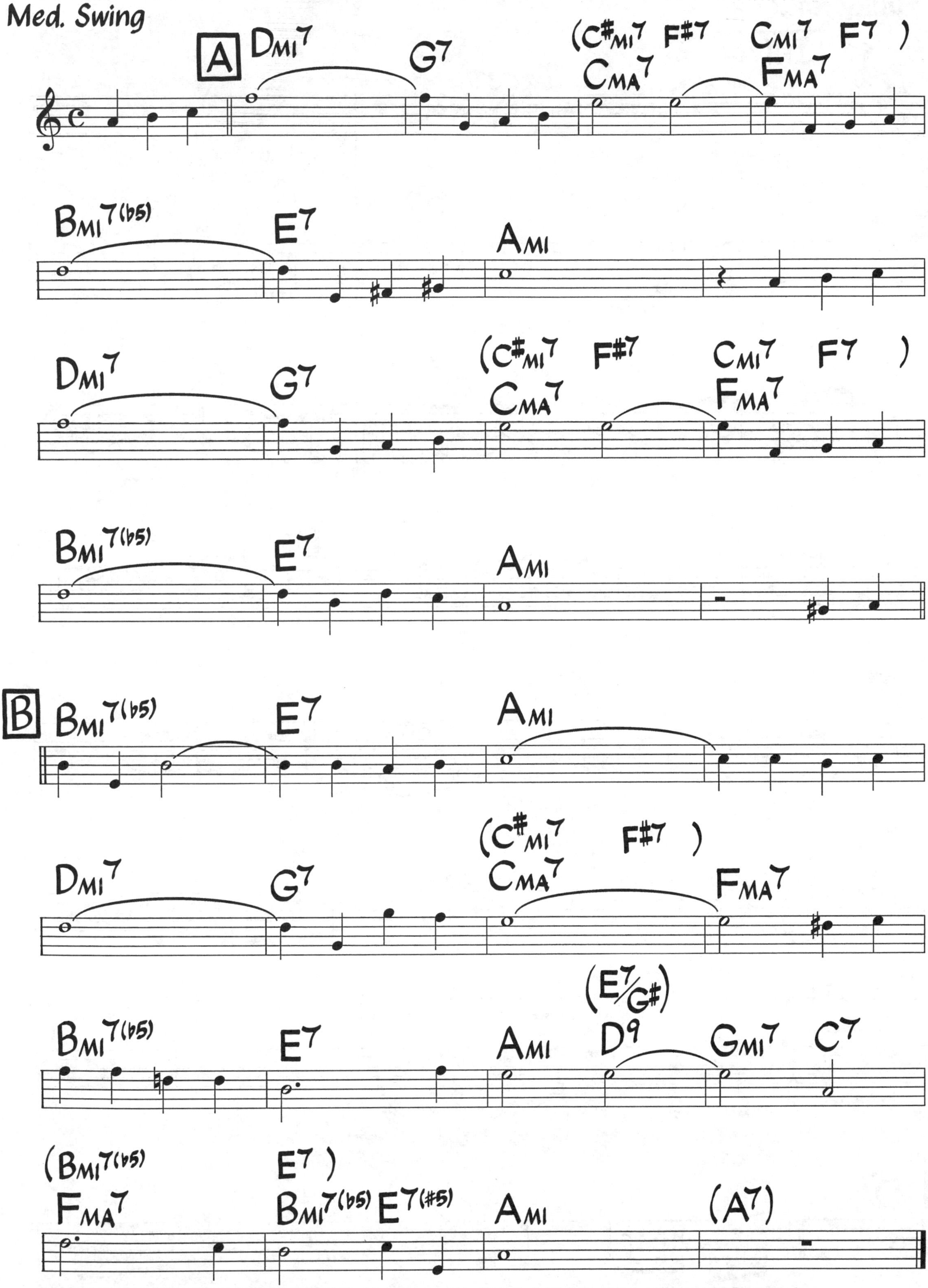

Baby, I Love You

Med.-Slow Funky Rock
♩ = 90 (Intro)

Ronnie Shannon
(As sung by Aretha Franklin)

©1967 Pronto Music & Fourteenth Hour Music. Used By Permission. All Rights Reserved.

Melody is freely interpreted.

Vamp & fade
(Lead vocal ad lib.)

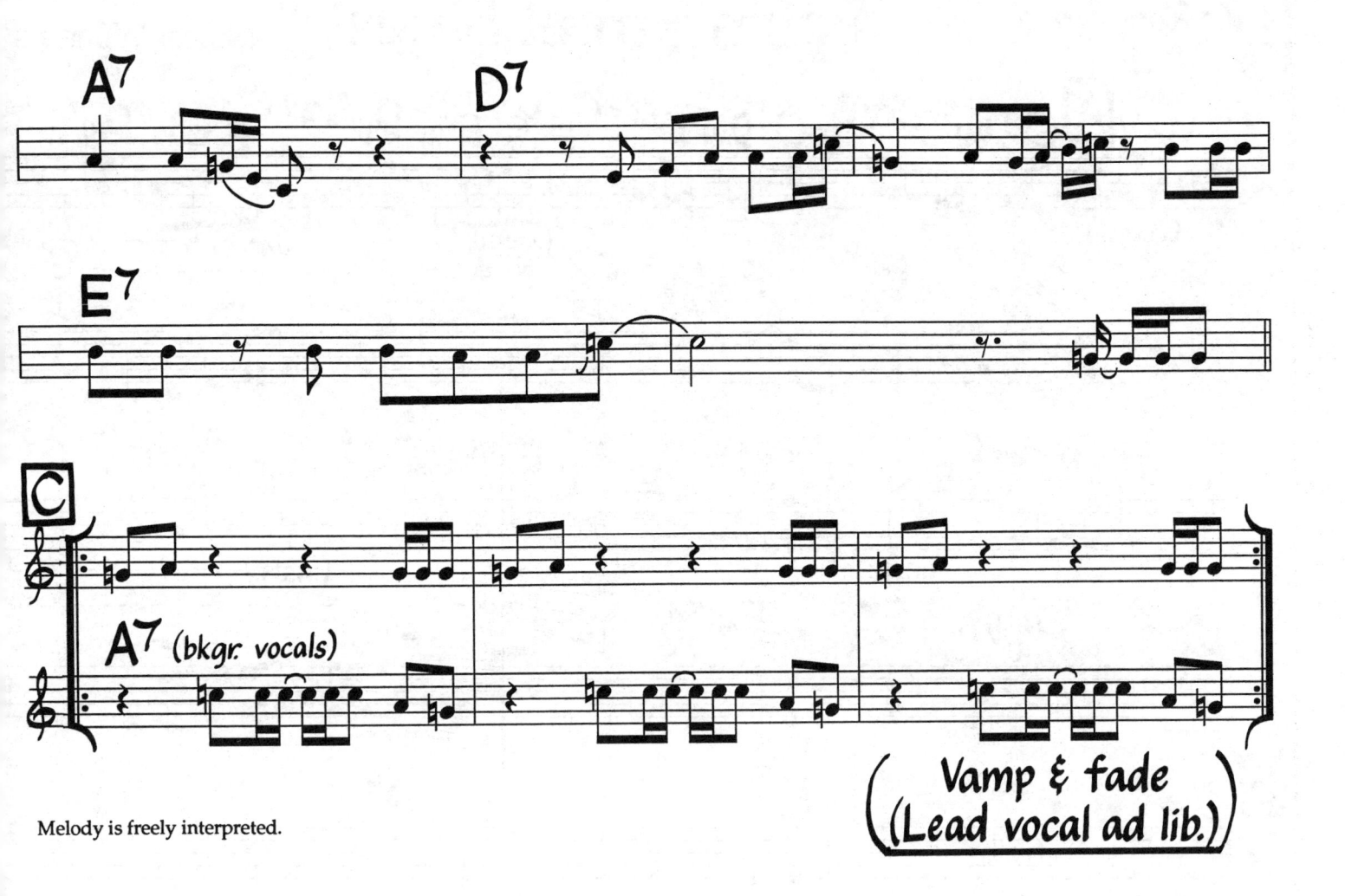

Basin Street Blues

Spencer Williams

Med.- Slow Swing (Dixieland)

Beautiful Love

Music by V. Young, W. King & E. Van Alstyne
Lyric by Haven Gillespie
(As played by Bill Evans)

Medium Swing

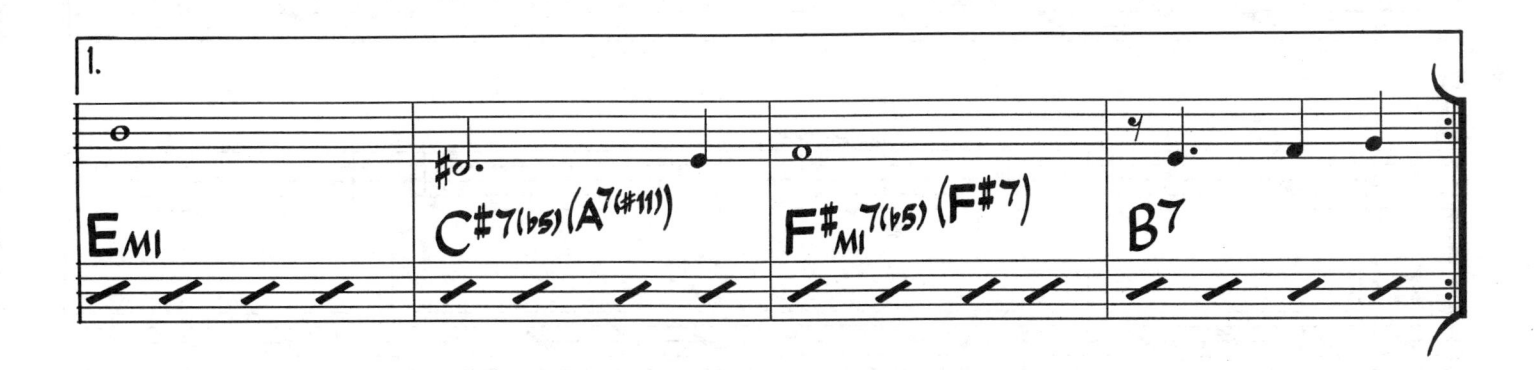

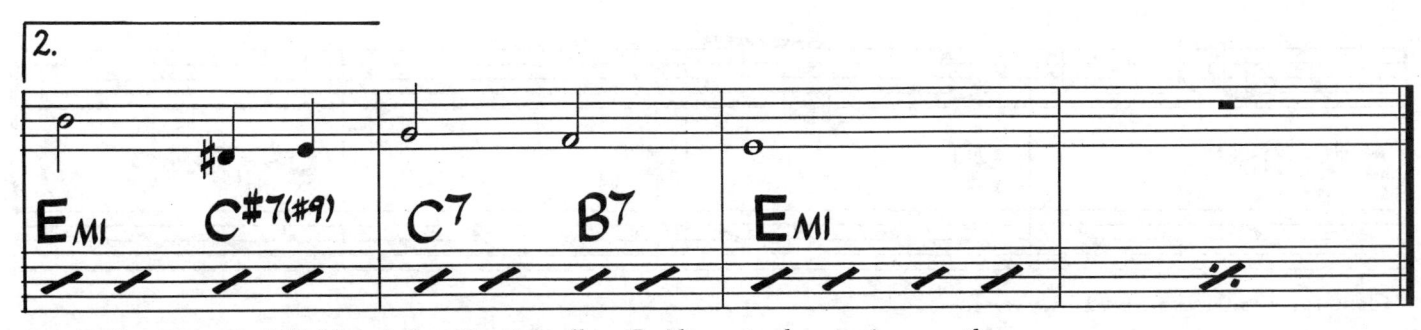

F#mi7(b5)	B7(#5)	Emi	(E7)
Ami7	D7	Gma7	F#mi7(b5) B7
Emi	Ami7	C7 (F#7)	B7

1.
| Emi | C#7(b5) (A7(#11)) | F#mi7(b5) (F#7) | B7 |

2.
| Emi C#7(#9) | C7 B7 | Emi | |

Originally written in 3/4. Note in bar 11 originally a G. Alternate changes in parentheses.

©1931,1959 Movietone Music Corp.NY,NY (Sam Fox Publishing Co., Inc. Santa Maria, CA - sole agents). Used By Permission.

Medium Swing

Bernie's Tune

Bernie Miller
(As played by Gerry Mulligan)

Chords in parentheses are used for solos.

Bird Food

Ornette Coleman

Fast Swing ♩=256

Solos in C, disregard the form

©1961,1988 by MJQ Music Inc., Rights assigned to Essex Musikvertrieb GmbH, Koln for Germany, Austria, Switzerland, Hungary, Bulgaria, Rumania, Czechoslovia, Yugoslavia, Poland, Greece, Turkey, Saudi Arabia, Iraq and Jordan. All Rights Reserved Including Public Performance For Profit. International Copyright Secured. Used By Permission.

Black Ice

Jeff Lorber

Medium-Up Funk
♩= 125 N.C.

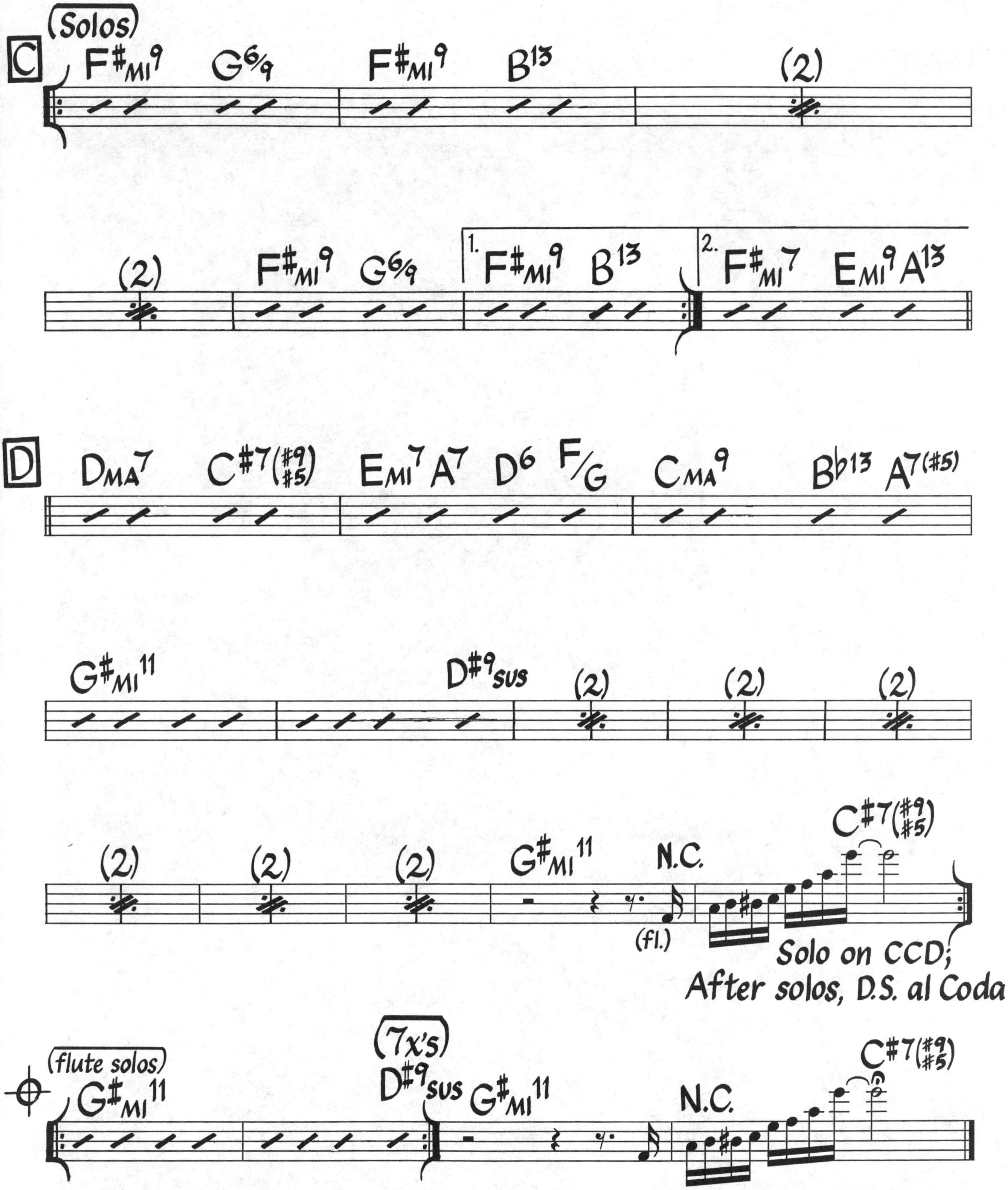

Flute sounds one octave higher than written.

JOE HENDERSON

Medium Jazz Waltz

Black Narcissus

Joe Henderson

Head is played twice before and after solos. Dynamics and kicks are used for solos.

Blizzard of Lies

Dave Frishberg
Samantha Frishberg

C#o7
DMI
C7/E
F
BbMA7A9
Ab13
F pedal (FMI7)
GMI7
C7
f (top note of pn. voicing)
(FMI7)
(vocal)
3rd x (in 4)
Bb9
Bo7
3
F/C
C#o7
DMI
break
(pn. fill)
Bb9
break
(pn. fill)
DMI
C13
Bb9
(A7 Ab13)
break
(G)
EbMA9(#11)
DMI(add 9)
(Ad lib.)

Blue Bossa

Kenny Dorham
(As played by Joe Henderson)

Medium-Up Bossa
♩ = 160

Blue Daniel

Frank Rosolino
(As played by Cannonball Adderley)

Medium Jazz Waltz
♩ = 132

A

(alto & trp.)

| E6 | D9 | C#mi7 | F#13 |

| C#mi9 | F#13(#11) | C#mi9 | F#13(#11) |

| Ami9 | D13 | Ema7 | D13(#11) |

| F#mi9 | B13sus   B13 |

(Ending)

| E6   D9 | C#mi7 | F#13(#11) | B13sus   B13 | Ema7 (trp.)(alto) |

©1959 Composer's Music. Used By Permission.

Blues Connotation

Ornette Coleman

Fast Swing ♩= 264

(alto & trp.)

Chords suggested only (no chordal instrument on recording).

©1962,1988 by MJQ Music Inc., Rights assigned to Essex Musikvertrieb Gmbh, Koln for Germany, Austria, Switzerland, Hungary, Bulgaria, Rumania, Czechoslovakia, Yugoslavia, Poland, Greece, Turkey, Saudi Arabia, Iraq and Jordan. All Rights Reserved Including Public Performance For Profit. International Copyright Secured. Used By Permission.

Solos in C; disregard the form.

Blues On The Corner

McCoy Tyner

Med. Swing

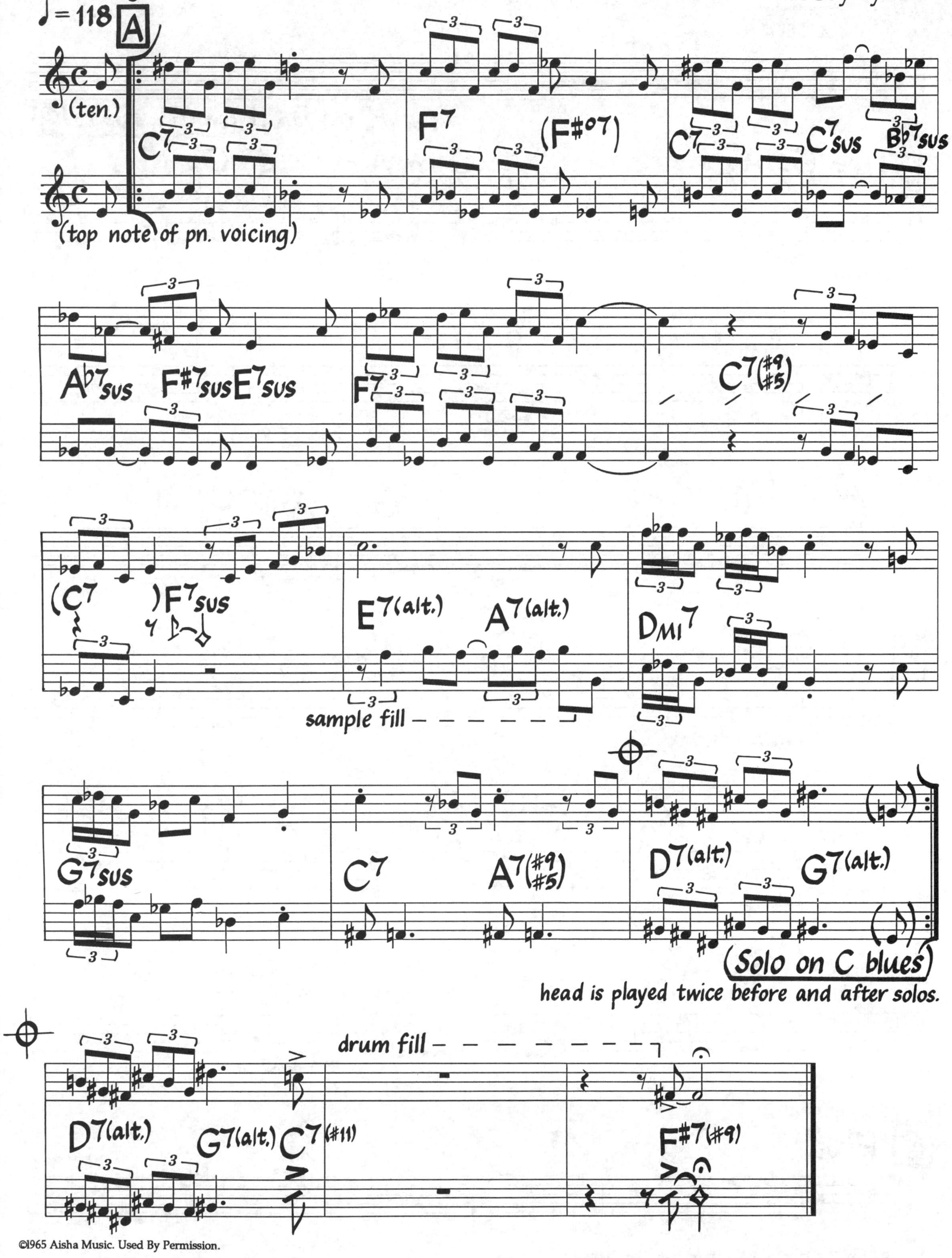

Boogie Down

Al Jarreau
Michael Omartian

Med. Funk
♩ = 114

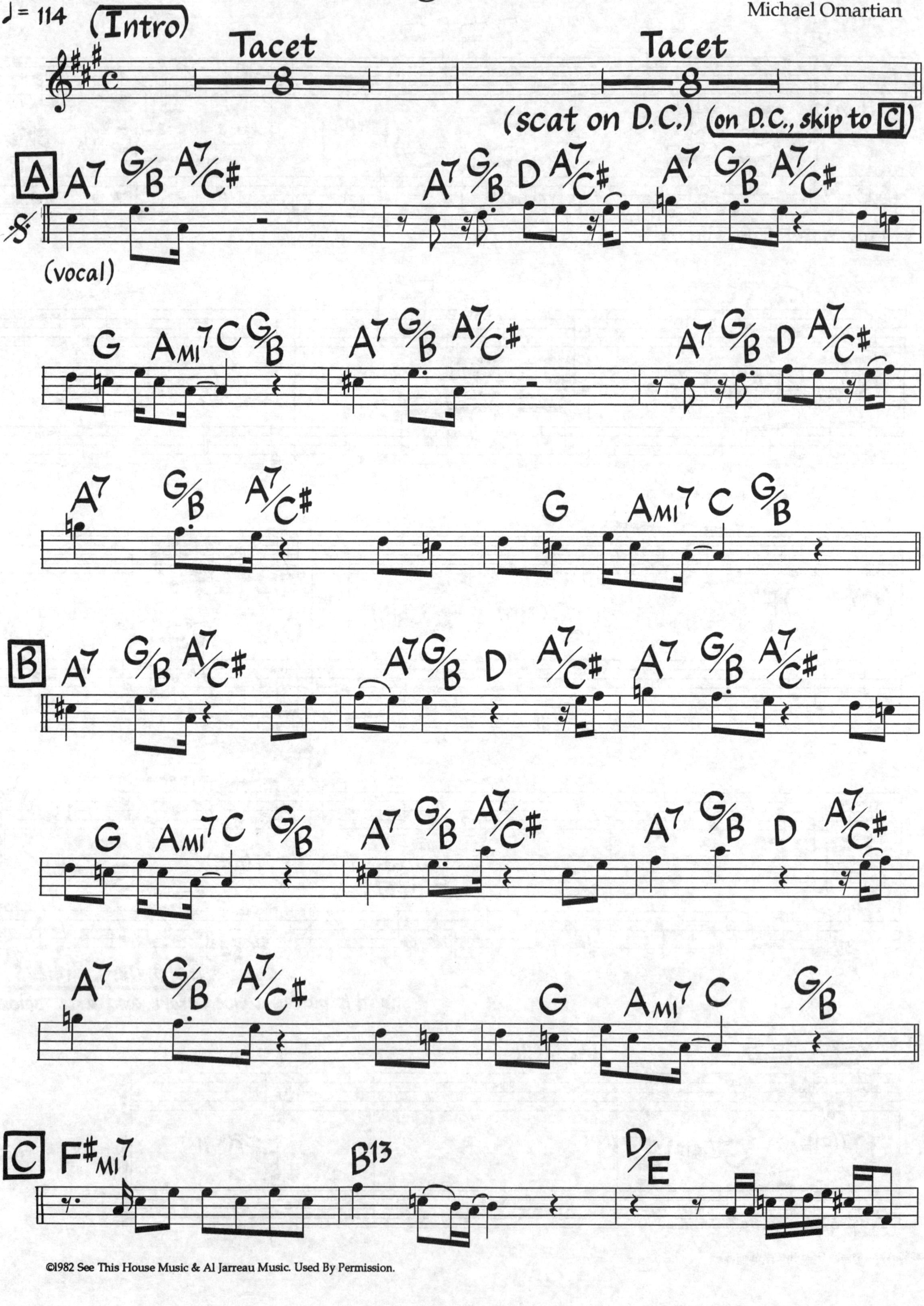

C#bass Dbass Ebass C#7(#5) F#MI11
DMA7
F#MI7 AMA7/E D#MI7(b5)
CMA7 BMI7 AMI7 D/E
D
A7 G/B A7/C#
A7 G/B D A7/C#
A7 G/B A7/C#
G AMI7 C G/B
A7 G/B A7/C#
A7 G/B D A7/C#
A7 G/B A7/C#
G AMI7 C G/B
D.C., play Intro, C, D, E
(1st x: tacet)
E
N.C.
(N.C.)
D.S., vamp & fade on A

Boogie Down (Brass)

MICHAEL BRECKER

Photo by Tom Copi ©1988

Both Sides Of The Coin

Michael Brecker
(As played by Steps Ahead)

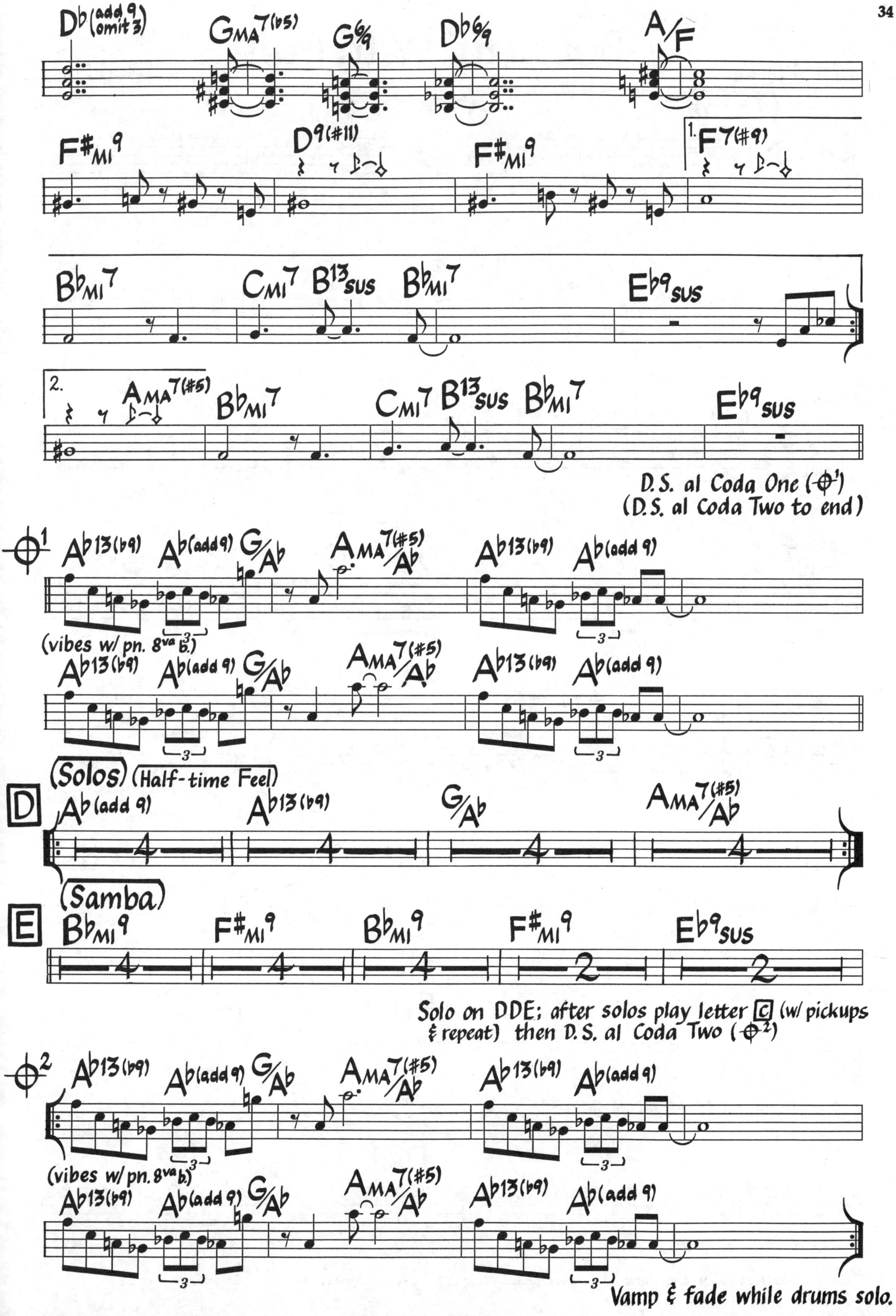
Db(add 9)(omit 3)
GMA7(b5)
G6/9
Db6/9
A/F
F#MI9
D9(#11)
F#MI9
1. F7(#9)
BbMI7
CMI7 B13SUS BbMI7
Eb9SUS
2. AMA7(#5)
BbMI7
CMI7 B13SUS BbMI7
Eb9SUS
D.S. al Coda One (⊕1)
(D.S. al Coda Two to end)
Ab13(b9) Ab(add 9) G/Ab AMA7(#5)/Ab Ab13(b9) Ab(add 9)
(vibes w/ pn. 8va b.)
Ab13(b9) Ab(add 9) G/Ab AMA7(#5)/Ab Ab13(b9) Ab(add 9)
(Solos) (Half-time Feel)
D
Ab(add 9) Ab13(b9) G/Ab AMA7(#5)/Ab
(Samba)
E
BbMI9 F#MI9 BbMI9 F#MI9 Eb9SUS
Solo on DDE; after solos play letter C (w/ pickups & repeat) then D.S. al Coda Two (⊕2)
Ab13(b9) Ab(add 9) G/Ab AMA7(#5)/Ab Ab13(b9) Ab(add 9)
(vibes w/ pn. 8va b.)
Ab13(b9) Ab(add 9) G/Ab AMA7(#5)/Ab Ab13(b9) Ab(add 9)
Vamp & fade while drums solo.

Bouncin' With Bud

Med. (-Up) Swing

Bud Powell

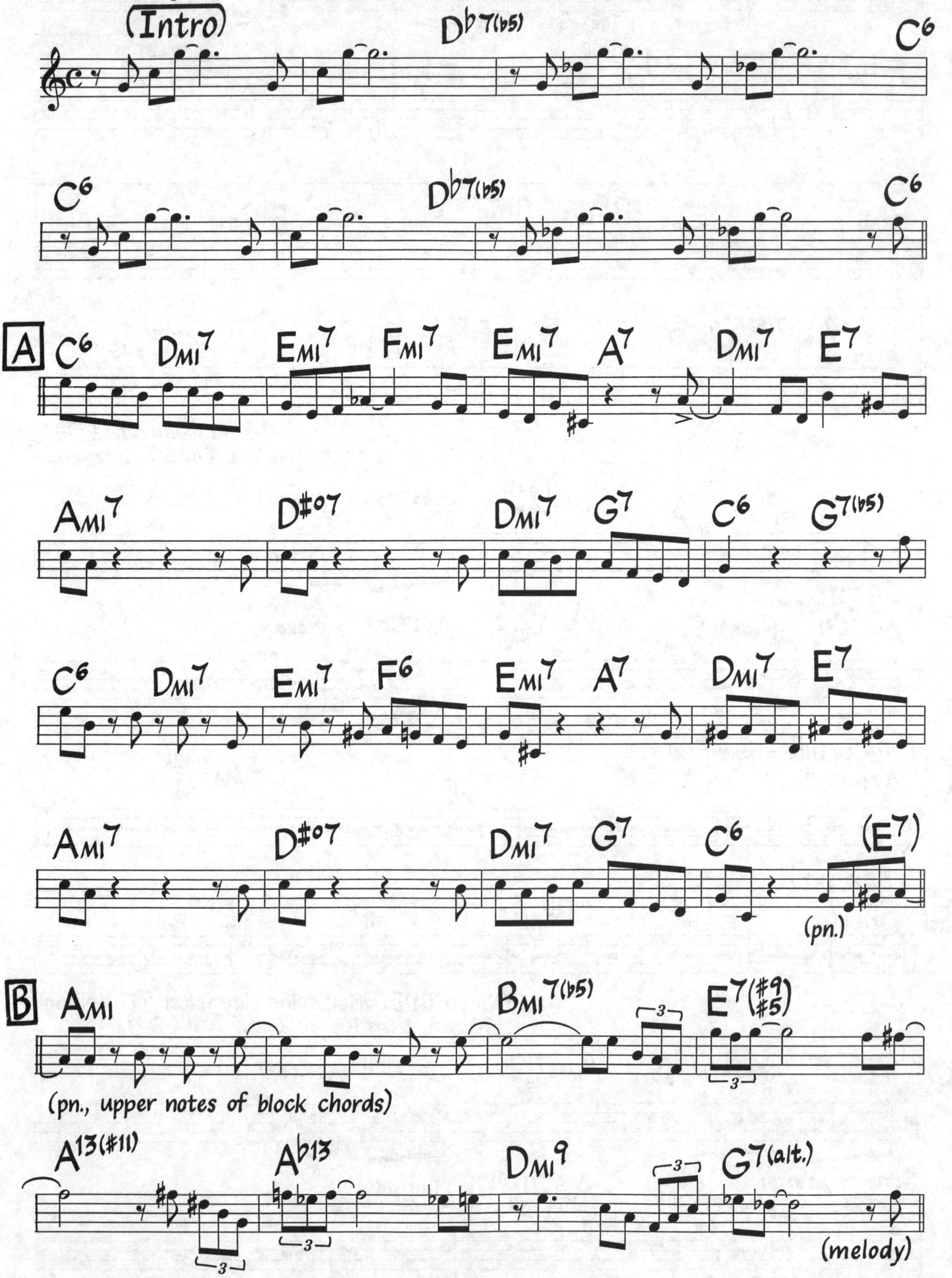

Solo on ABC;
After solos, D.C. al Coda.

background echoes at 5 & 6 and 13 & 14
of letter A and bars 5 & 6 of letter C:

(pn., w/ 8va)

Breakfast Wine

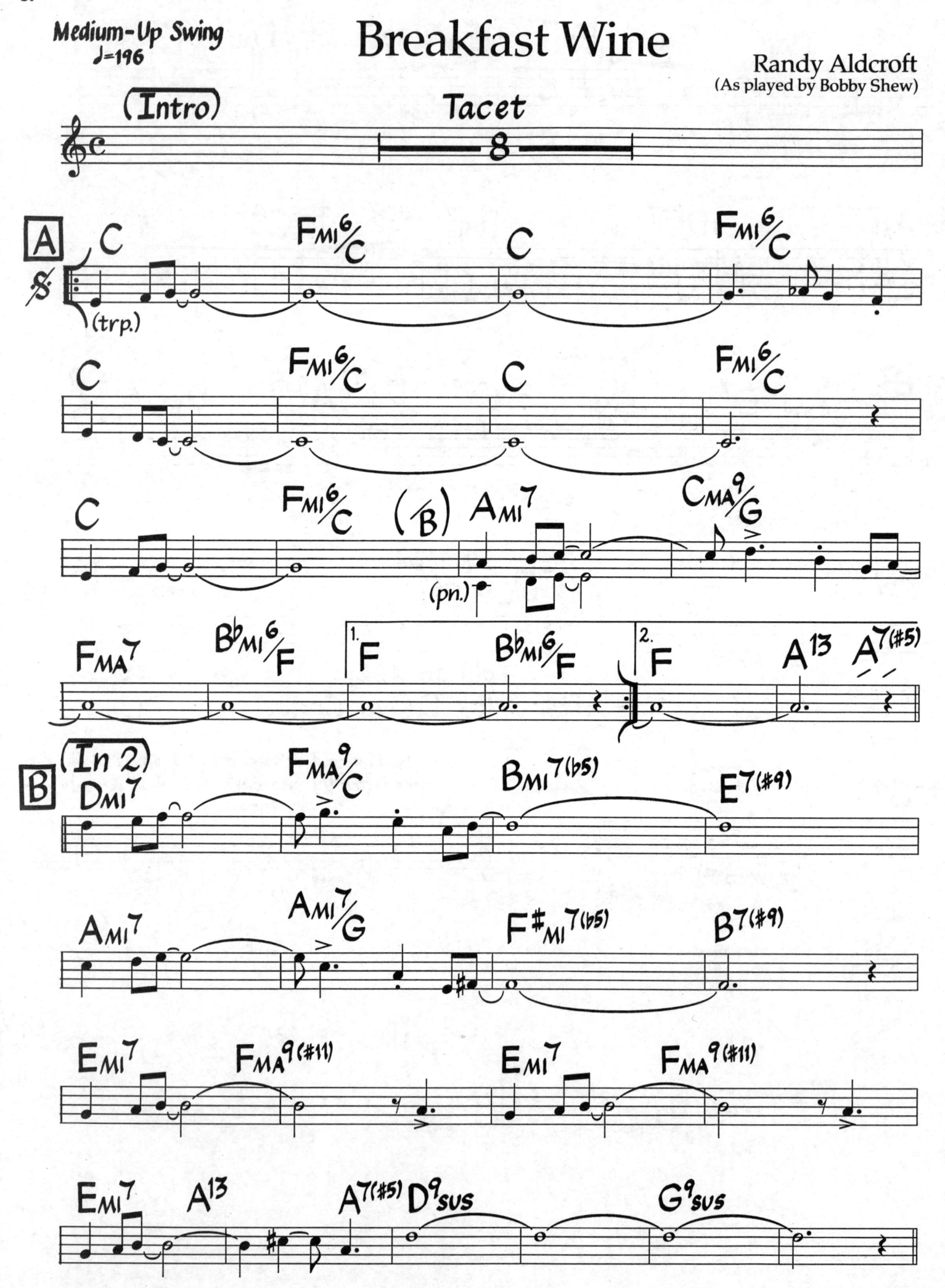

Randy Aldcroft
(As played by Bobby Shew)

Medium-Up Swing ♩=196

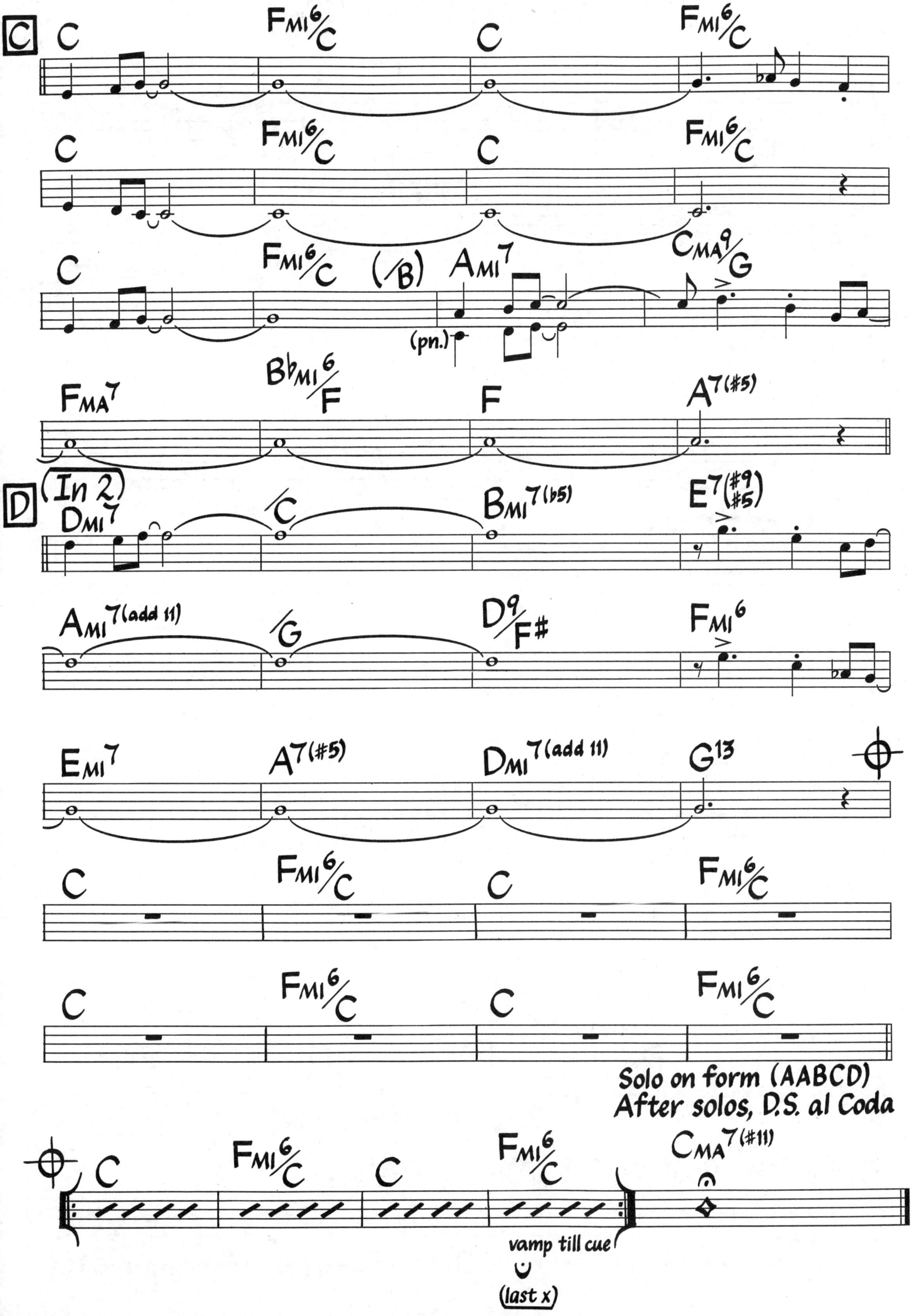
C
C
FMI6/C
C
FMI6/C
(/B)
AMI7
CMA9/G
(pn.)
FMA7
BbMI6/F
F
A7(#5)
(In 2)
D
DMI7
/C
BMI7(b5)
E7(#9 #5)
AMI7(add 11)
/G
D9/F#
FMI6
EMI7
A7(#5)
DMI7(add 11)
G13
Solo on form (AABCD)
After solos, D.S. al Coda
CMA7(#11)
vamp till cue
(last x)

Breakin' Away

Al Jarreau
Tom Canning
Jay Graydon

mf
(trp., 2nd x only)
G13sus
F#13sus
G13sus
(trb.)
G13sus
1.
F#13sus
2.
F#13sus
(vocal)
f
FMI7
BbMI7
EbMI7
GMI7 C7(b9)
FMA7
(shake - -)
FMA7 F7(b9)
BbMI9 BbMI7
FMI7
Ab9sus
(trp.)
cresc.
Ab/Gb
AMI7
DMI7 D7(b9)
BbMI9 BbMI7
FMI7
Vamp & Fade

MARK MURPHY

But Beautiful

Music by Jimmy Van Heusen
Lyric by Johnny Burke

Med. Ballad

Chain Of Fools

Don Covey
(As sung by Aretha Franklin)

Med. Rock
♩ = 114
(Intro)

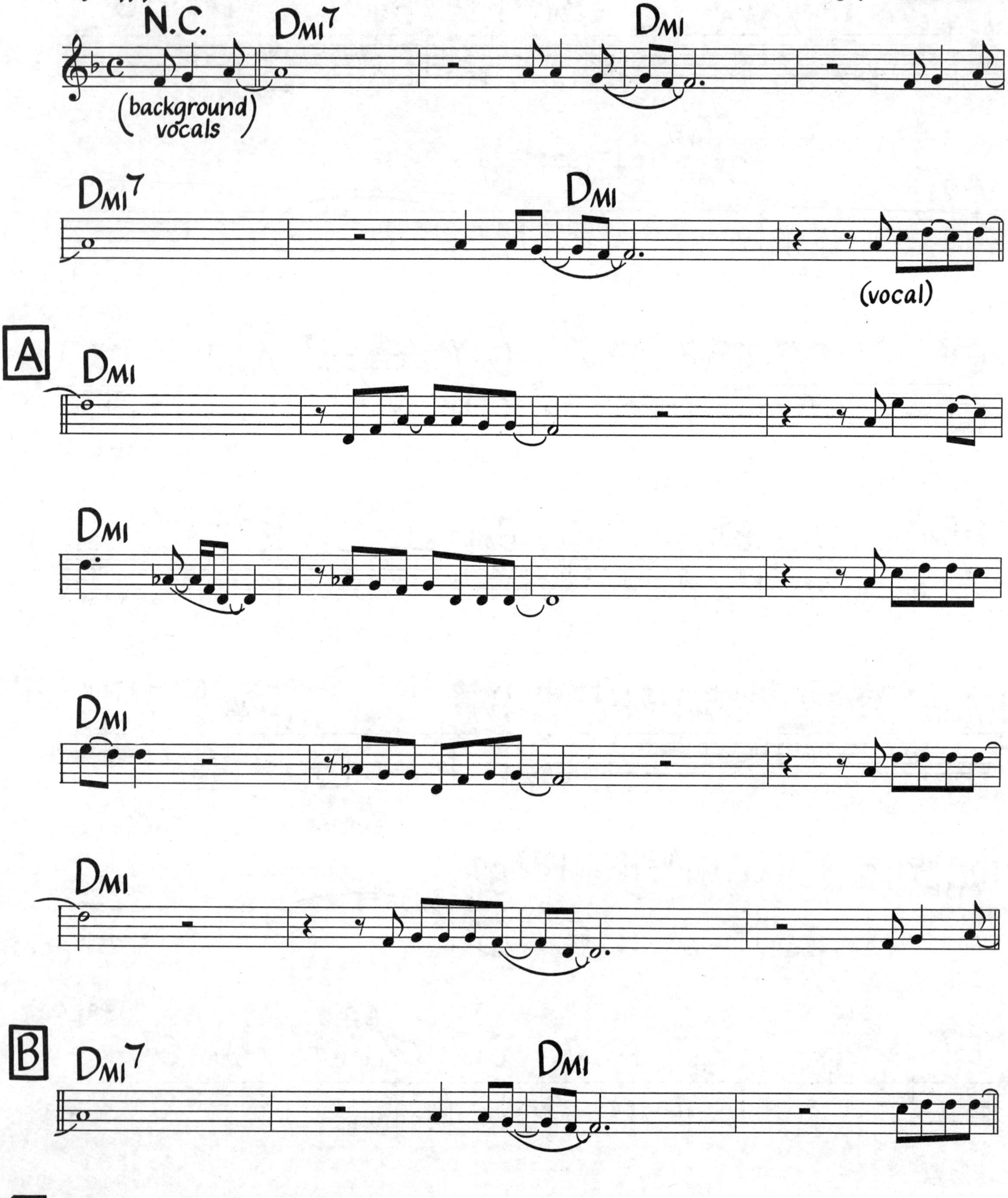

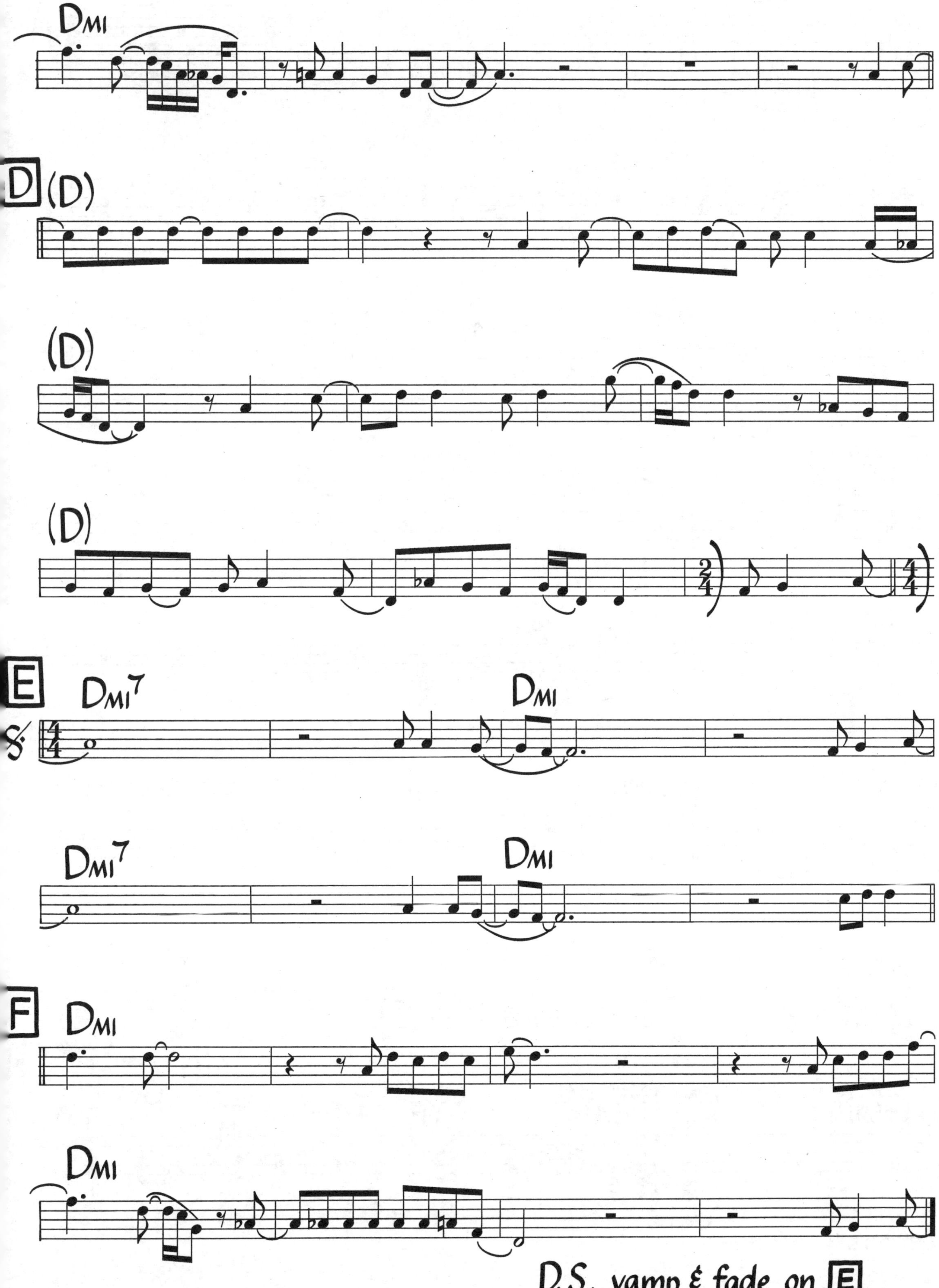
DMI
D
(D)
(D)
(D)
E
DMI7
DMI
DMI7
DMI
F
DMI
DMI
D.S., vamp & fade on E

Medium Swing
♩= 132

Change Of Mind

Bob Mintzer
(As played by Peter Erskine)

Chords in brackets are used for solos.

Solo on ABC
After solos, play letter D (w/ pickup)
then D.S. al Fine

Chega De Saudade
(No More Blues)

Music by Antonio Carlos Jobim
Lyric by Jon Hendricks & Jessie Cavanaugh

Med. Bossa Nova

C
EMA7
C#7(#5)/F
F#MI7
B9SUS
B7
E°7
EMA7
G#MI7
G°7
F#MI7
F#9
AMI6
B7
D
EMA7
C#MI7
F#7
G#7
C#MI7
CMI7
BMI7
E7
AMA7
AMI7
G#MI7
C#13
C#7(#5)
F#9
B13SUS
(G#7)
G#MI7
C#7(#5)
F#9
B9SUS
E6
(B7(#5))

Chelsea Bridge

Billy Strayhorn

Med. Ballad

A
N.C.
CMI(MA 7)
B♭MI(MA 7)
CMI(MA 7) B♭MI(MA 7) C7
FMI9
B♭13
E♭6
1. E♭6 (D7 D♭7)
break
2. E♭6
C♯7
B
G♯MI7 C♯7
F♯MA7 D♯MI7 G♯MI7 C♯7(♭9 ♯5) C♯MI7 F♯7
(BMI7 E7)
BMA7 D7
AMA7
AMI D9
E♭7(♯11)(D7 D♭7)
break
C
CMI(MA 7)
B♭MI(MA 7)
CMI(MA 7) B♭MI(MA 7) C7
FMI9
B♭13
E♭6
E♭6(D7 D♭7)

©1941,1942, renewed 1966 Tempo Music. Used By Permission.

F9(♯11) may be substituted for CMI(MA 7) and E♭9(♯11) for B♭MI(MA 7) throughout, in which case bar 8 of A, B and C may be played: E♭ D7 D♭7 C7

Come Sunday

Med.- Slow Gospel Ballad

Duke Ellington

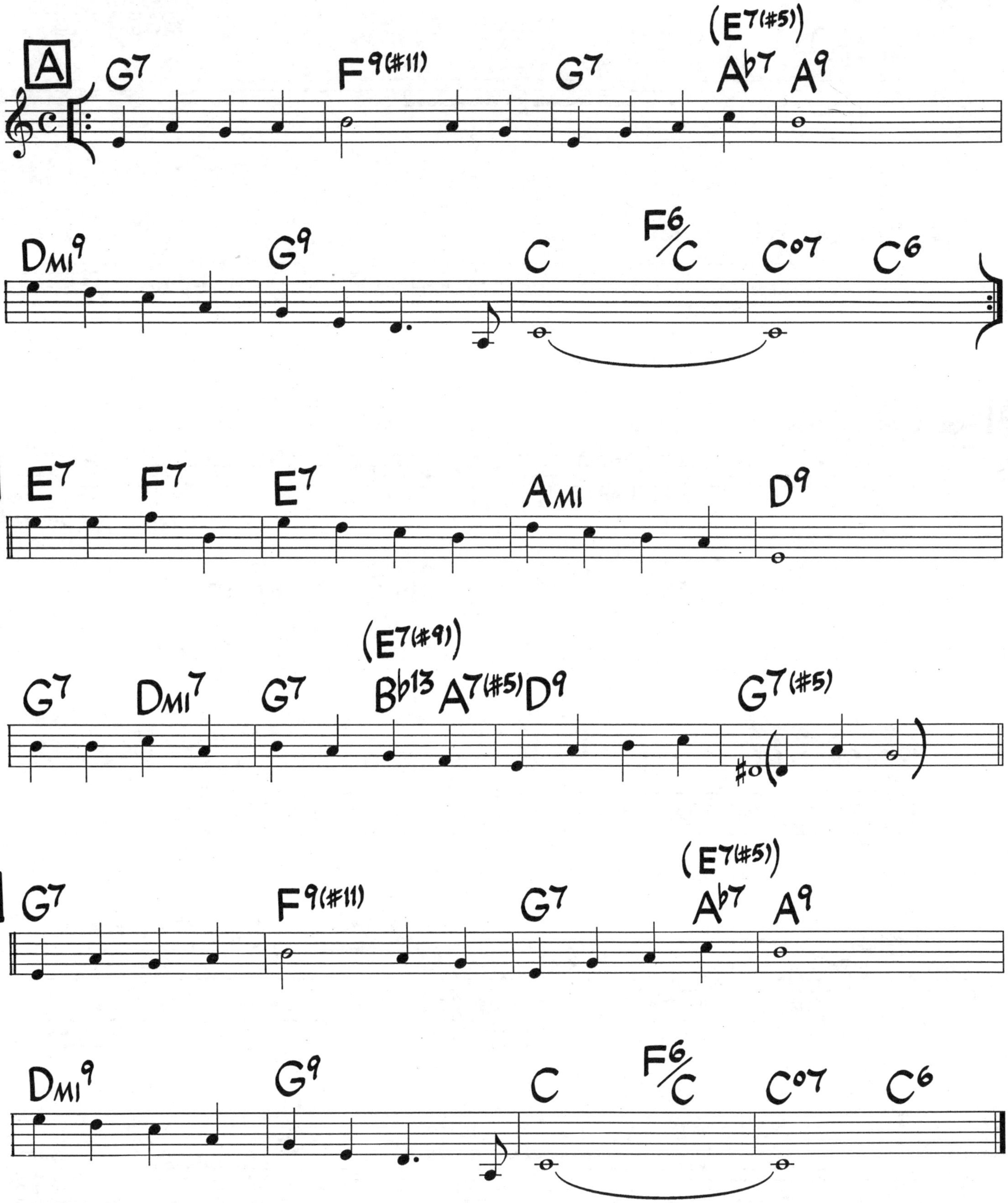

Compared To What

Med. Gospel/Rock
♩= 144

Eugene McDaniels
(As sung by Les McCann)

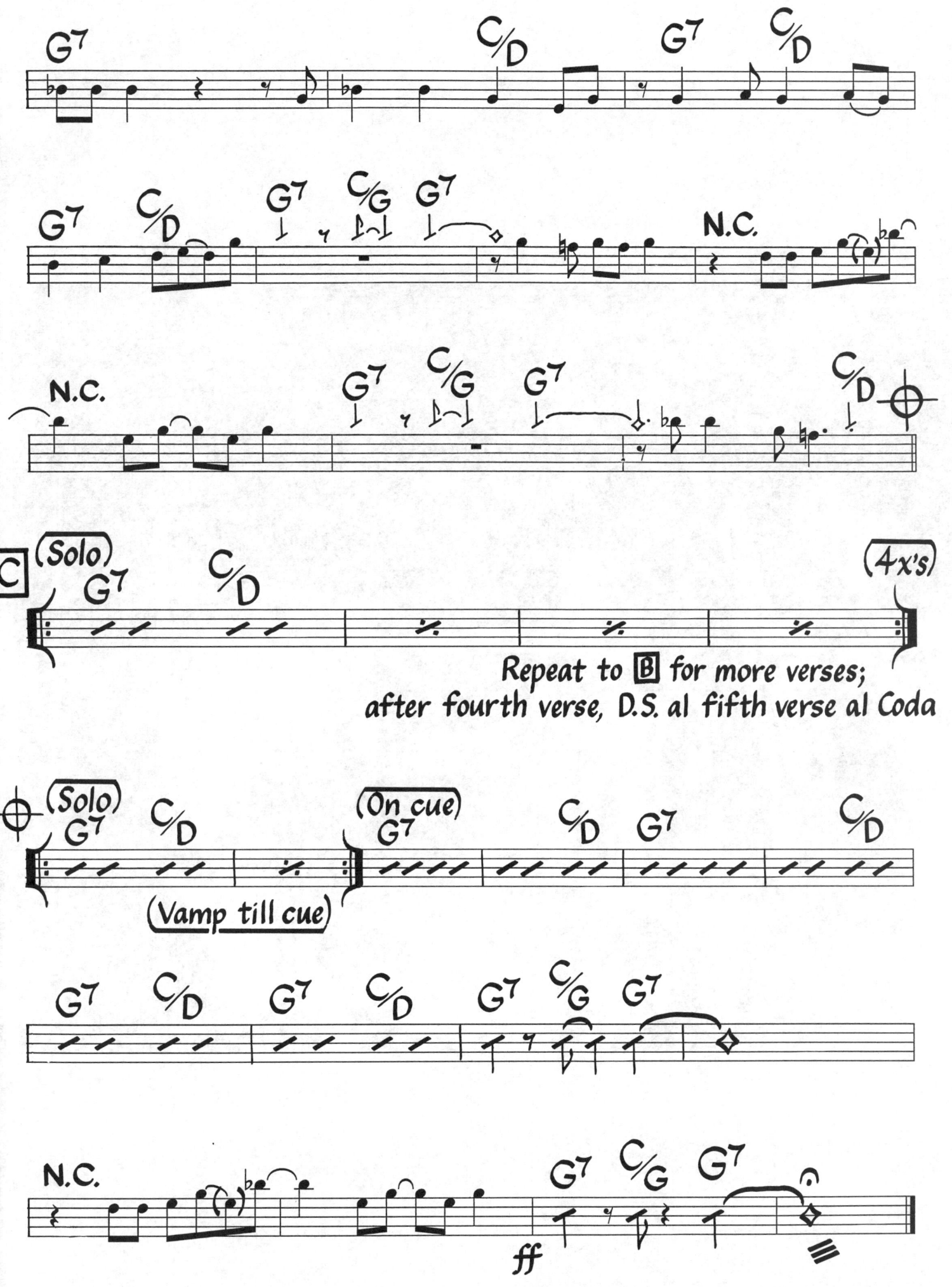

Repeat to **B** for more verses;
after fourth verse, D.S. al fifth verse al Coda

Melody is freely interpreted and varies with each verse.
Coda vamp is played 24 times on recording (three 16 bar phrases).

AIRTO

Bright Samba
𝅗𝅥 = 272

Creek

Victor Brasil
(As played by Airto)

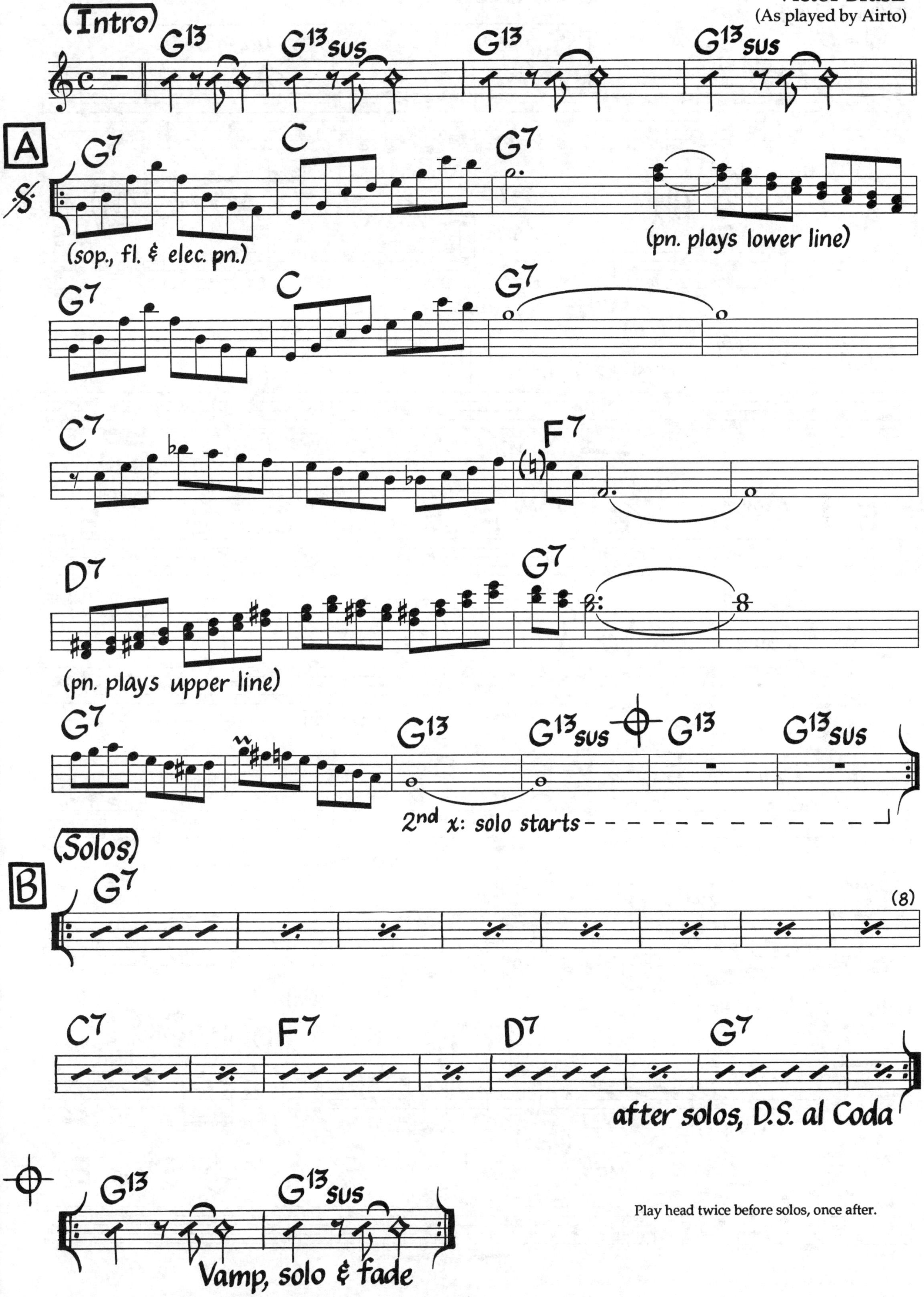

Crystal Love

Makoto Ozone

C
(Solos - Samba-Like Feel)
AMA7 Bb/A G#o7/A AMA7 G#13(#11) C#7(alt.)
FMA7 E7(#9 #5) AMI7 G FMI(MA7) 1. 2. FMI(MA7)
D
E AMI6/E F#/E AMI6/E E AMI6/E F#/E AMI6/E
E C#MI7 F#MI7 Go7 C/Ab
suspended time feel
G B7 EMI7 AMI7 Bbo7 D#/B GMI7 FMI7
suspended time feel
C#MA7 C#7(#11 b9) F#MI D(add 9)/F# DMI6/F
AMA7/E D#MI7(b5) DMI7 E/C CMA7 BMI7(add 11) E7
Solo on CCD; after solos
D.C. al Coda
E9sus E7 AMA7 Bb/A G#o7/A AMA7 Ab13(#11)
(unis.)
(pn.)
(unis.)
Ab13(#11) C#7(#9 b9 #5) FMA7 E7(#5) AMI7 G FMI(MA7)
rit.

Medium-Up
Funky Latin

Cubano Chant

Ray Bryant

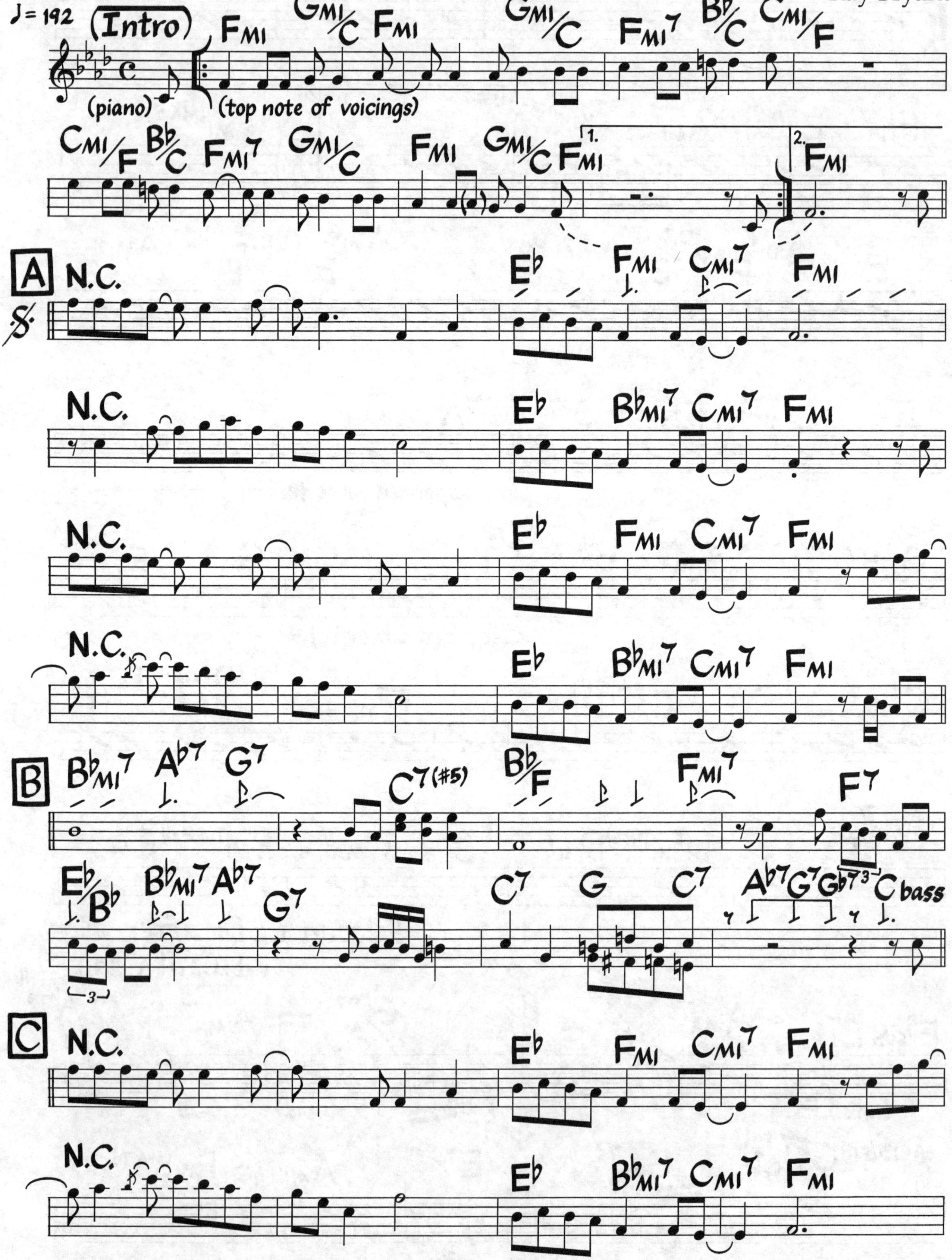

Eb Bbmi7 Cmi7 Fmi Bb7 Eb7 Ab7 Db7
Db7 Gbma7(b5) C7sus (omit 5) Fmi6 Dmi7(b5) G7(#5) C7 F7
solo break
D
(Solos)
Fmi7 Dmi7(b5) G7 C7 Fmi7 Dmi7(b5)
G7 C7 F7 F7/A Bb7 Bo7
1. F7/C D7 G7 C7
2. F7/C C7 F7
E
Bb7 F7
Bbmi7 Ab7 G7 C7 Bb7 Ab7 Gb7
F
Fmi7 Dmi7(b5) G7 C7 Fmi7 Dmi7(b5) G7 C7
F7 F7/A Bb7 Bo7 F7/C D7 G7 C7
Solo on DDEF
After solos, D.S. al Coda
N.C. C7sus (omit 5) Fmi6 Dmi7(b5) G7(#5) C7 F7 Bb7
Eb7 Ab7 Db7 Gbma7(b5) C7sus (omit 5) Fmi6 Dmi7(b5) G7(#5) C7 F7
(tremolo chord)

RICHIE BEIRACH

Photo by Tom Copi ©1988

Darn That Dream

Med. Ballad

Music by Jimmy Van Heusen
Lyric by Eddie DeLange

A

| A6 | Cmi7 F7 | Bmi7 C#7(b5) | F#mi7 (B/D#) E7 | Dmi6 C#mi7(b5) F#7 |

| Bmi7 G9 | C#mi7 Cmi7 | Bmi7 E7 | C#mi7 C7 Bmi7 E7 |

| A6 | Cmi7 F7 | Bmi7 C#7(b5) | F#mi7 (B/D#) E7 | Dmi6 C#mi7(b5) F#7 |

| Bmi7 G9 | C#mi7 Cmi7 | Bmi7 E13 | A6 Gmi7 C7 |

B

| Fma7 | Dmi7 Gmi7 | C7 | Ami7 G#mi7 C#7 Gmi7 C7 |

(Bmi7(b5) E7 Ami)

| Fma7 | Dmi7 Ami | Bmi7 E7 | Cmi7 F7 Bmi9 E13 |

C

| A6 | Cmi7 F7 | Bmi7 C#7(b5) | F#mi7 (B/D#) E7 | Dmi6 C#mi7(b5) F#7 |

| Bmi7 G9 | C#mi7 Cmi7 | Bmi7 E13 | A6 (Bmi7 E7) |

Bars 6 & 14 of A and bar 6 of C originally played: C#mi7 C°7

©1939, renewed 1969 Lewis Music Publishing Co., Inc., Scarsdale Music Publishing Co. All Rights Reserved. Used By Permission.

Delevans

Jeff Lorber

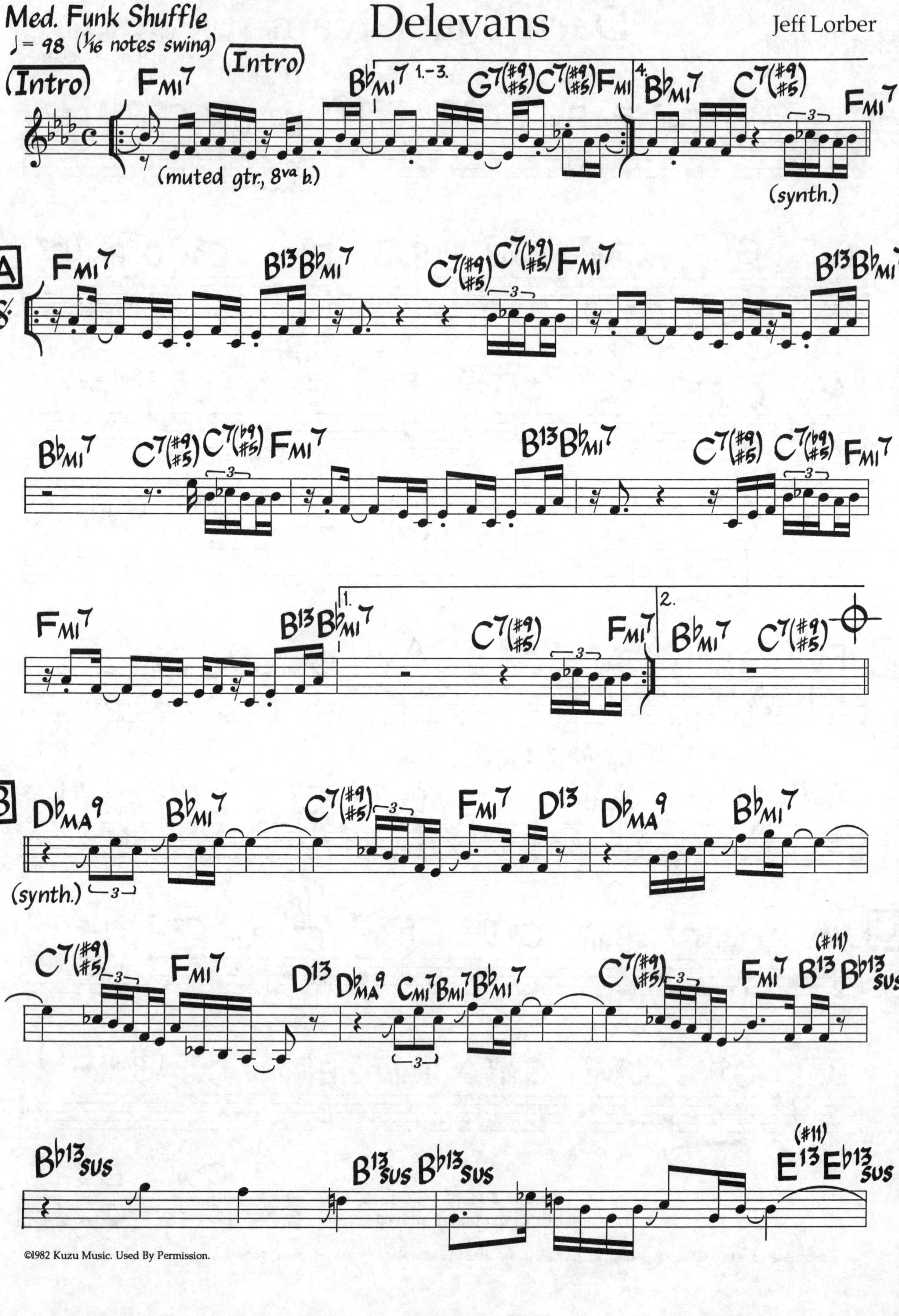

Eb13sus
E13sus Eb13sus
solo break
FMI7
to DS:
[D.S. al Coda (after solos)]
(Solos)
C
FMI7
B13 BbMI7
C7(#9 #5) C7(b9 #5) FMI7
(2)
(2)
FMI7
B13 BbMI7
1.
C7(#9 #5)
FMI7
2.
BbMI7
C7(#9 #5)
Bb13sus
D
Bb13sus
B13sus C13sus Db13sus
(solos continue)
(Db13sus)
B13sus Bb13sus
Ab13sus
G13sus
Ab13sus A13sus Bb13sus
C7(#9 #5)
FMI7
Solo on CCD; after solos play letter B, then D.S. al Coda.
(Synth. solo)
FMI7
BbMI7
C7(#9 #5) C7(b9 #5) FMI7
(2)
(2)
FMI7
BbMI7
C7(#9 #5)
FMI7
Vamp, solo & fade

Desafinado

Music by Antonio Carlos Jobim
Lyrics by Jon Hendricks & Jessie Cavanaugh

BMA7 G#MI7 C#MI7 F#7
DMA7 D#°7 EMI7 A7
AMI7 FMI6 A7 D7(b9)
C
GMA7 A7(b5)
AMI7 D7 BMI7(b5) E7
AMI7 CMI6 GMA7 (A7) EMI7
(AMI7) A7 F9
A7 AMI7 D7 G6 (D7)

Desire

Tom Scott

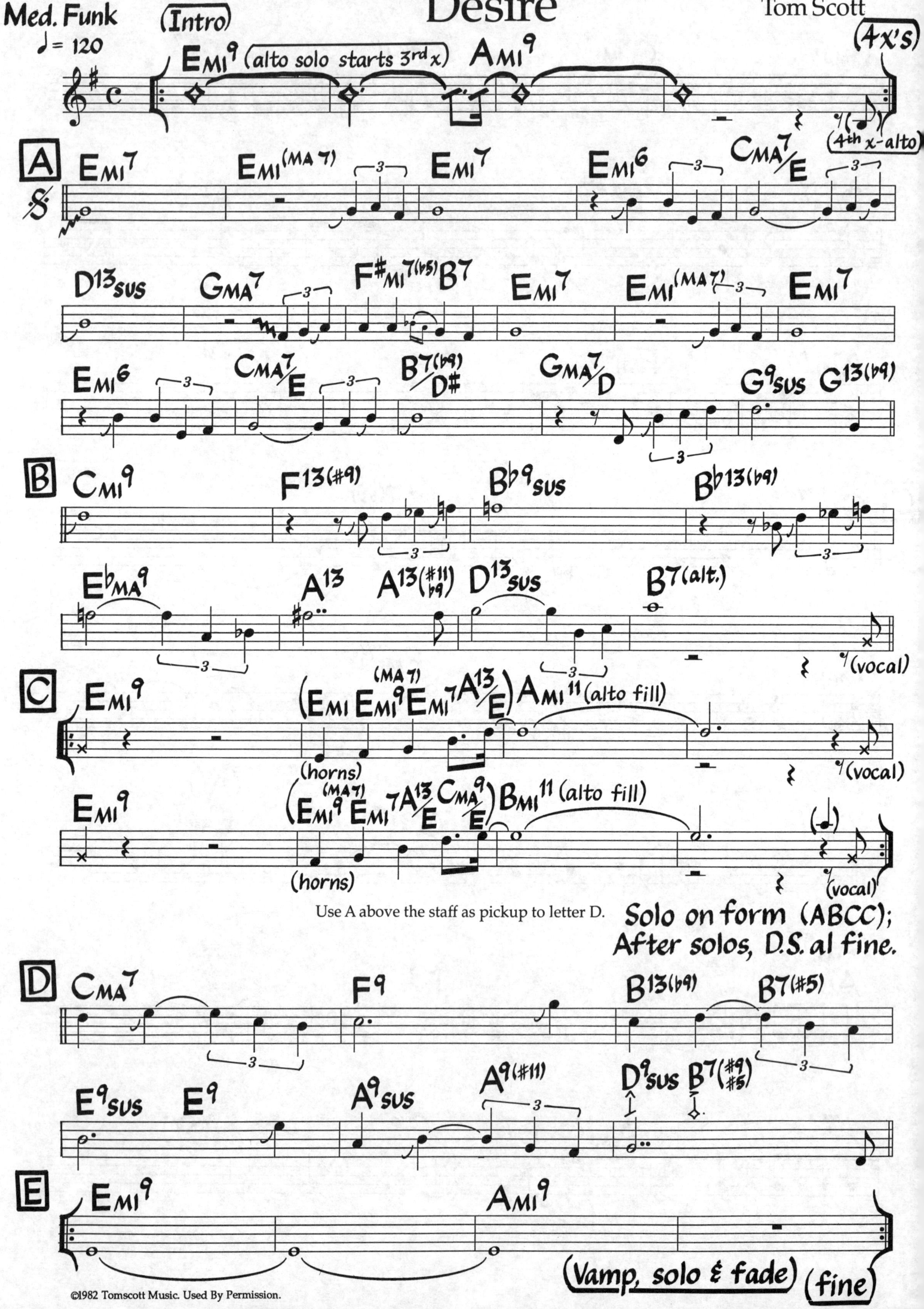

Dig

Miles Davis

Medium-Up Swing ♩=240

Based on "Sweet Georgia Brown" changes.

©1964 Prestige Music. Used By Permission.

Dindi

Music by Antonio Carlos Jobim
English Lyric by Ray Gilbert

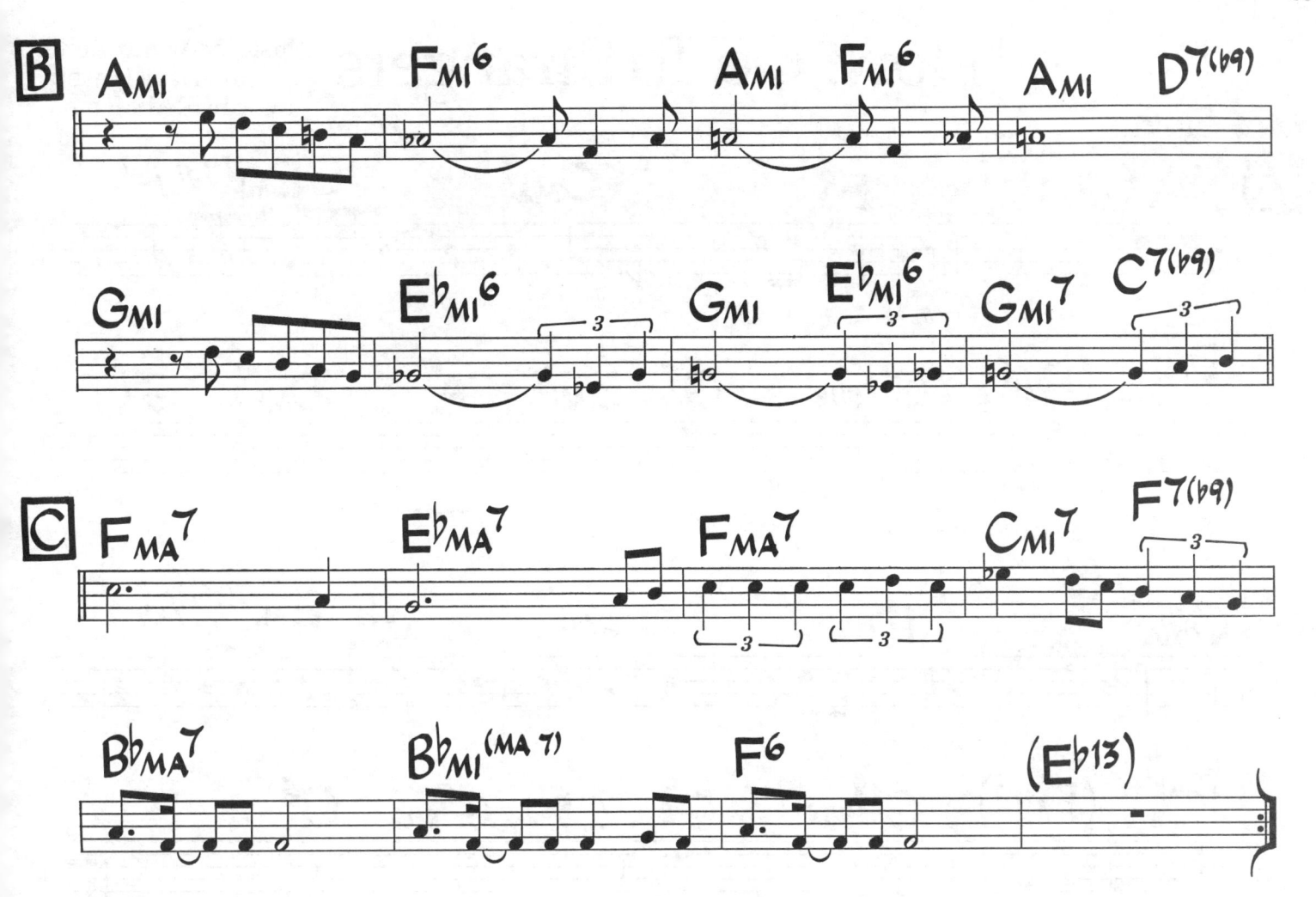

Eb13(#11) may be substituted for Bbmi(ma7) in letters A and C.

Don't Go To Strangers

Music by Arthur Kent
and Dave Mason
Lyric by Redd Evans

Med. Straight 1/8's
(quasi 1/16-note March)

Doors

Mike Nock

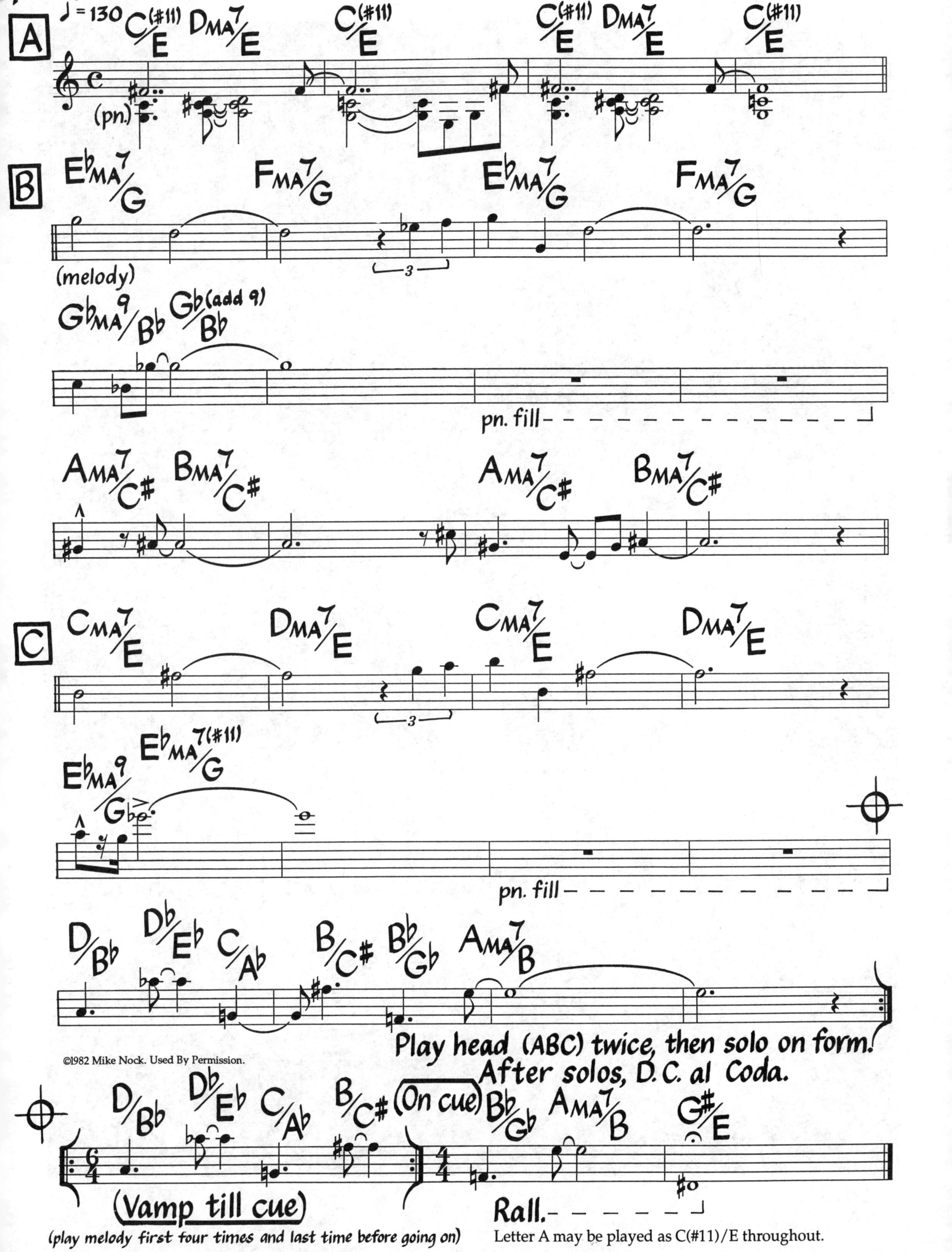

Letter A may be played as C(#11)/E throughout.

STAN GETZ

Photo by Jerry Stoll

Early Autumn

Music by Ralph Burns & Woody Herman
Lyric by Johnny Mercer

Easy

Al Jarreau
Tom Canning
Jay Graydon

Medium Funk/Samba
♩= 114

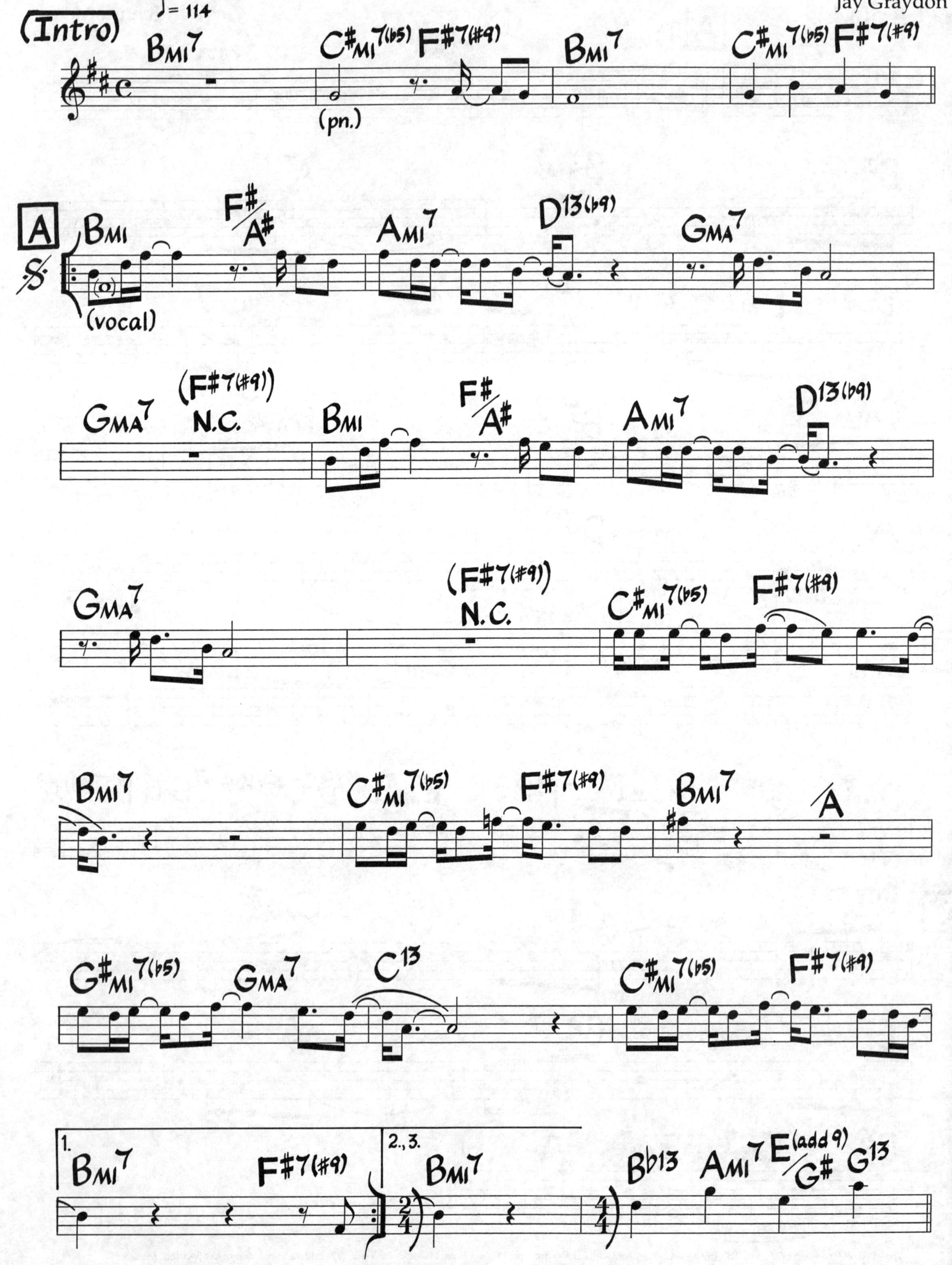

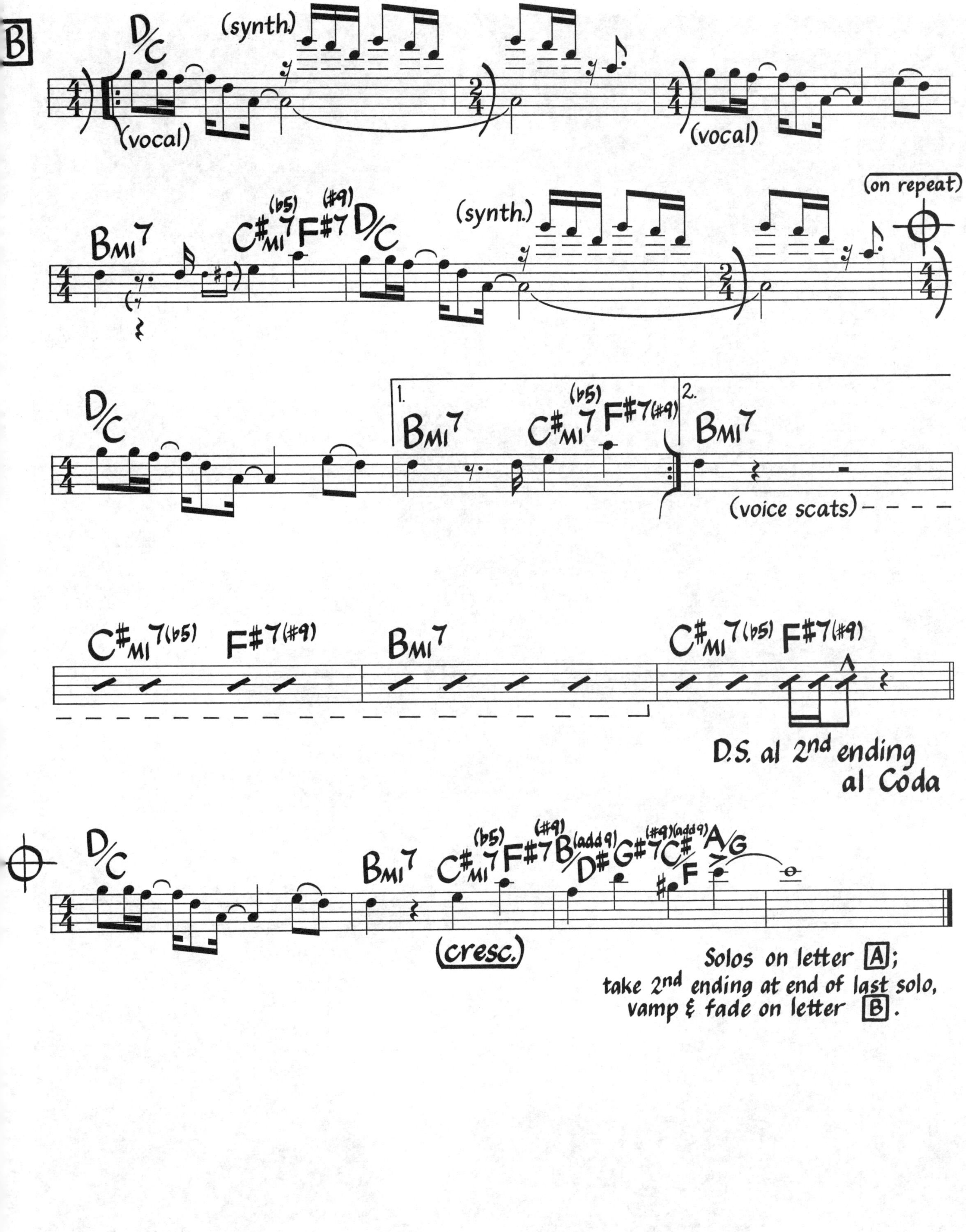
B
D/C
(synth.)
(vocal)
(vocal)
BMI7
C#MI7(b5)
F#7(#9)
D/C
(synth.)
(on repeat)
D/C
1.
BMI7
C#MI7(b5)
F#7(#9)
2.
BMI7
(voice scats)
C#MI7(b5)
F#7(#9)
BMI7
C#MI7(b5)
F#7(#9)
D.S. al 2nd ending
al Coda
D/C
BMI7
C#MI7(b5)
F#7(#9)
B(add9)/D#
G#7(#9)
C#(add9)/F
A/G
(cresc.)
Solos on letter A;
take 2nd ending at end of last solo,
vamp & fade on letter B.

MILES DAVIS

Photo by Jerry Stoll ©1988

Eighty One

Ron Carter
(As played by Miles Davis)

Med. Latin/Rock
♩=140

Chords in parentheses are optional.
Each solo progresses from Latin to swing feel.
'Sus' chords are sometimes played as dominant 9th chords (with 3rd).

After solos, D.C. al Coda

Vamp & fade till cue

©1965 Retrac Productions Inc. Used By Permission.

Med.- Slow
Straight-Eighths
♩= 110

Elm

Richie Beirach

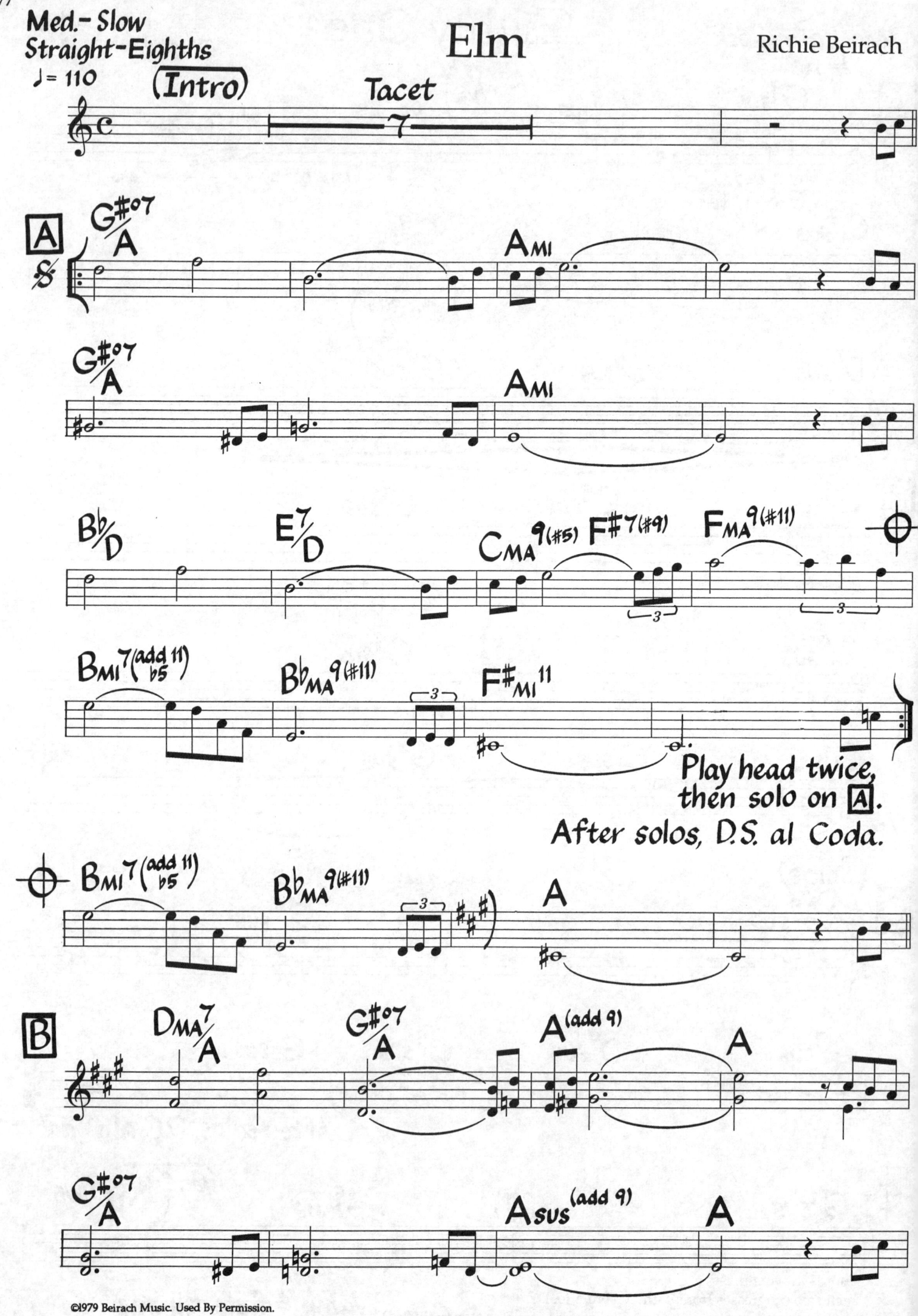

Medium Funk
♩= 110

Endangered Species

Wayne Shorter
Joseph Vitarelli

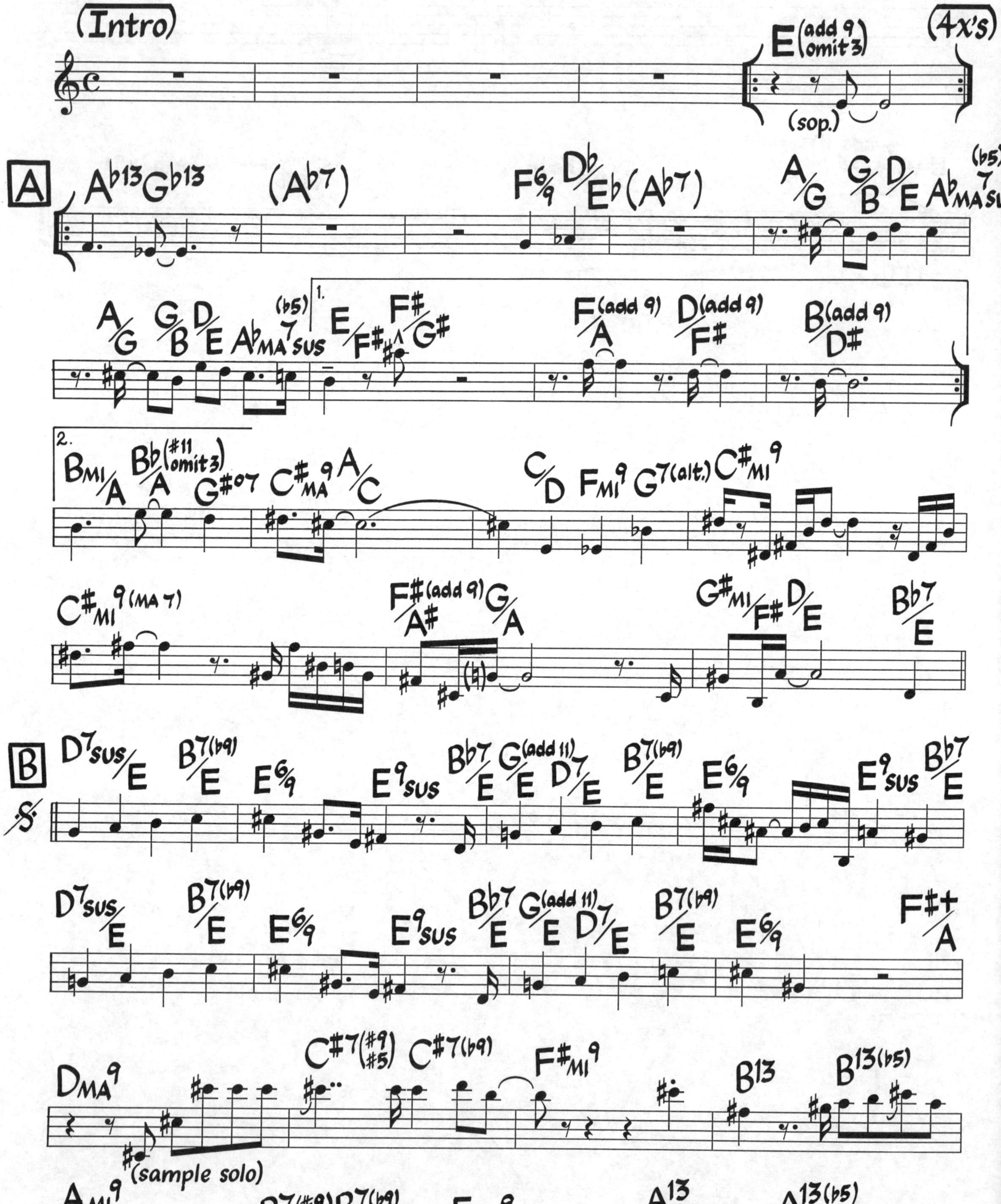

Some chord names have been simplified (see piano part).

WAYNE SHORTER

Photo by Jim Marshall ©1988

Fast Swing
♩= 268

E.S.P.

Wayne Shorter
(As played by Miles Davis)

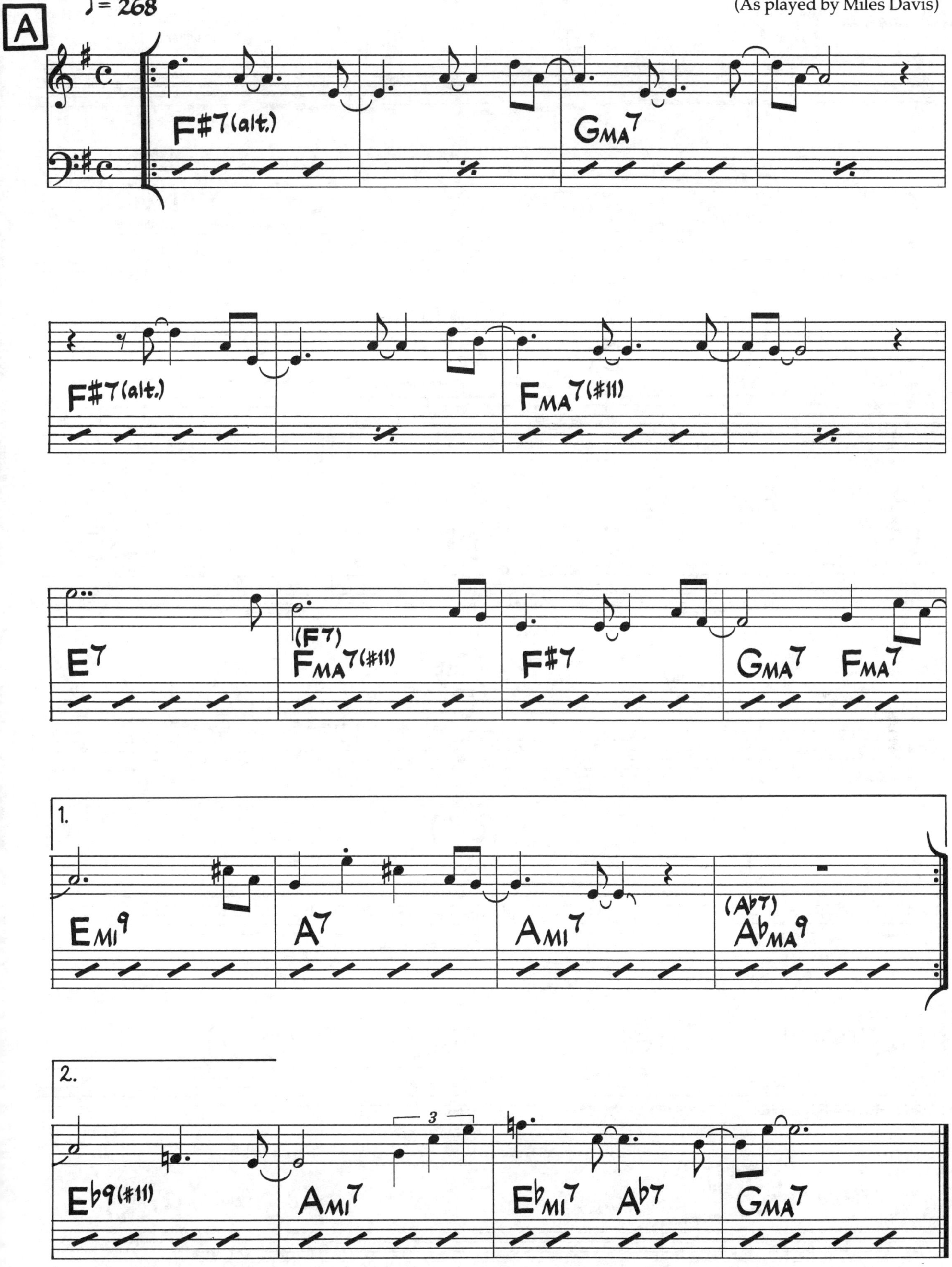

Everything Happens To Me

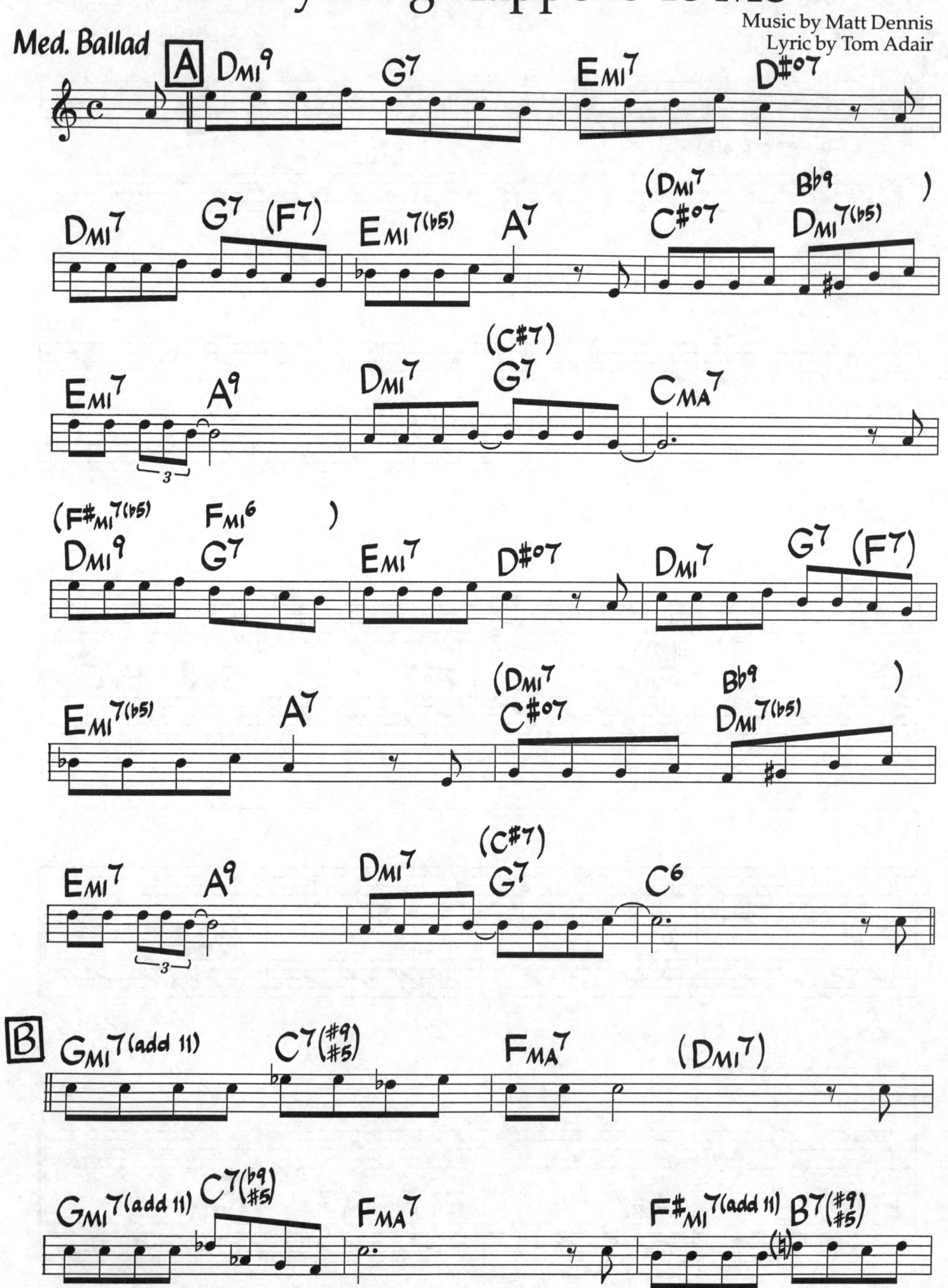

Music by Matt Dennis
Lyric by Tom Adair

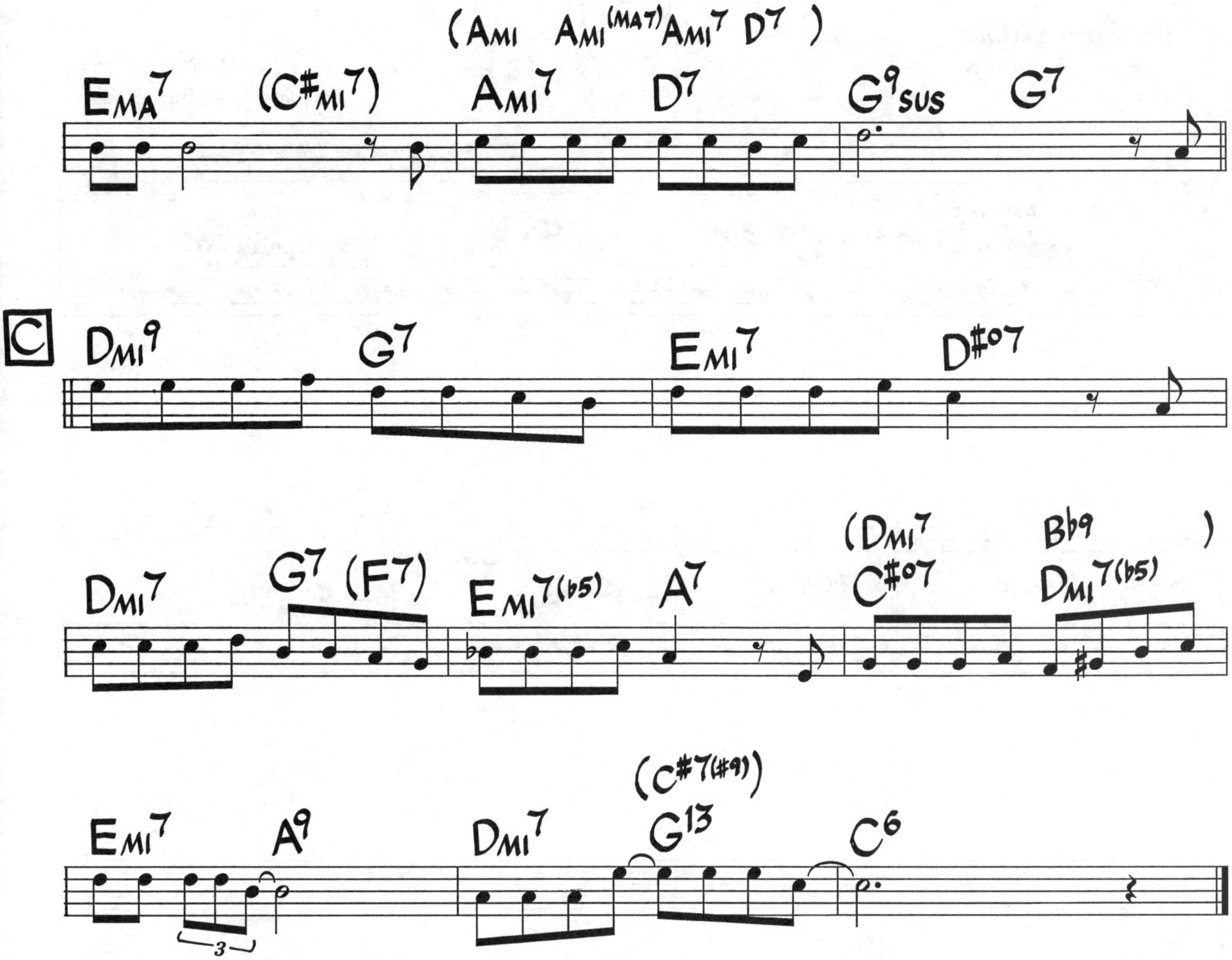
(AMI AMI(MA7) AMI7 D7)
EMA7 (C#MI7)
AMI7 D7
G9SUS G7
C
DMI9 G7
EMI7 D#O7
DMI7 G7 (F7)
EMI7(b5) A7
(DMI7 Bb9)
C#O7 DMI7(b5)
(C#7(#9))
EMI7 A9
DMI7 G13
C6
3

Fall

Medium Ballad
(with triplet undercurrent)
♩ = 82

Wayne Shorter
(As played by Miles Davis)

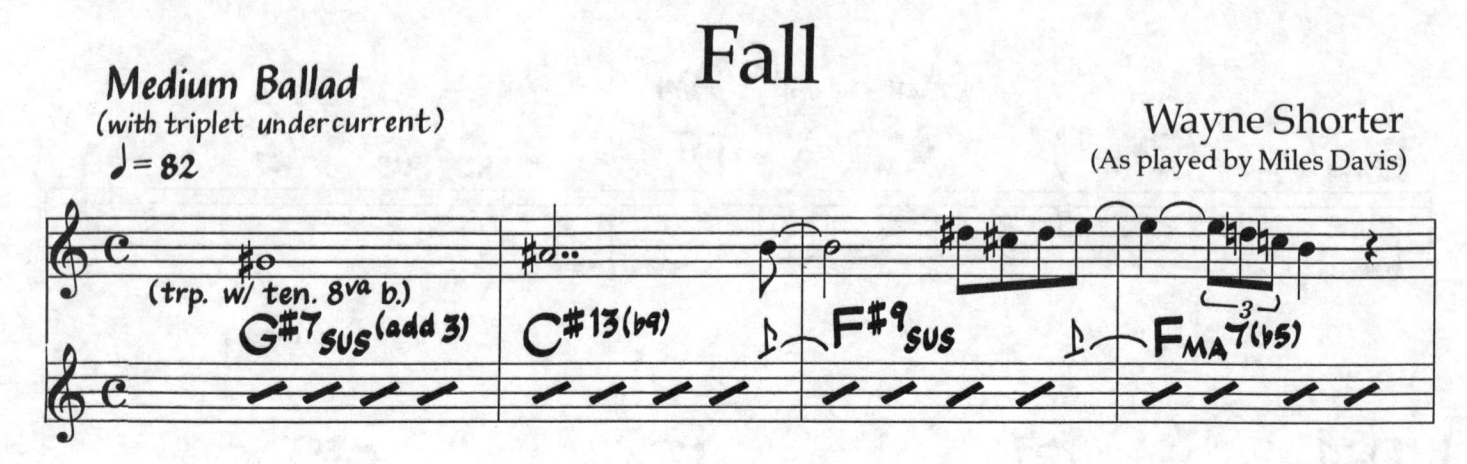

(trp. w/ ten. 8va b.)

According to the composer, the bass line is the melody. The treble line given here continues underneath solos.

©1968 Miyako Music. Used By Permission.

Farmer's Market

Music by Art Farmer
Lyric by Annie Ross

Med.-Up Swing

N.C. (Intro - optional)

(trp. w/ ten. 8va b.)

A G6 | Ami7 D7 | G6 |
Dmi7 G7 | Cma7 | Cmi7 F7 |
Bmi7 | E7(b9) | Ami7 |
D7(b9) | G6 | BbMA7 | EbMA7 Ab7 |

B G6 | Ami7 D7 | G6 |
Dmi7 G7 | Cma7 | Cmi7 F7 |
Bmi7 | E7(#5) | Ami7 Eb7 |
D7(#5) | G6 solo break — — — — — |

(fine)

Solos on G blues
After solos, D.S. al fine

©1952, renewed 1980 Raybird Music Inc. & Art Farmer Music. International Copyright Secured. Used By Permission.

Favela

Antonio Carlos Jobim

Med. Bossa Nova

G/A may be replaced by Emi7 throughout

©1965 Ipanema Music. Used By Permission.

Feel Like Makin' Love

Medium Latin/Rock ♩= 92

Eugene McDaniels
(As sung by Roberta Flack)

Gmi9 | C13sus | Fma7 Eb7 | Eb7 D7 | Gmi9 | C13sus | Fma7 | B7(b5) | Bbma7 | Ami7 | Gmi7 | Dmi7 | Bbma7 | Ami7 | Eb7 | Dmi7 | F7 F#7 G7 | drum fill

To end, sing first verse and fade.

©1973 Skyforest Music. Used By Permission.

Fire

Joe Henderson

Med. Latin ♩= 110

On cue, D.S., play head (A), continue to next solo, after last solo, D.S. al Coda

Vamp at letter B is long, vamp at letter C much shorter.
Melody may be doubled by other instruments.

©1974 Johen Music. Used By Permission.

First Light

Medium Latin
♩ = 154

Freddie Hubbard

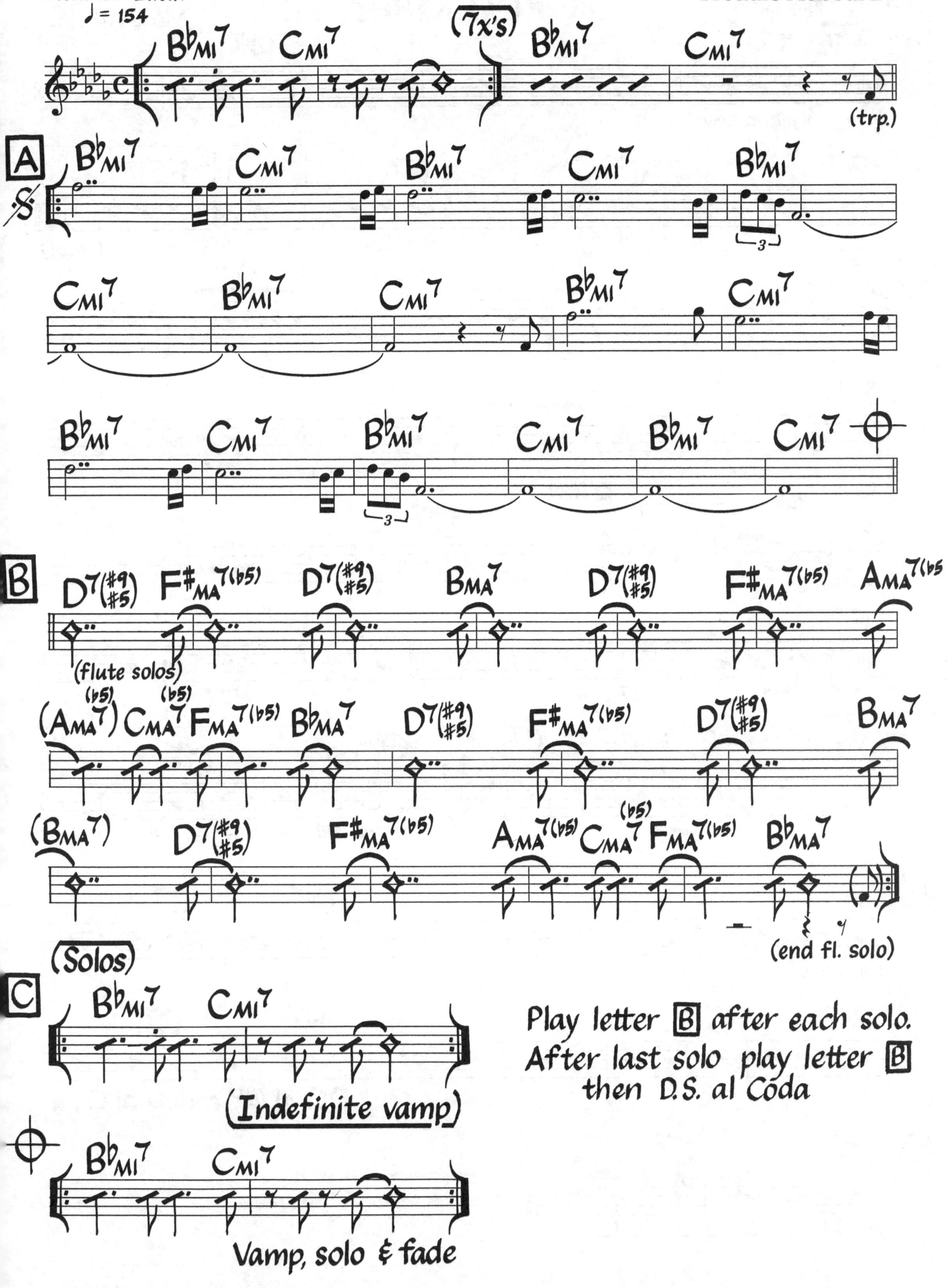

Foolkiller

Mose Allison

Melody varies with each verse.

©1961 Audre Mae Music. Used By Permission.

Footprints

Wayne Shorter

Upper line is melody. Harmony line is optional.

Four

Music by Miles Davis
Lyric by Jon Hendricks

Med. Swing
♩ = 178

©1963 Prestige Music. Used By Permission.

Solo on form (AB)
After solos, D.C. al Coda

Chords in parentheses are used for solos. Solos are straight ahead (no breaks or stop-time) except for solo break before each solo.

Four Brothers

Jimmy Giuffre
(As played by Woody Herman)

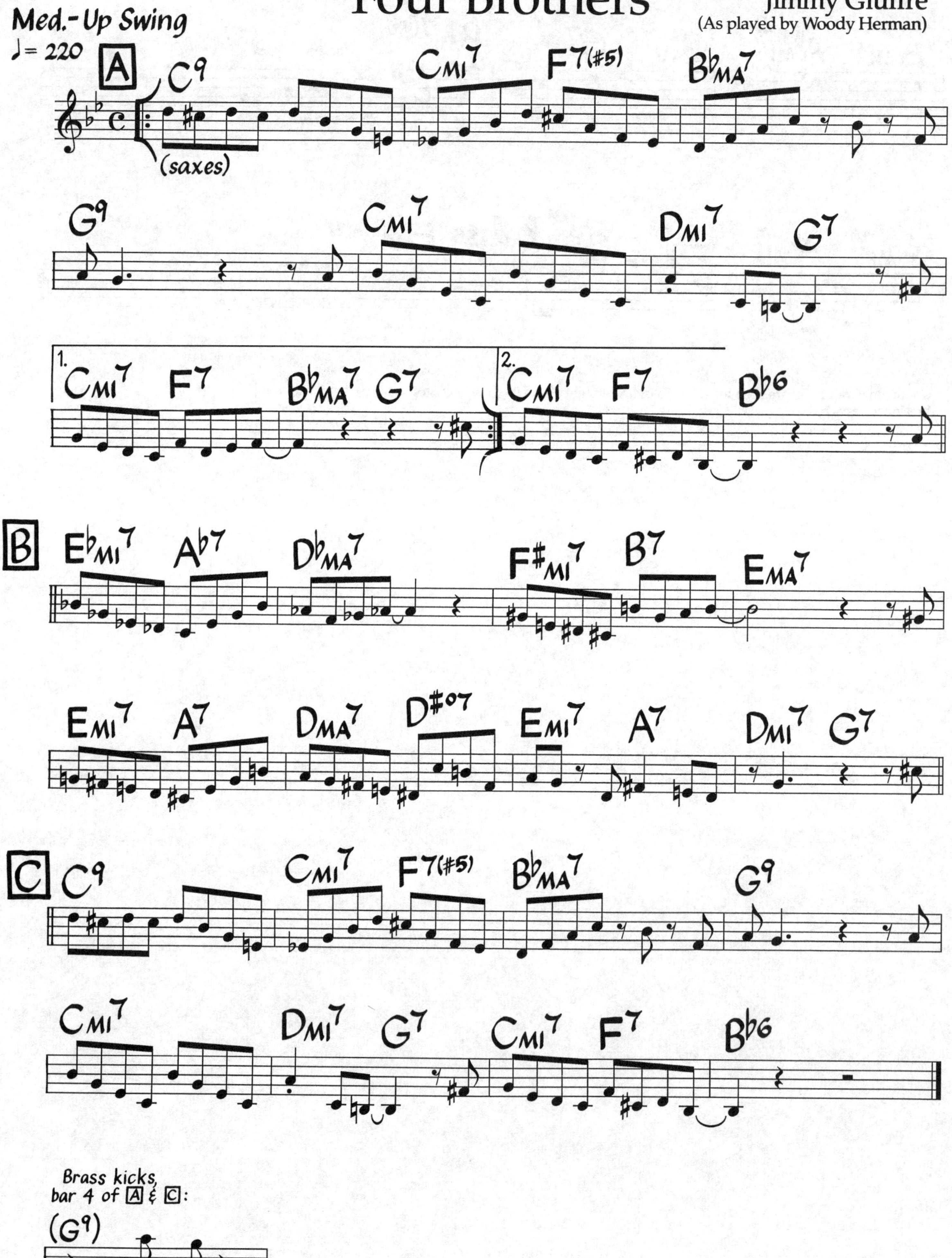

Four On Six

John L. "Wes" Montgomery

Medium-Up Swing ♩= 230

Friends And Strangers

William Jeffrey
(As played by Dave Grusin)

Med. Funk

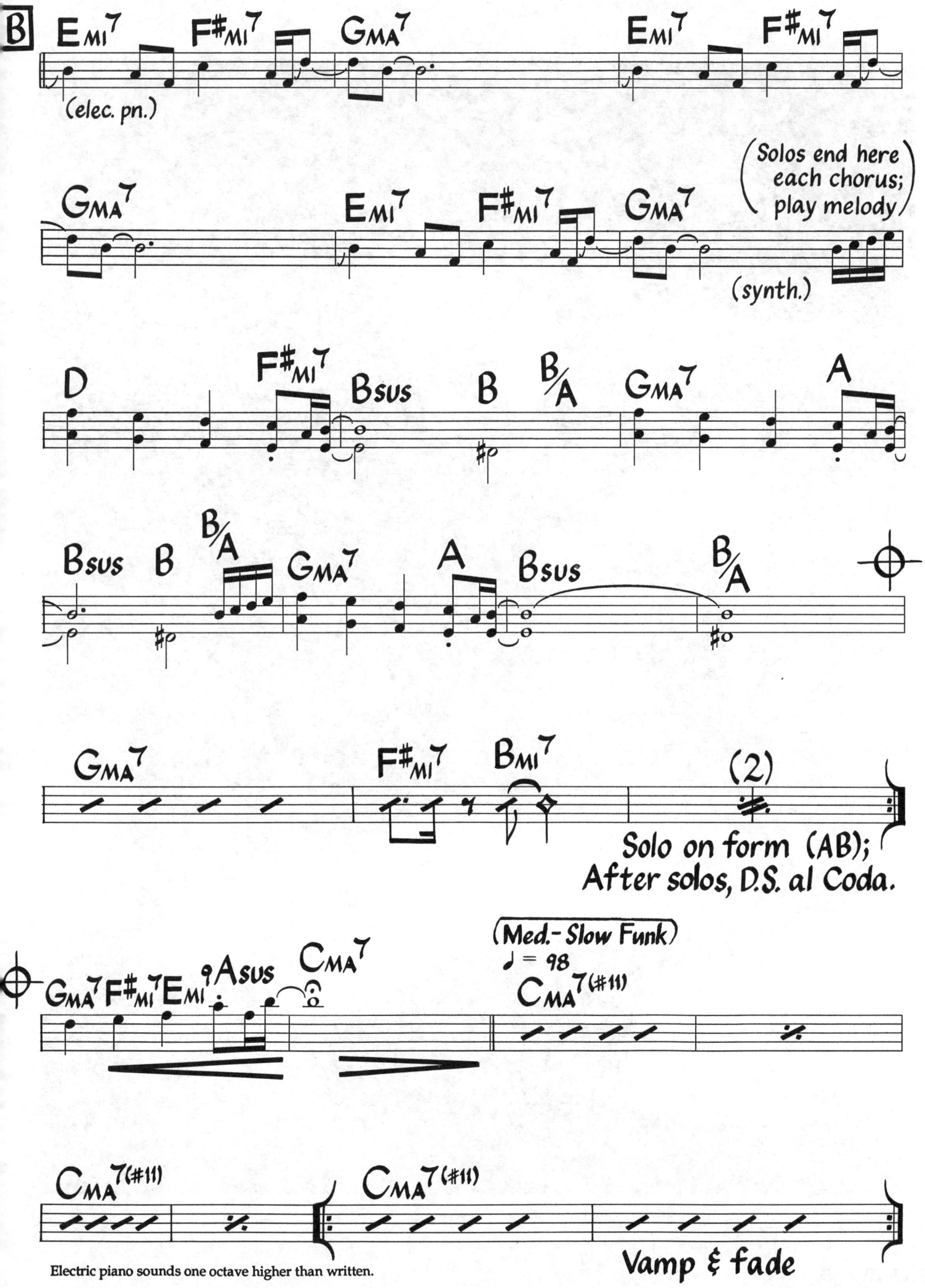

Electric piano sounds one octave higher than written.

BILL EVANS

Funkallero

Bill Evans

Med.-Up Swing ♩ = 213

Gaviota

Clare Fischer

Medium Latin (Bolero-Guajira) ♩= 112

1st solo on letter C (indef.)
2nd solo on ABC

After solos, play head (AB); vamp, solo & fade on letter C

These are only the top voices of the piano score.

LOUIS ARMSTRONG & CARMEN McCRAE

Gee Baby, Ain't I Good To You

Music by Don Redman
Lyric by Don Redman & Andy Razaf

Med.- Slow Swing (Bluesy)

Melody is freely interpreted, in a blues style.

©1929 Michael H. Goldsen, Inc. Renewed 1944 Michael H. Goldsen, Inc. Used By Permission.

Gemini

Bright Jazz Waltz ♩= 220 (Intro)

Jimmy Heath
(As played by Cannonball Adderley)

D.S. al solos; solo form is A (once) B (indef.). After solos, D.S. al Coda.

(Solo till cue)
play letter C before 2nd solo
and letter D before last solo;
D.S. before other solos.

Chords in parentheses are optional. Melody in bars 16-18 of letter D is slightly different than Cannonball's recorded version, at the composer's request.

Flute sounds one octave higher than written.

BILL EVANS

Gloria's Step

Scott LaFaro
(As played by Bill Evans)

Chords in parentheses are used for solos.

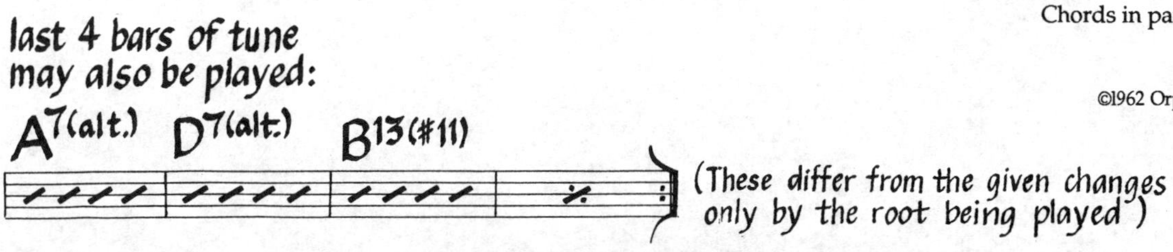

Goin' Home

Russ Ferrante
(As played by The Yellowjackets)

Med.-Slow Funk

(sample fill)
(D.S. (gtr. solo) al Coda)
(Synth. solo)
Till Cue
On Cue
(Vamp till cue)
((synth.; end solo))
C
8va (etc.)
(2nd x:)
(sample fill)
(Vamp & fill till cue)
On cue
rit.

JOHN ABERCROMBIE

Gone With The Wind

Music by Allie Wrubel
Lyric by Herb Magidson

Med. Swing

The Goodbye Look

Donald Fagen

Med. Caribbean Feel
♩=106

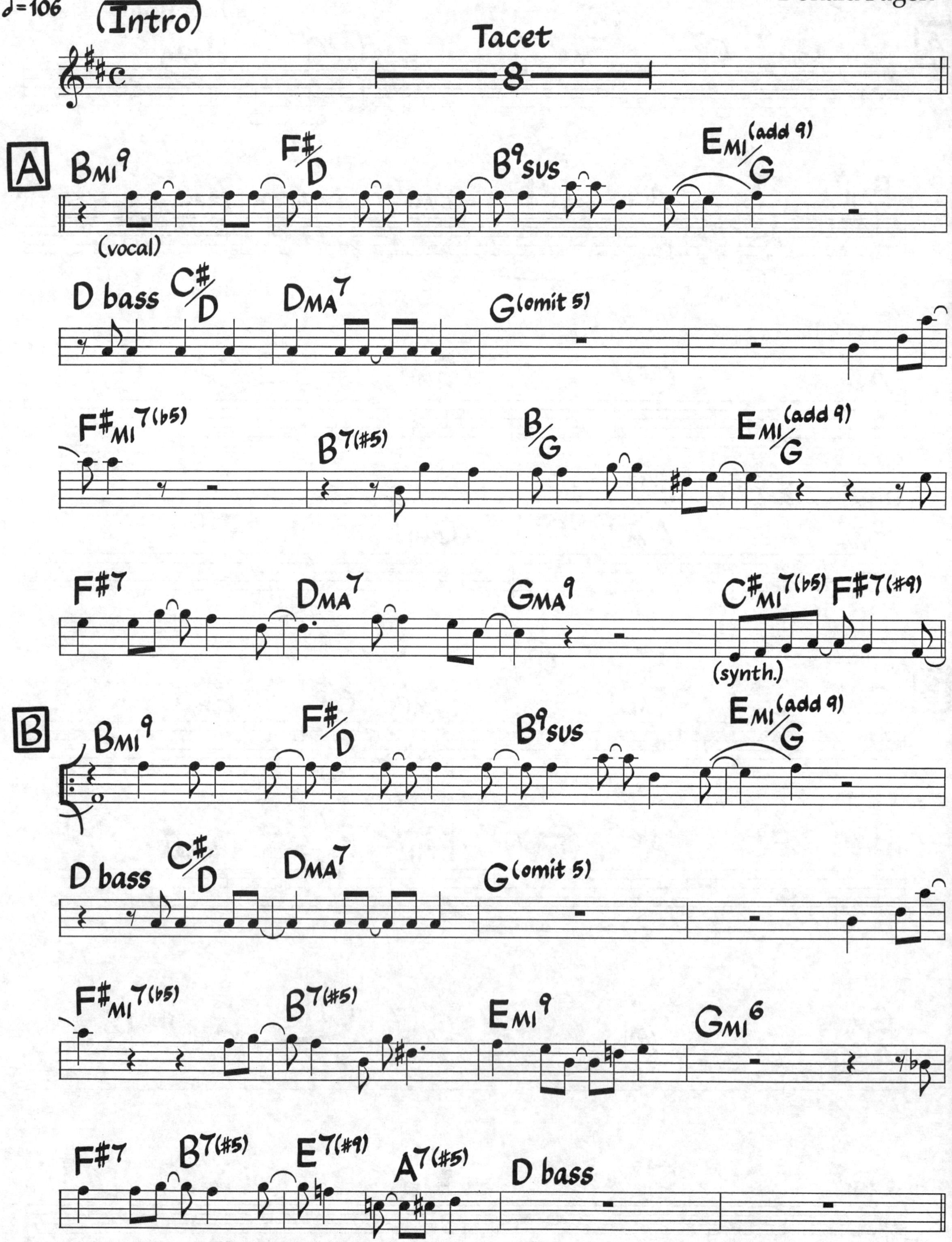

(Continued on next page)

V.S.

E
D bass
(synth.; gtr. doubles top line)
GMA7/A
gtr. fill
D bass
B(add 9)
EMI9
GMI6/9
(gtr. solo)
1.
F#MI7
FMI7
Bb7
EbMA7
AbMA7
DMA7
2.
F#7
B7(#5)
E7
A7(#5)
D bass
(end solo)
F
G
DMA7
(vocal)
G
DMA7
C#7(#9/#5)
F#MI7
B7(#5)
EMI7
A13
GMA7
F#7(#9)
G
BMI9
F#/D
B9SUS
EMI(add 9)/G
D bass
C#/D
DMA7
G(omit 5)
F#MI7(b5)
B7(#5)
EMI9
GMI6

F#7
B7(#5)
E7(#9)
A7(#5)
D bass
H
GMA9
C#7(#9 #5)
CMA7(add 13)
B7(#5)
EMI11
A9SUS
F#MI7(b5)
B7
EMI7(add 11)
C#7(#9 #5)
F#7(#9)
F#MI7(b5)
B7
GMA7
C#7(#5)
CMA7(add 13)
B7(#5)
3
(gtr.)
EMI7(add 11)
A9SUS
BMI9
AMA9
GMA9
D13
GMA9
GMI(MA 7)
(elec. pn.– top note of voicing)
(Synth. solo)
(D)
BMI A
(D)
BMI A
Vamp, solo & fade

Guarujá

Randy Brecker

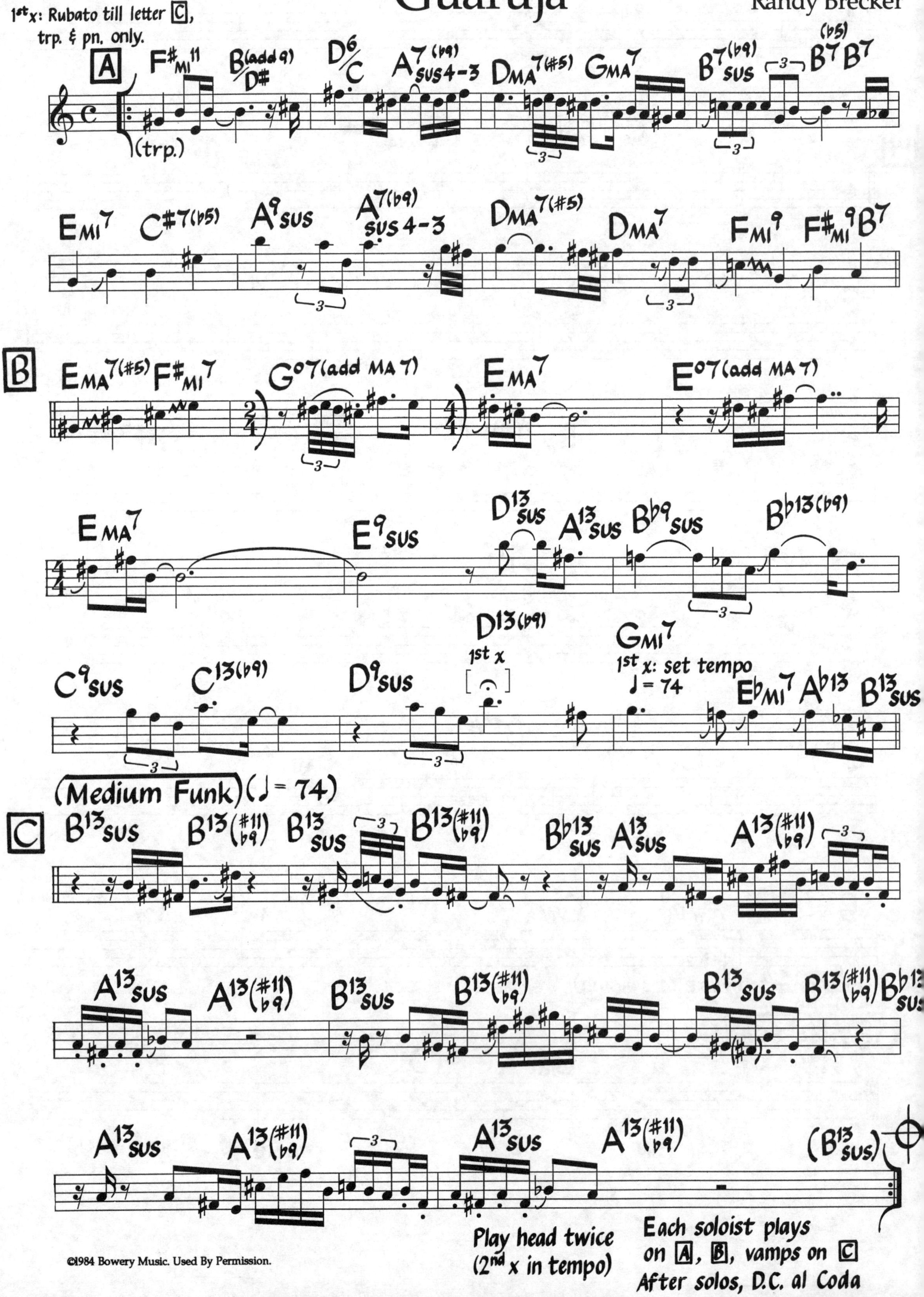

Vamp & Solo till cue

Kicks hold for solos. Letters A & B are more subdued, letter C is funkier.

Hallucinations

Bud Powell

Bright Bebop

(Solos)
E
(C#MI7(b5))
G6 C7 B7 E7 A7 D7 G6 G7
C7 C#o7 G7/D E7 AMI7 D7
1. G6 D7
2. G6 (F7)
F
EMI7 A7 DMI7 G7 CMI7 F7 BMI7 E7
AMI E7/B C6 D7 G6 E7 AMI7 D7
G
(C#MI7(b5))
G6 C7 B7 E7 A7 D7 G6 G7
C7 C#o7 G7/D E7 AMI7 D7 G6 D7
Solo on EEFG; after solos, D.C. al Coda.
G6 G7 C7 C#o7 G7/D E7(b5) A7SUS A7 (D7(b9)) Ab7(#9) GMA9
Melody may be played one octave lower.
alternate letter D:
C#MI7(b5) F#7 BMI7(b5) E7 AMI7 D7 G6
solo break

DUKE ELLINGTON

Photo by Jim Marshall ©1988

Haunted Ballroom

Music by Victor Feldman
Lyric by Milo Adamo

Med. Swing (in 2)
♩ = 131

Solos in 4. Changes on 1 & 3 (not anticipated).

©1977 Good Vibes Music & Hampstead Heath Music. Used By Permission.

Havona

Bright Funk/Samba

Jaco Pastorius
(As played by Weather Report)

Here's That Rainy Day

Med. Ballad

Music by Jimmy Van Heusen
Lyric by Johnny Burke

A

| Ama7 | C7 | Fma7 | Bbma7 |

| Bmi7(add 11) | E7 | Ama7 | Emi7 A7(b9) |

| Dmi7 | (Dmi7 G#9 G7) G7 | Cma7 | (F#9) Fma7 |

| Bmi7 | (Bmi7 F9 E7) E7 | Ama7 F#mi7 | Bmi7 E7 |

B

| Ama7 | C7 | Fma7 | Bbma7 |

| Bmi7(add 11) | E7 | (Bbmi7 Eb7) Ama7 | Emi7 A7 |

| Dma7 | Bmi7 E13/D (D13) | C#mi7 F#mi7 | B13 (C°7) |

| Bmi7(add 11) | E7 | A6 | (F#mi7 Bmi7 E7) |

©1949, 1953 by Burke & Van Heusen, Inc., assigned to Bourne Co. and Dorsey Bros. (Music Sales Corp.). Copyright renewed. International Copyright Secured. All Rights Reserved. Used By Permission. Rights for Japan assigned to Chappell/Intersong K.K. Used by permission of JASRAC License #8670719.

Hideaway

Dave Sanborn

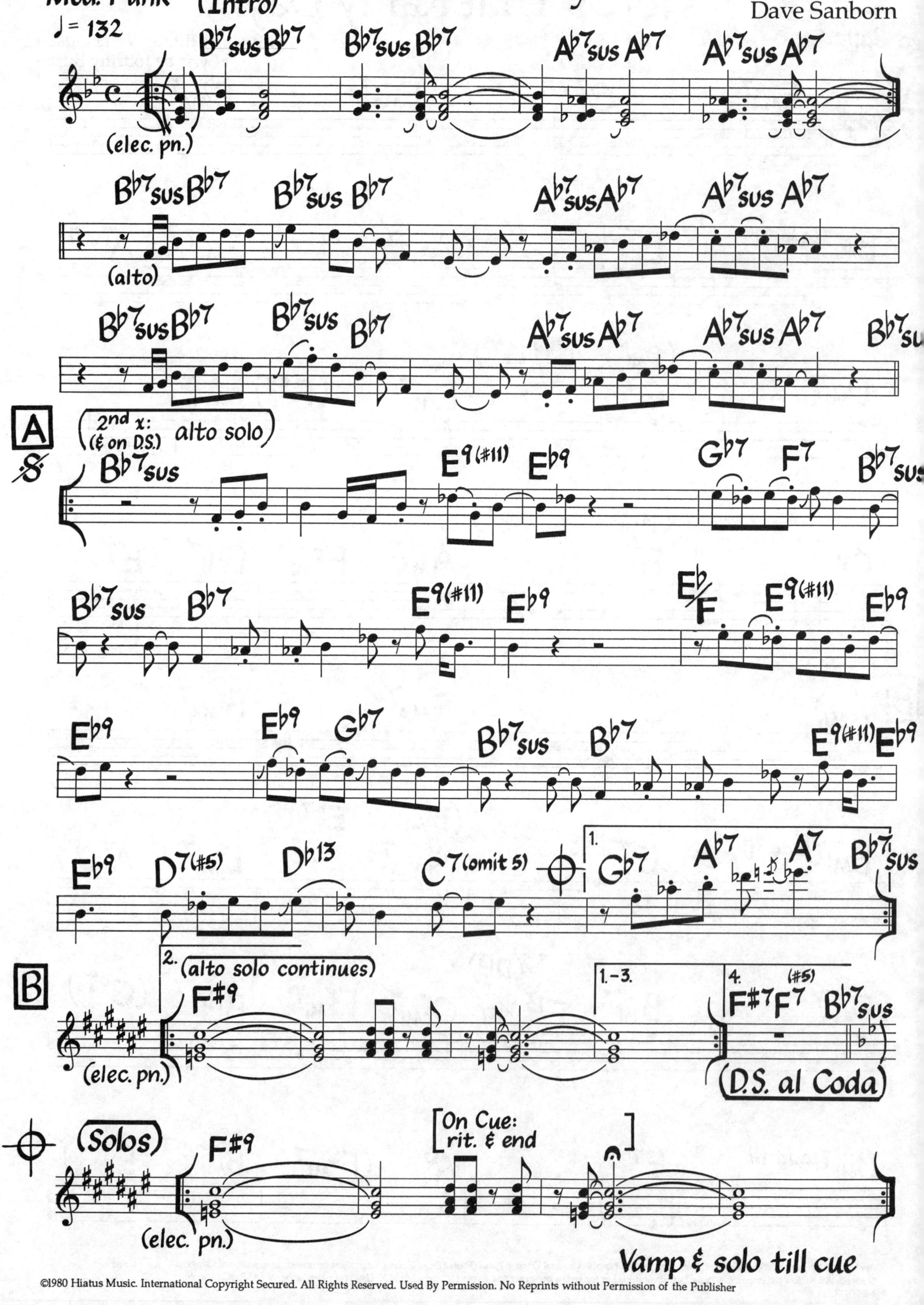

I Love Lucy

Eliot Daniel
(As played by Richie Cole)

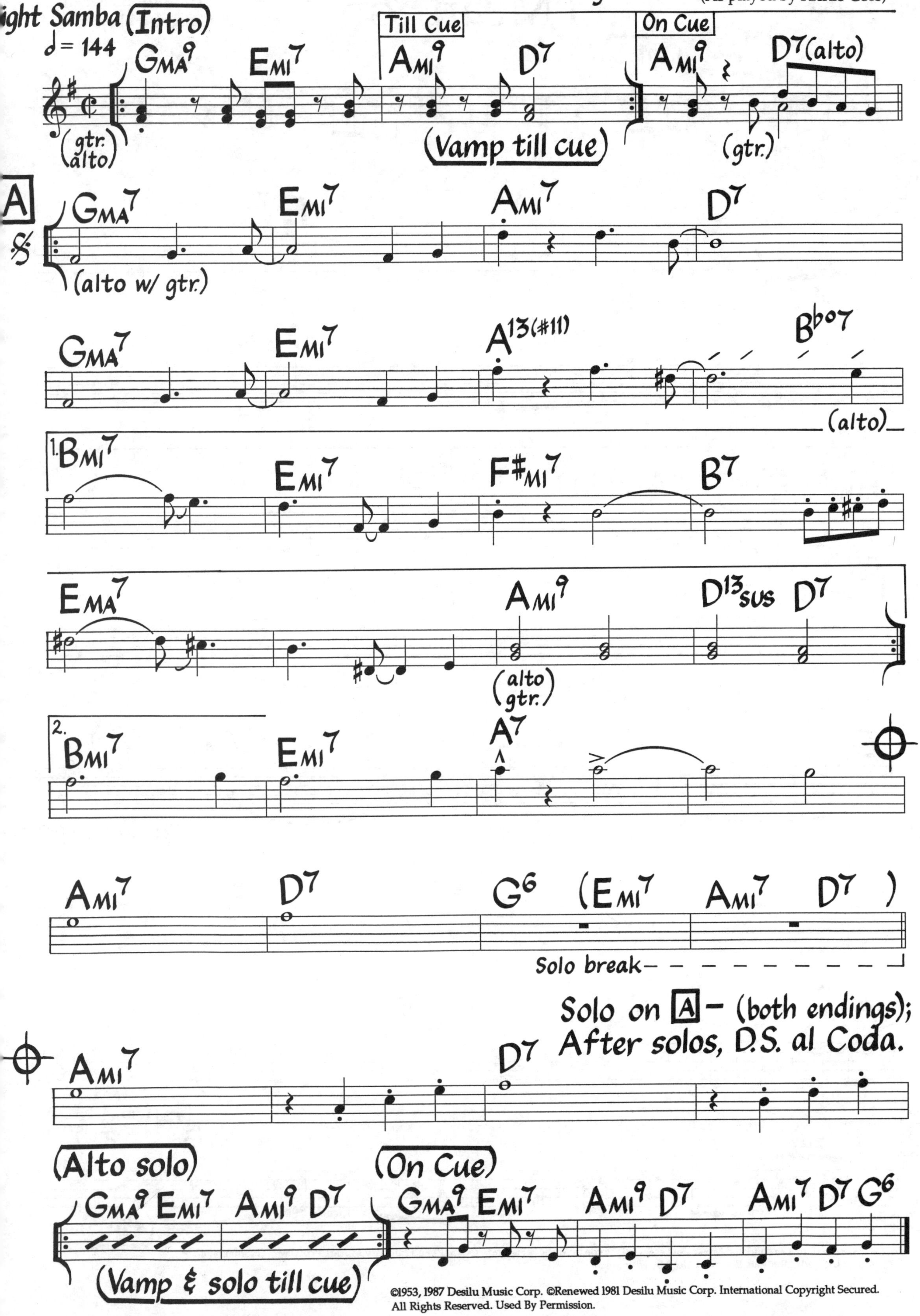

Med. Swing

I Mean You

Thelonious Monk
Coleman Hawkins

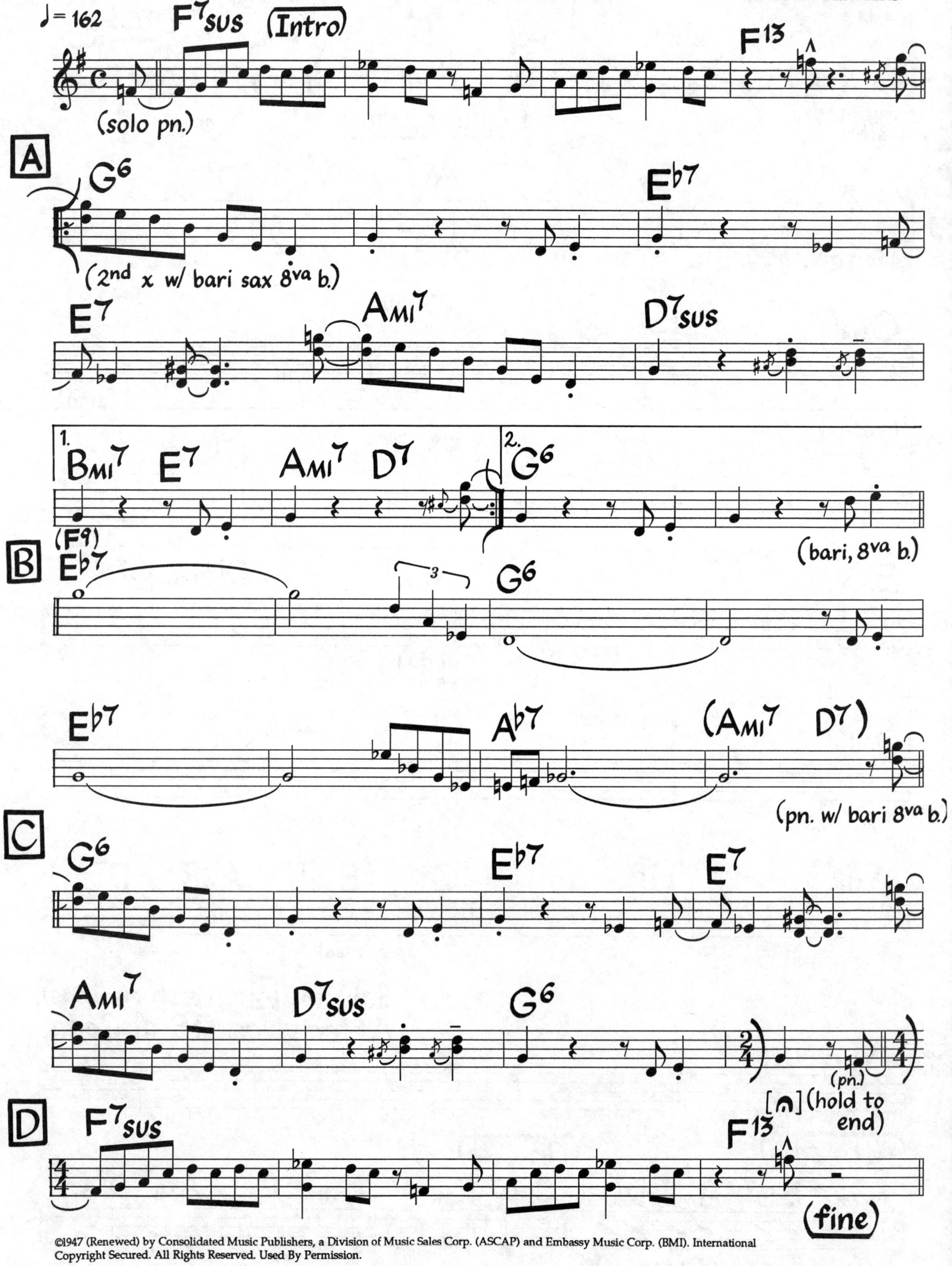

128

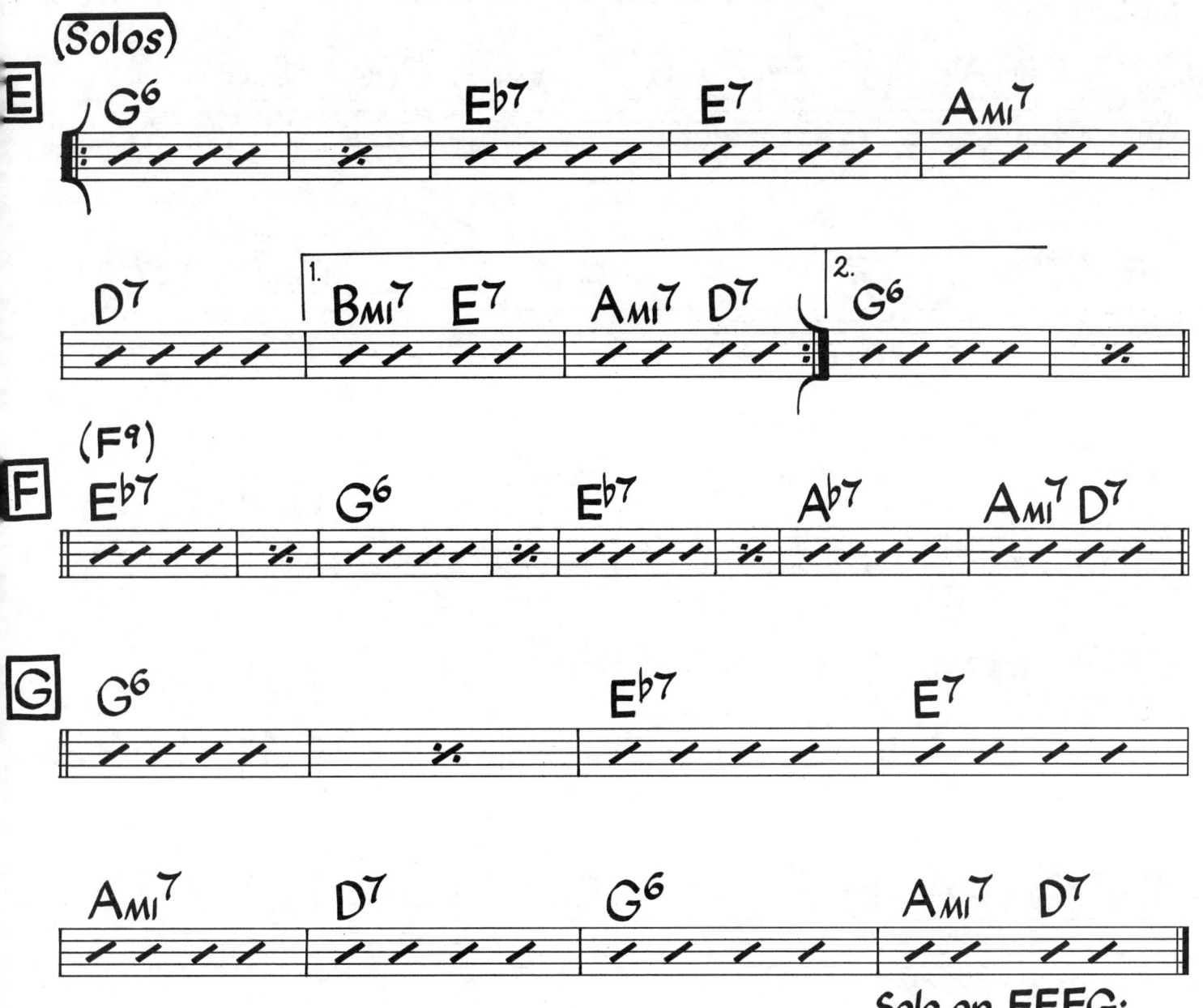

E (Solos)

| G6 | Eb7 | E7 | Ami7 |

| D7 | 1. Bmi7 E7 | Ami7 D7 | 2. G6 | |

F (F9)

| Eb7 | G6 | Eb7 | Ab7 | Ami7 D7 |

G

| G6 | | Eb7 | E7 |

| Ami7 | D7 | G6 | Ami7 D7 |

Solo on EEFG;
After solos, D.C. al fine.

I Should Care

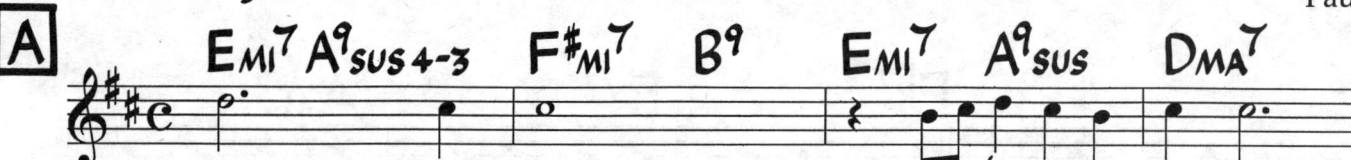

Sammy Cahn
Axel Stordahl
Paul Weston

Med. Swing *

A | Emi7 A9sus 4-3 | F#mi7 B9 | Emi7 A9sus | Dma7 |
F#mi7(b5)	B7	Emi7 Gmi7	C9
Dma7	C#mi7(b5) F#7	Ami7 D7	Gma7
C#mi7(b5) F#7(b9) Bmi7	Bmi7 E9	Emi7 A9

B | Emi7 A9sus 4-3 | F#mi7 B9 | Emi7 A9sus | Dma7 |
F#mi7(b5)	B7	Emi7 Gmi7	C9
Dma7	C#mi7(b5) F#7	Bmi	(E7 F°7) E7
Emi7	A7	D6	(G7 F#mi7 B7)

*also played as a ballad

Alternate changes for first four bars of letters A & B:
| G#7(#11/#9) C#13(b9) | F#7(#9) B13 | E7(#9) A13 | Dma7 G13(#11) |

I Thought About You

Med. Ballad

Music by Jimmy Van Heusen
Lyric by Johnny Mercer

If I Were A Bell

Med. Swing

Frank Loesser
(As played by Miles Davis)

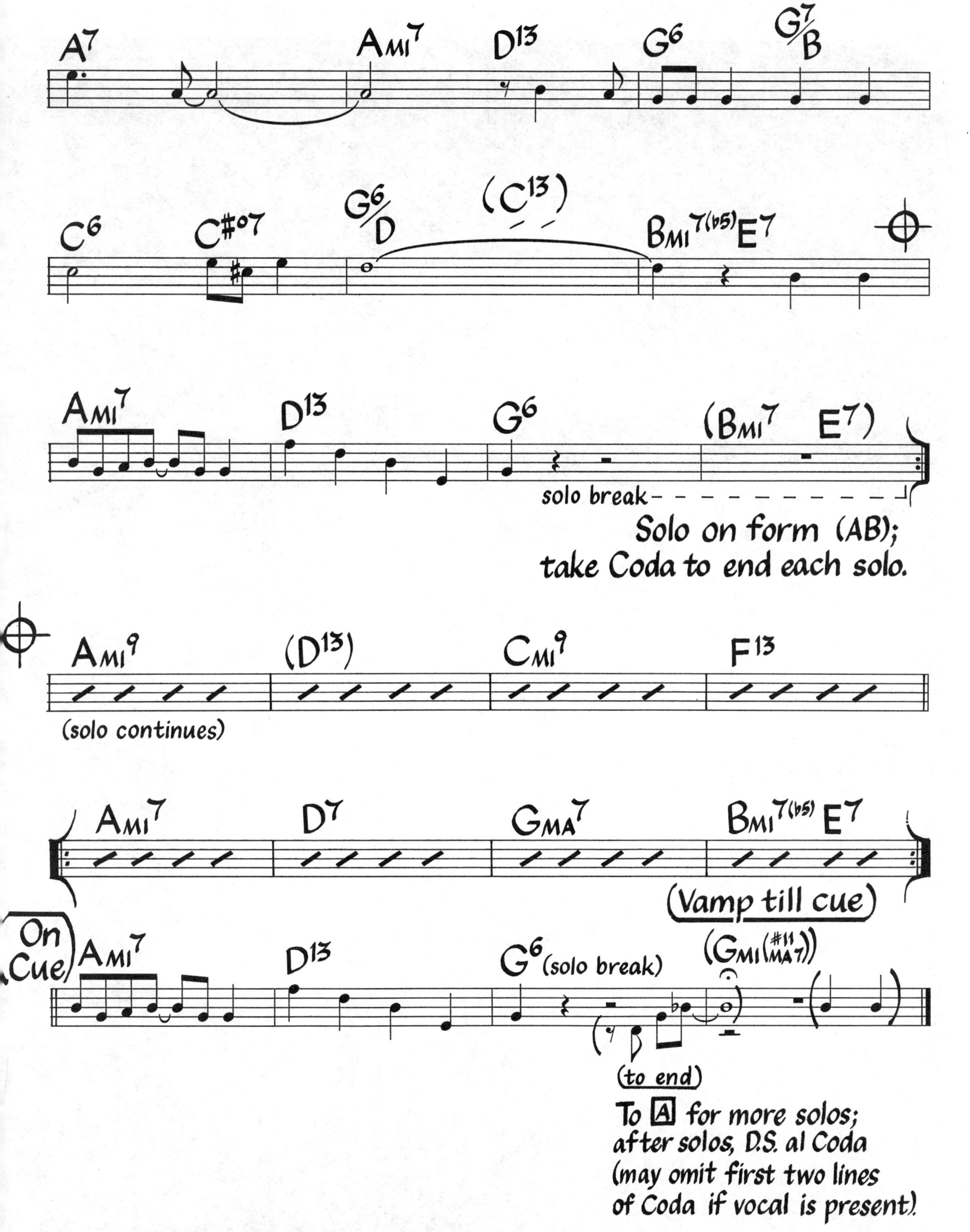

Bass walks in 4 for solos (no kicks or breaks). Original melody has been slightly altered to conform to common practice.
Last line of Coda is played by each soloist to cue end of vamp.

ANTONIO CARLOS JOBIM

If You Never Come To Me

Med.-Slow Bossa Nova

Music by Antonio Carlos Jobim
English Lyric by Ray Gilbert

I'll Take Romance

Bright Jazz Waltz

Music by Ben Oakland
Lyric by Oscar Hammerstein II

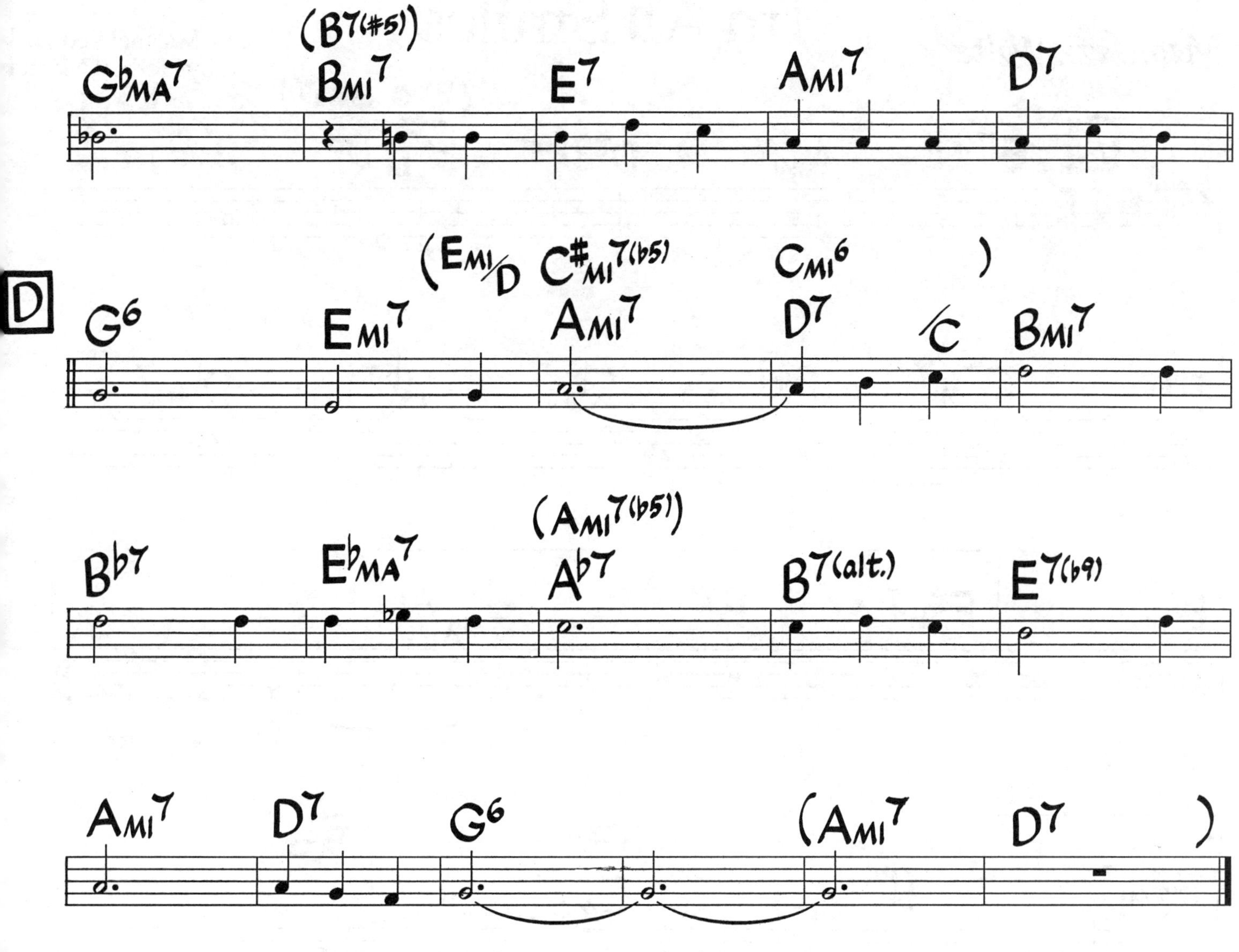
(B7(#5))
G♭MA7 BMI7 E7 AMI7 D7
D
(EMI/D C#MI7(♭5) CMI6)
G6 EMI7 AMI7 D7 /C BMI7
(AMI7(♭5))
B♭7 E♭MA7 A♭7 B7(alt.) E7(♭9)
AMI7 D7 G6 (AMI7 D7)

I'm All Smiles

Med. Jazz Waltz

Music by Michael Leonard
Lyric by Herbert Martin

C
(F#/G GMA7)
E7(#9) AMI7 D#7(#9) C#6/D D6 BMI7
E9 C#MI7 F#9 EbMI7 Ab9
DbMA7 BbMI7 F#MI7 B7 EMA7
E7 Ab/A AMA7 F#7/A# B7 B7/A
G#MI7 C#MI7 F#MI7 B9SUS B7/A G#7
3
C#MI7 F#MI7 B9SUS B7 E6

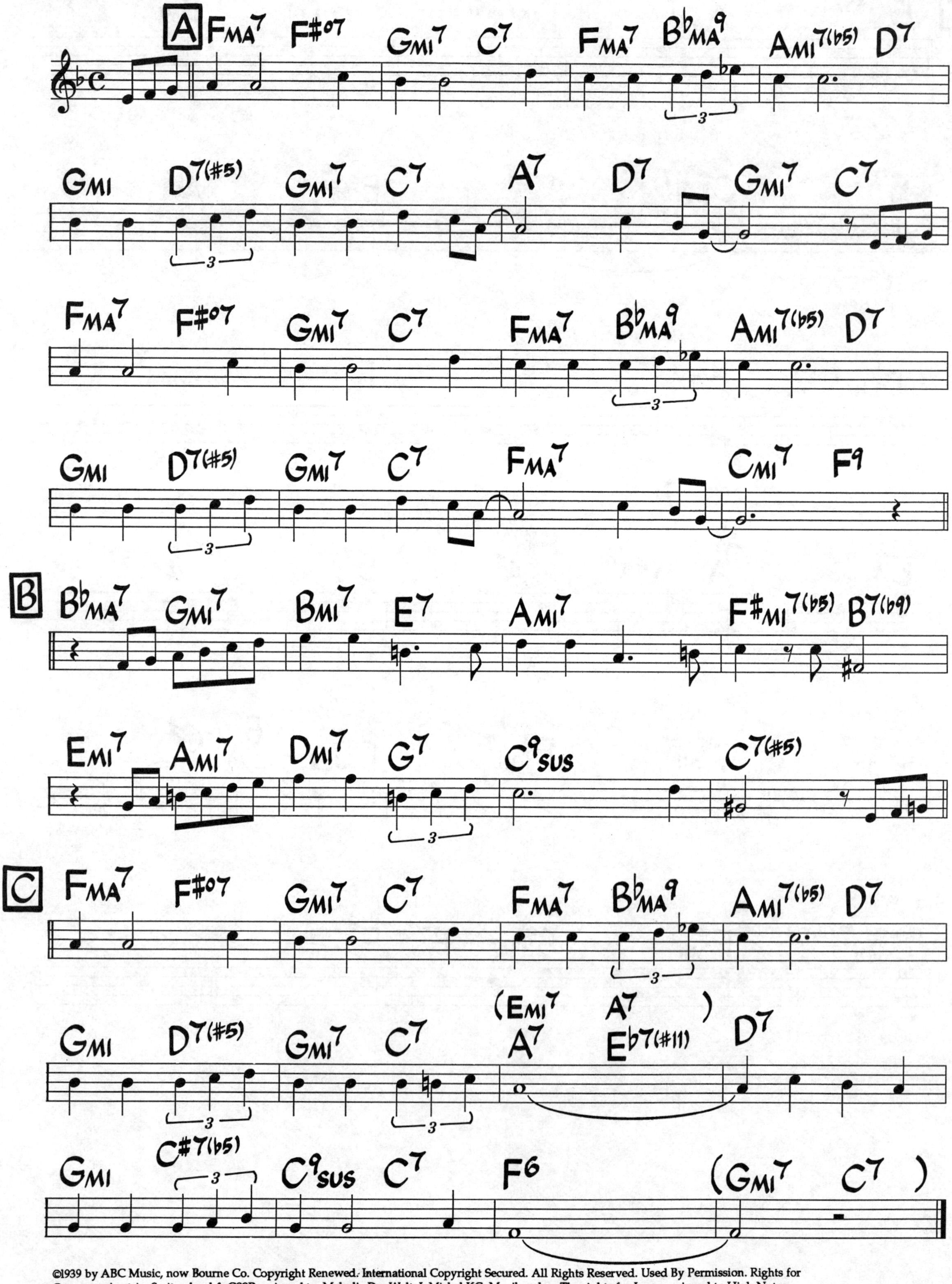

In Walked Bud

Med. Swing — Thelonious Monk

Tenor plays the B natural in bar 6 of letters A and C.

Alternate countermelody, bars 3 & 4 and 7 & 8 of letter B:

©1948 (Renewed) by Embassy Music Corp. (BMI). International Copyright Secured. All Rights Reserved. Used By Permission.

The Island

Music by Ivan Lins
& Vitor Martins
English Lyric by
Alan & Marilyn Bergman
(As sung by Mark Murphy)

Med. Latin

Melodic rhythm is freely interpreted. Tune starts quietly and grows slowly louder throughout.

Med-Slow
Funk/Latin

It Happens Every Day

Joe Sample
(As played by The Crusaders)

Melody may be doubled by piano and guitar. Intro is from Hubert Laws' "Say It With Silence."

TEDDY WILSON, JO JONES & LESTER YOUNG (At recording session playback)

Jersey Bounce

Bobby Plater
Tiny Bradshaw
Edward Johnson
(As played by Benny Goodman)

Med. Bounce
(Swing)

Joshua

Victor Feldman
(As played by Miles Davis)

Tenor plays lower line of all two part writing.

EMI9 DMI9 CMI9 DMI9 EMI9
(Solos)
D
EMI7
8
EMI7 DMI7 CMI7 DMI7 EMI7
1.
2.
AMI7 D7
E
GMA7 GMI7 C7(#9 #5) FMA7 FMI7 Bb7(#9 #5)
EbMA7 A7(#9 #5) DMI7 CMI7 F#7(#9 #5) B7(#9 #5)
(3x's)
F
EMI7
8
EMI7 DMI7 CMI7 DMI7 EMI7
Solo on DDEEEF
After solos, D.S. al Coda
EMI11 AMI7 (CMI7 Eb/A F9) Eb/A (add 9 b5) EMI11
(ten. loco)
EMI11
(6)
mp
(bass only)

Keep That Same Old Feeling

Wayne Henderson
(As played by The Crusaders)

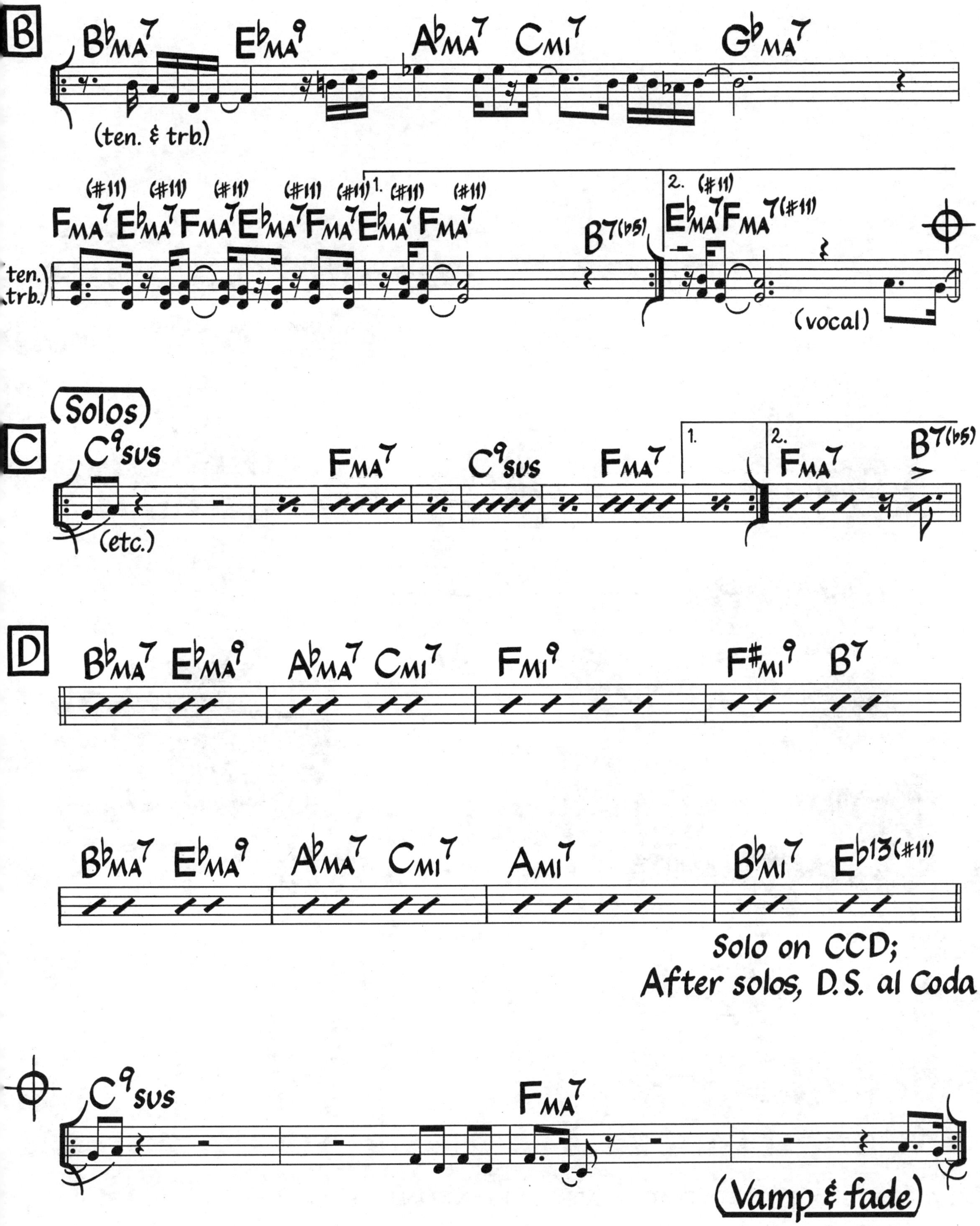

Horns may play riff from letter A during Coda.

SARAH VAUGHN, ROBERTA FLACK & ARETHA FRANKLIN

Killing Me Softly With His Song

Med. Rock/Latin Ballad
♩ = 118

Music by Charles Fox
Lyric by Norman Gimbel
(As sung by Roberta Flack)

(Intro) Tacet — 8 bars

A: | Cmi7 | F9 | Bb | Ebma7 | Cmi7 | F9 | Gmi | Cmi7 | F7 | Bb | D7 |

B: | Gmi | Cmi7 | F | Bb (Eb/Bb Bb(omit 3) F7) | Gmi | C/E | F | Eb | Bb | Eb | Abma7 | G |

(fine)

©1972 Fox-Gimble Productions, Inc. Used By Permission.

La Samba

Medium-Slow Samba
♩ = 90

Ray Obiedo
(As played by Andy Narell)

Esus chords imply Dorian mode for soloing

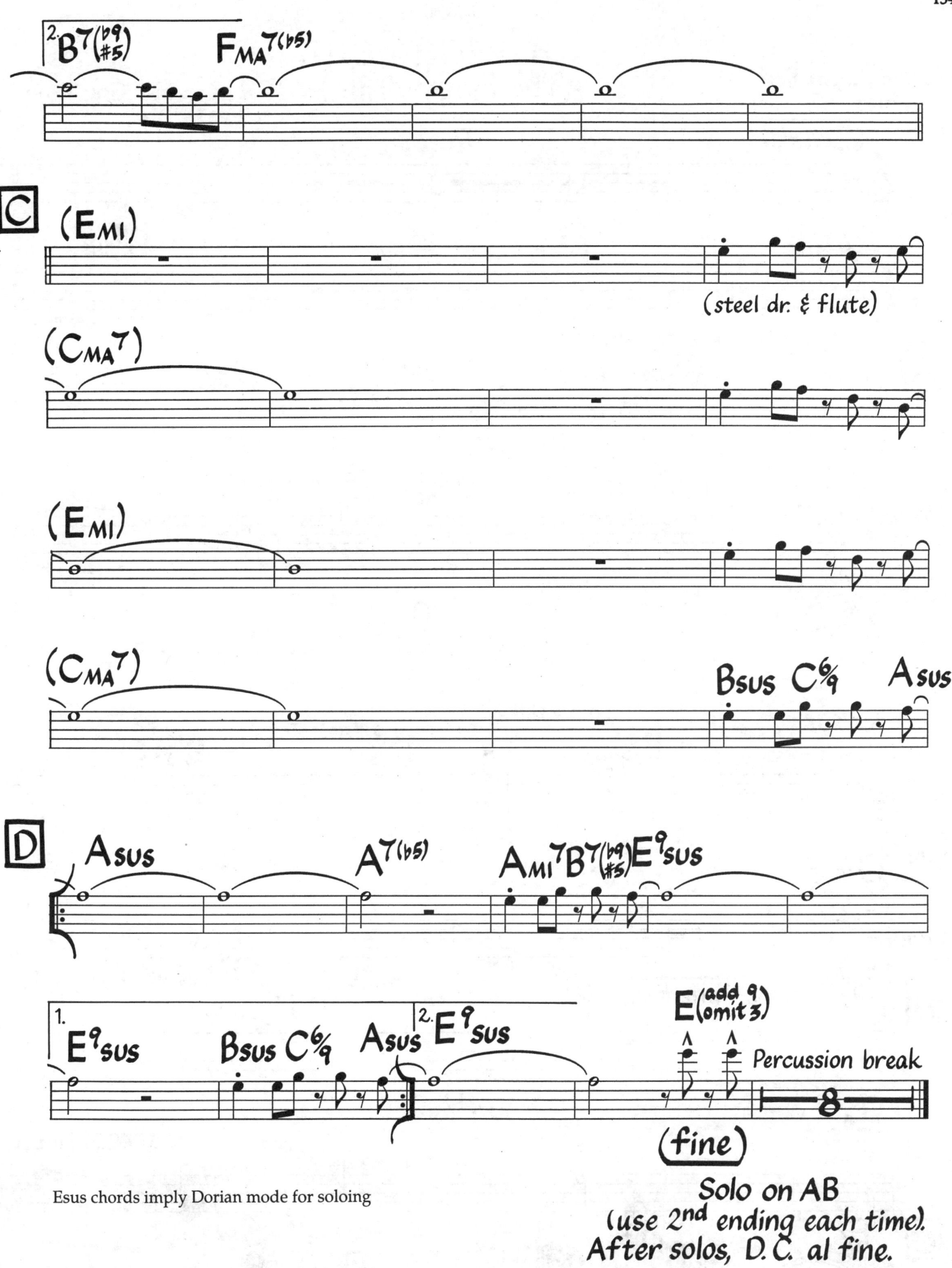

Solo on AB
(use 2nd ending each time).
After solos, D.C. al fine.

La Vida Feliz
(The Happy Life)

McCoy Tyner

Medium Latin/Rock
♩=162

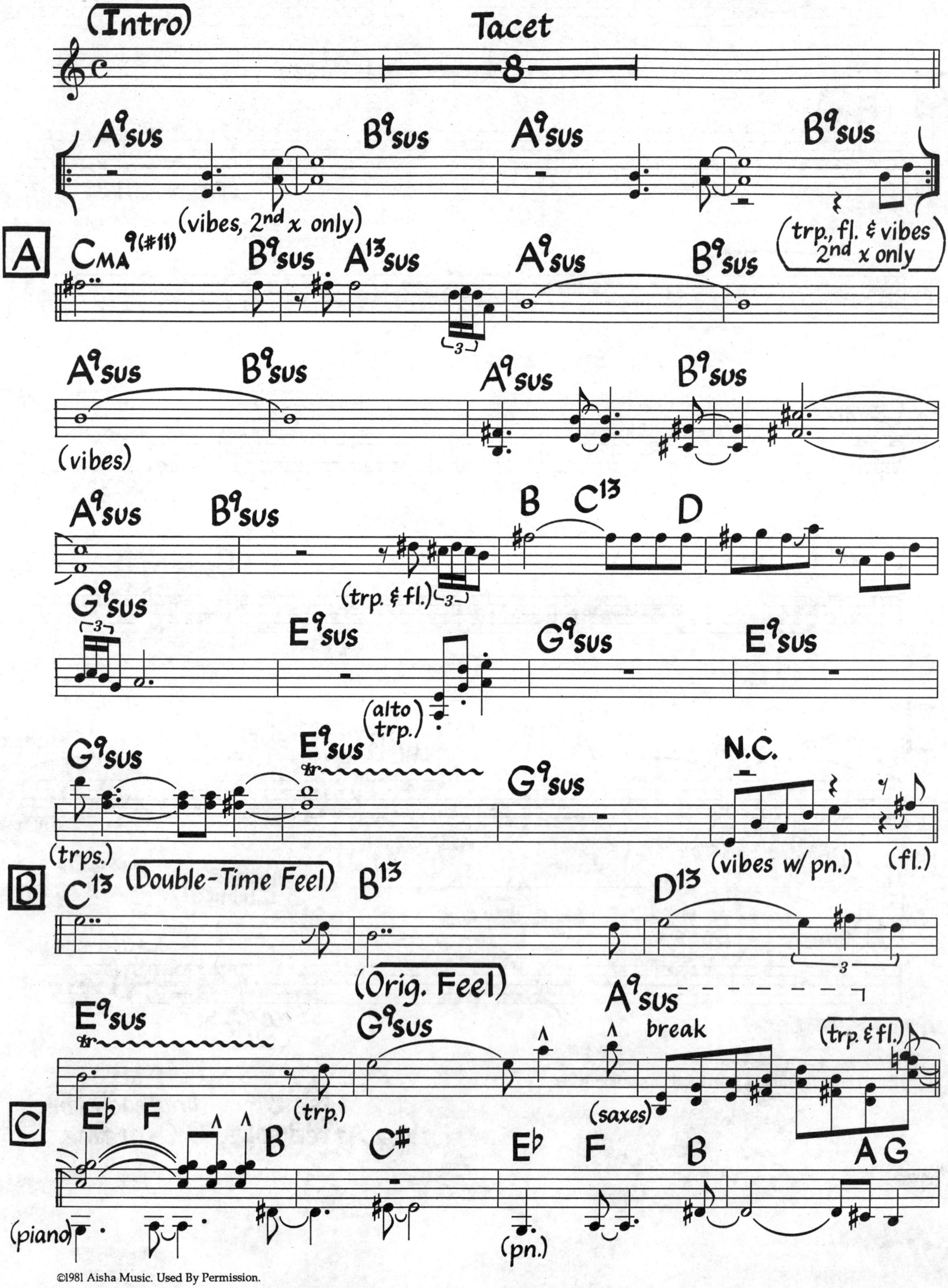

156

Lady Bird

Tadd Dameron
(As played by Miles Davis)

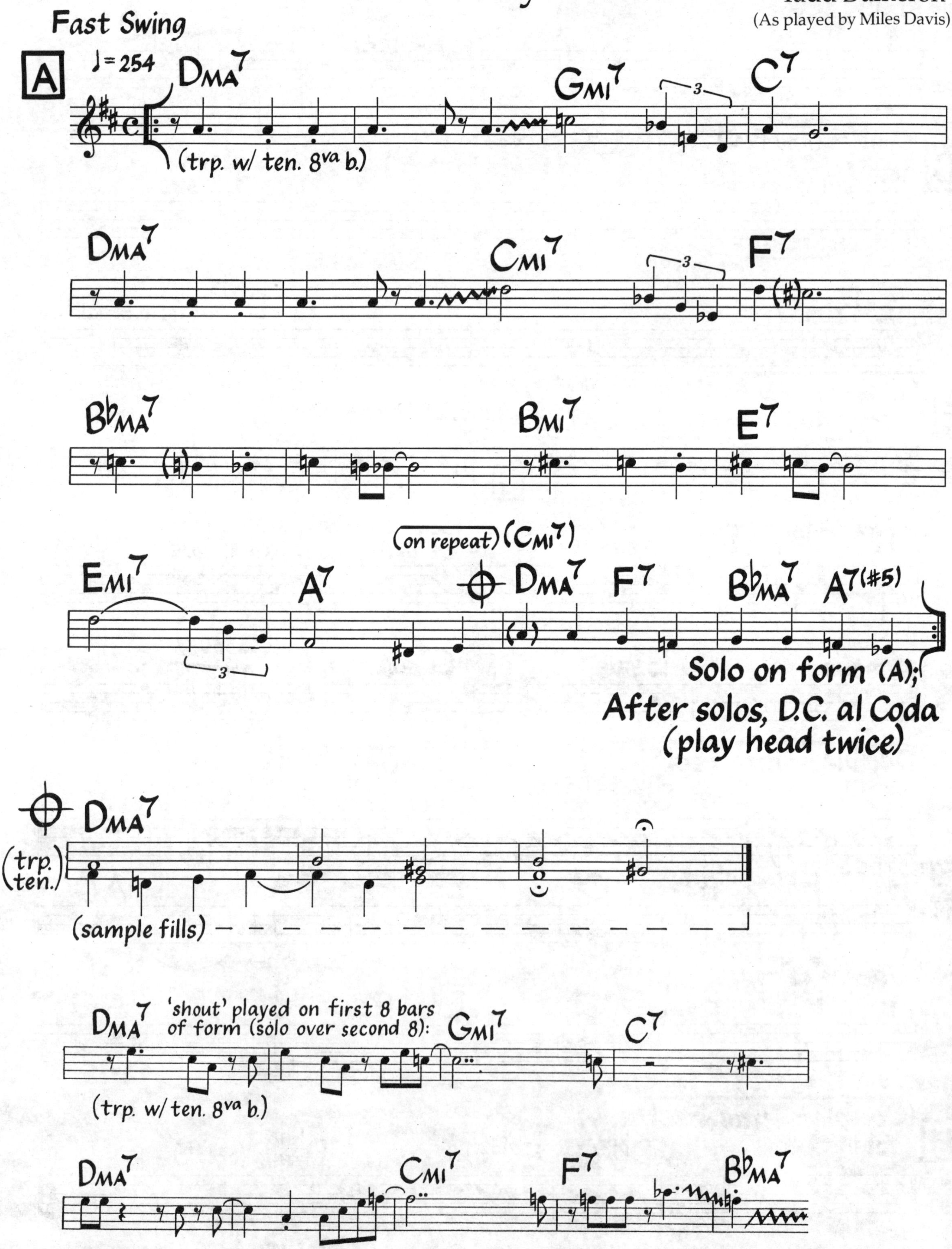

Lady Bird (Alternate Version)

Med.-Up Swing
♩= 174
(Intro)

(As played by Fats Navarro & Tadd Dameron)

Use chords in parentheses for solos; no kicks during solos.

Last First

Gary Peacock

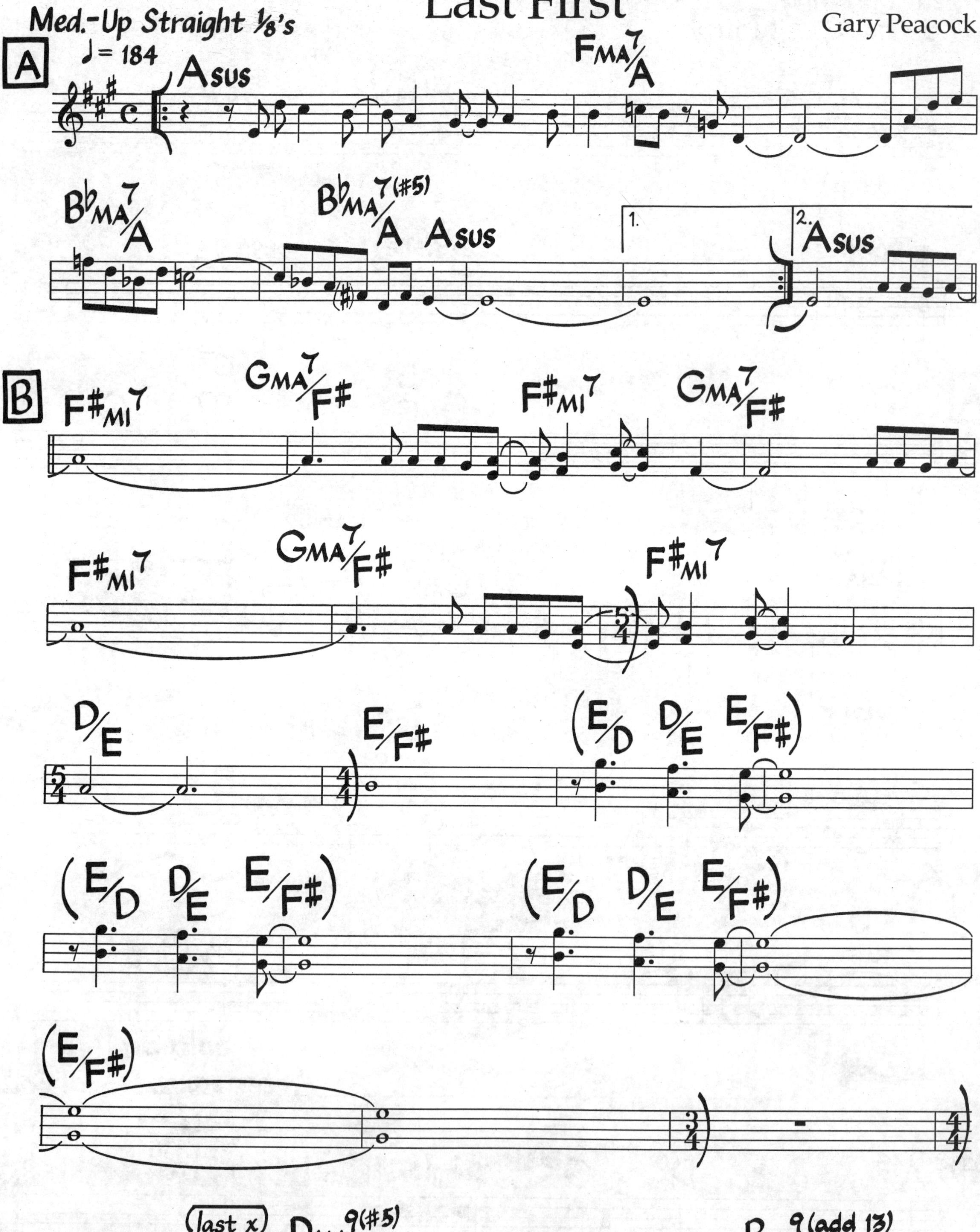

160

Solo on CCD; continue to E to end each solo.

Return to C for more solos; after solos, D.C. al fine.

Use A Major scale on Asus chords for solos.

Last Train From Overbrook

James Moody

Chords in parentheses are used for solos.

Laurie

Bill Evans

Medium
Funk Ballad
♩= 77

Let Me Be The One

Angela Bofill
Rick Suchow
Alan Palanker

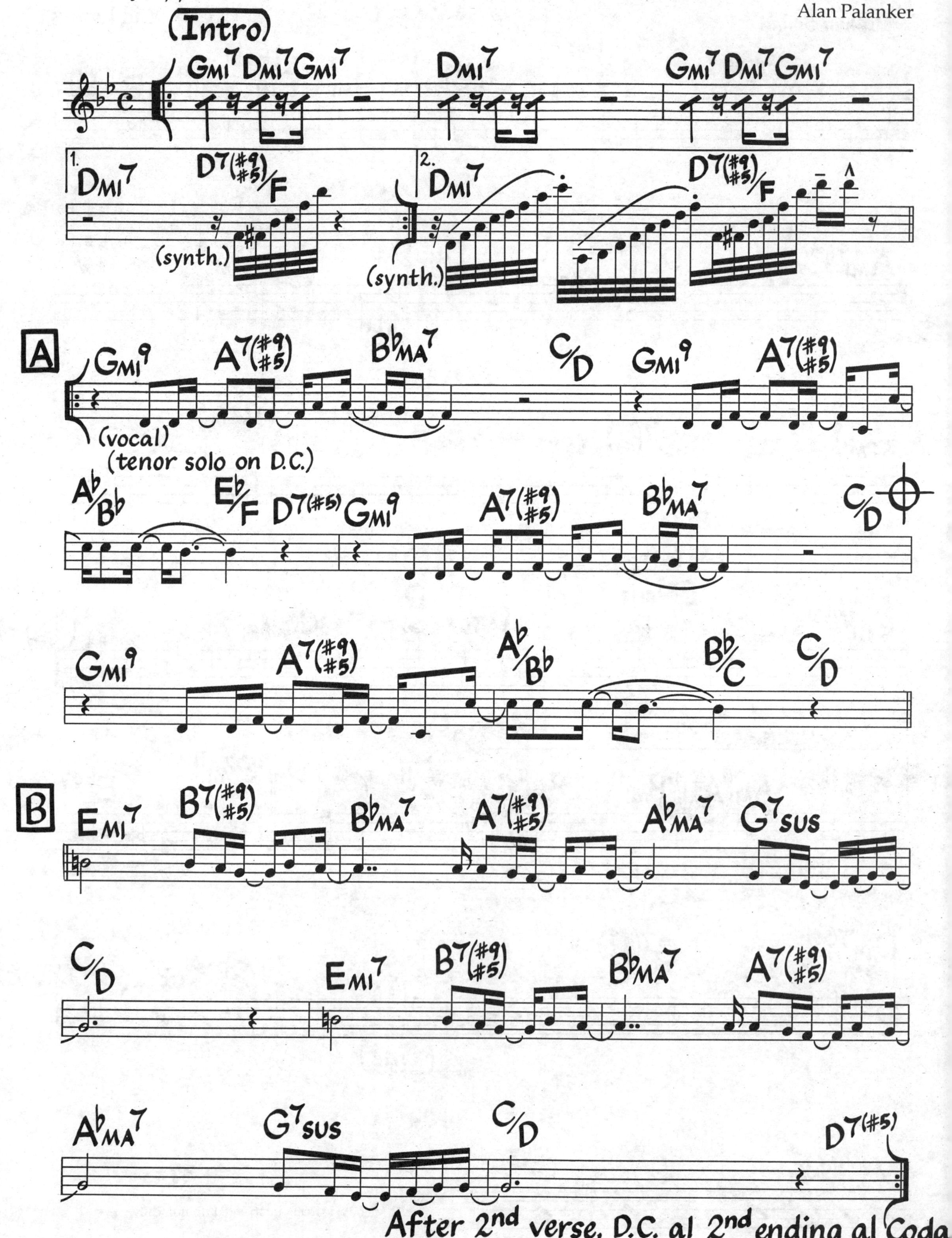

164

Let's Go Dancin'

Victor Feldman

Bright Samba ♩= 146

Flute sounds one octave higher than written. Use chords in parentheses for solos.

Solo on AAB; after solos play head (AABA) to fine.

Like Someone In Love

Music by Jimmy Van Heusen
Lyric by Johnny Burke

Med. Swing

A

| Dma7 | F#7/C# | Bmi7 | Bmi7/A | E7/G# | G9(#11) | F#mi7 | B7 |

| Emi7 | (G#mi7 C#7) A7 | Dma7 | Ami7 D7 |

| Gma7 | C#mi7 F#7 | Bma7 | |

| Bmi7 | E7 | Emi7 | A7(#5) |

B

| Dma7 | F#7/C# | Bmi7 | Bmi7/A | E7/G# | G9(#11) | F#mi7 | B7 |

| Emi7 | (G#mi7 C#7) A7 | Dma7 | Ami7 D7 |

| Gma7 | C#mi7 F#7 | Bma7 | E7 F°7 |

| F#mi7 B7 | Emi7 A7 | D6 | (Emi7 A7) |

All changes get 2 beats each when 2 to the bar.

©1949 by Burke & Van Heusen, now Bourne Co and Dorsey Bros. Music. Copyright Renewed. All Rights Reserved. International Copyright Secured. Used By Permission. Rights for Germany, Austria, Switzerland & CSSR assigned to Melodie Der Welt, J. Michel KG, Musikverlag. Rights for Japan assigned to Chappel/Intersong K.K. - used by permission of JASRAC License #8670719.

Line For Lyons

Gerry Mulligan

Medium Swing

Head is in 2, solos are in 4. Sounds one octave lower than written.

Solo on form (AABC); After solos, D.C. al Coda

©1954, renewed 1982 Atlantic Music Corp. Used By Permission.

Little Sunflower

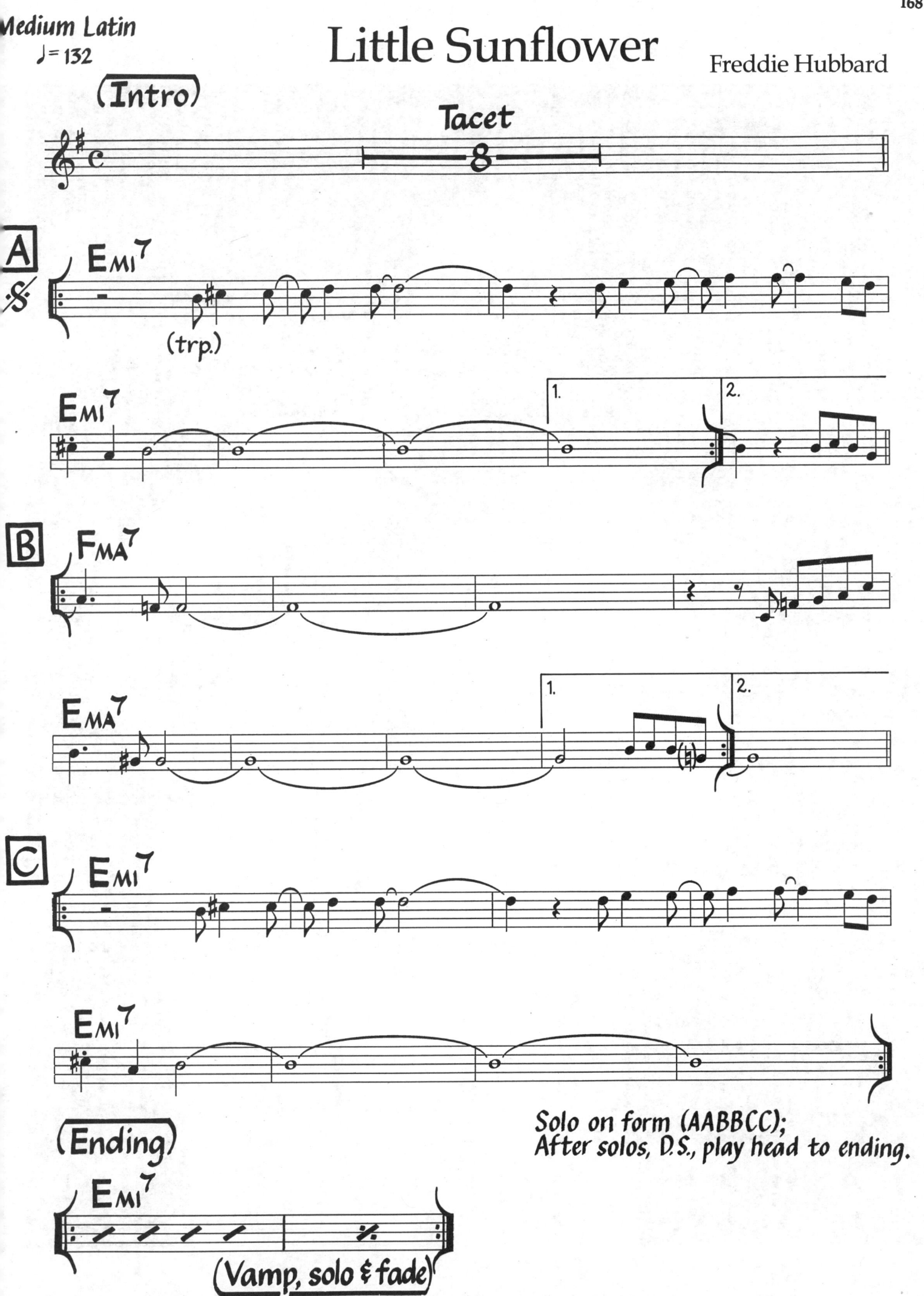

Freddie Hubbard

Medium Latin ♩= 132

(Intro) Tacet

A E_mi7 (trp.)

E_mi7

B F_ma7

E_ma7

C E_mi7

E_mi7

(Ending) E_mi7

(Vamp, solo & fade)

Solo on form (AABBCC);
After solos, D.S., play head to ending.

Letter B may be played as a double-time feel samba.

©1972 Hubtones Music. Used By Permission.

SARAH VAUGHN

A Little Tear

Med. Bossa Nova
♩ = 94

Music by Eumir Deodato & Paulo Valle
English Lyric by Ray Gilbert
(As sung by Sarah Vaughn)

©1966 Rio-Cali Music. Used By Permission.

Vamp & fade

Little Waltz

Med.-Slow Jazz Waltz

Ron Carter

Melody at A and C may
also be played with this rhythm:

Love Came On Stealthy Fingers

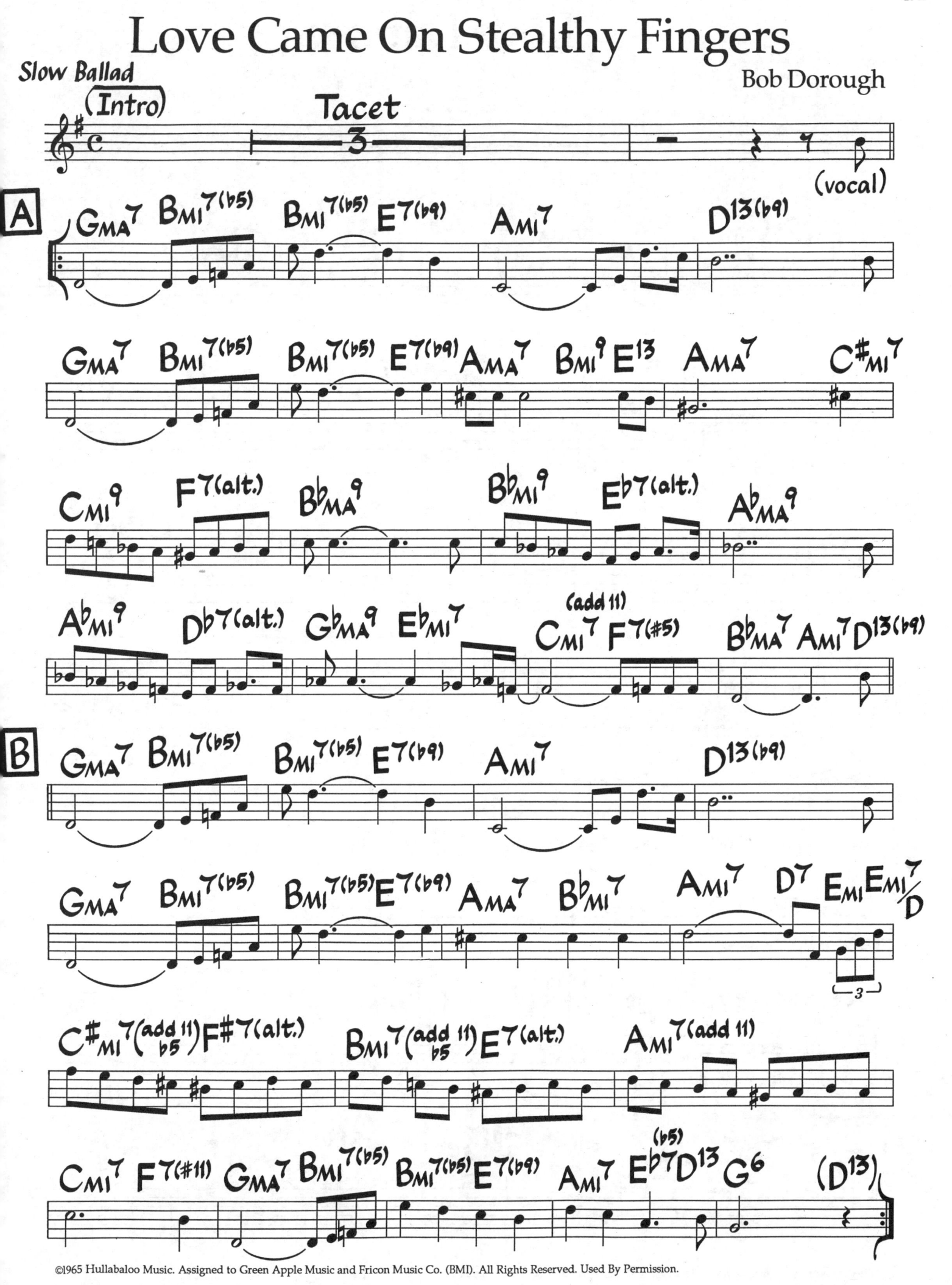

Bob Dorough

Slow Ballad

Love Dance

Med. Funk Ballad
♩ = 57

Music by
Ivan Lins & Gilson Peranzzetta
English Lyric by Paul Williams
(As sung by Diane Schuur)

(Intro) Tacet — 4 bars

A FMA7 | Gmi7 Ami7 | BbMA7 Eb13sus | Eb13 | Ami7 | Dmi7

G13sus | G13 | C13sus | C/Bb | A13 | A7(#5)

D9sus | D7(#9#5) | G13sus | G13 | C13sus | C13sus(b9)

G6/F | Bbmi7/F | [1.] G6/F Eb13sus | [2.] G6/F Eb13sus B7(b5)

B (tenor solo on D.S.) Emi7(b5) A7(#5) | Dmi7(add 11) Dmi7/C | Bmi7(add 11 b5) E7(alt.) | AMA7

G#mi7(b5) C#7(#5) | F#mi7(add 11) F#mi7/C | G13sus G13 | C13sus C13sus(b9)
(end solo)

C FMA7 Gmi7 Ami7 | BbMA7 Eb13sus | Eb13 | Ami7 | Dmi7

©1980 Kidada Music, Inc., Brammus Music, State Of The Arts Music & Hobsong Music. Used By Permission.

(D.S. al Coda)

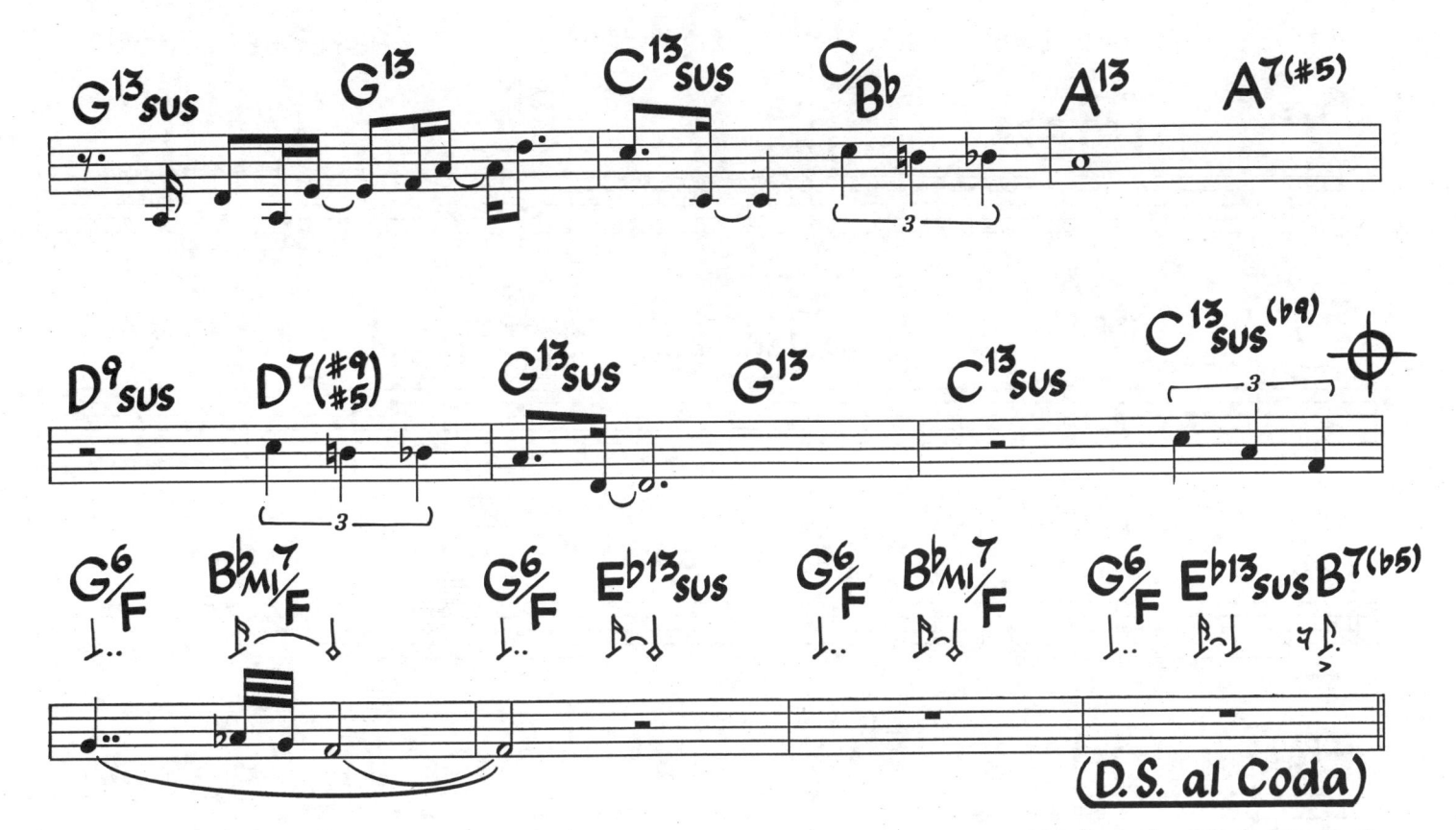

Melodic rhythm is freely interpreted.

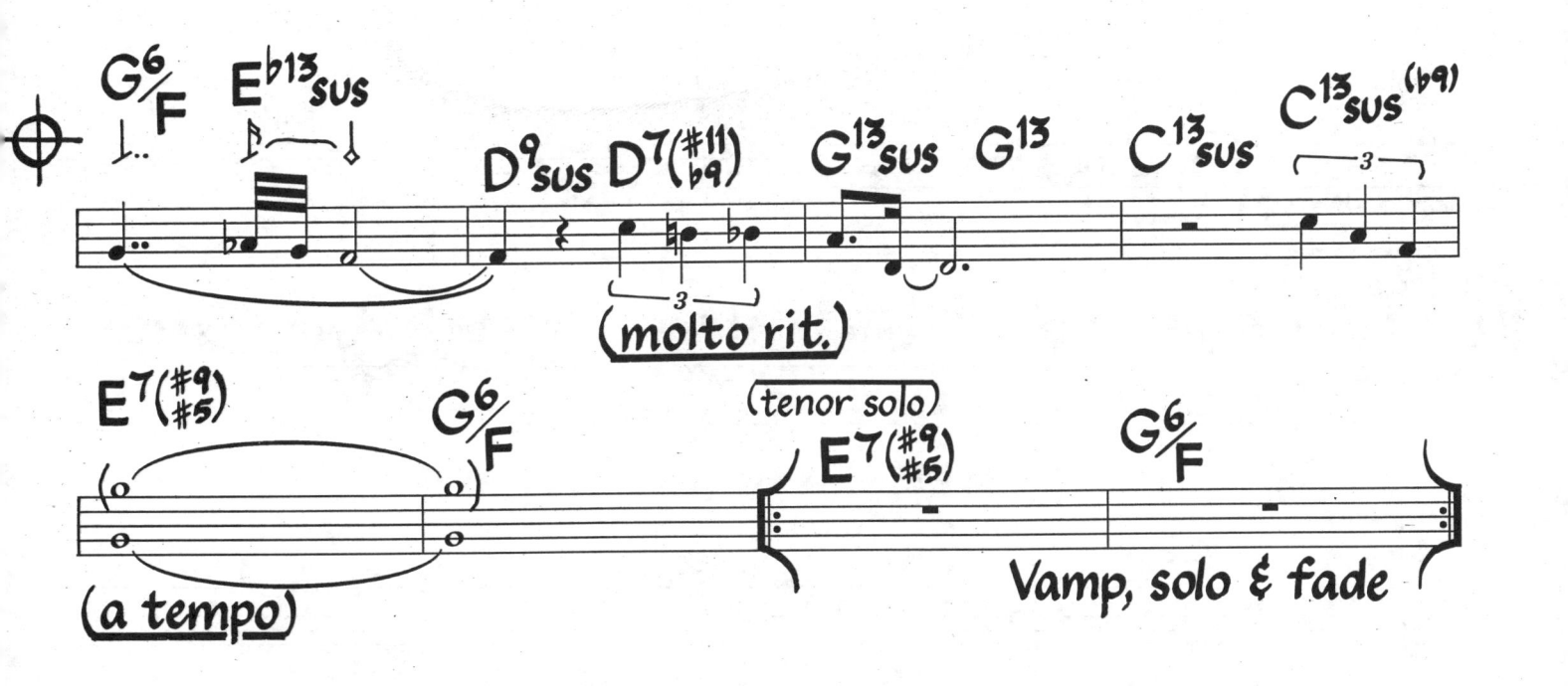

(molto rit.)

(a tempo)

(tenor solo)

Vamp, solo & fade

Lush Life

Billy Strayhorn
(As played by John Coltrane)

(Med. Ballad)
♩≈ 58
C
E♭MA7 E13(♯11) E♭MA7 E13(♯11) E♭6 A♭MI7 D♭13 G♭MA7 E13(♯11)
E♭MA7 E13(♯11) E♭MA7 E13(♯11) E♭6 E♭9 D13 GMA7 B13
B♭MA7 F7(♯9 ♯5) B♭MA7 F♯MI7 B7 EMA7 EMI7 A7 DMA7 B♭13
D
E♭MA7 E13(♯11) E♭MA7 E13(♯11) E♭6 D7(♯11 ♯9) D♭13 GMI (add 11) C7
A♭MI9 D♭13 B9(♯5) B♭13 E♭MA7 A♭13
GMI7 C7 A♭MI9 D♭13 B9(♯5) B♭13
(Double-time Feel)
B♭7(♯9) B7(♯9) C7(♯9) C♯7(♯9) D7(♯9) E13(♯11) E♭MA7 B♭13 E♭MA7 E13(♯11) E♭MA7 E13(♯11)
(First solo begins here)
Solo on CD; after solos, D.S. al Coda
Solos are in double-time feel swing.
B♭7(♯9) B7(♯9) C7(♯9) C♯7(♯9) D7(♯9) E13(♯11) E♭MA7
(molto rit.)

Madagascar

Richie Beirach
(As played by
John Abercrombie)

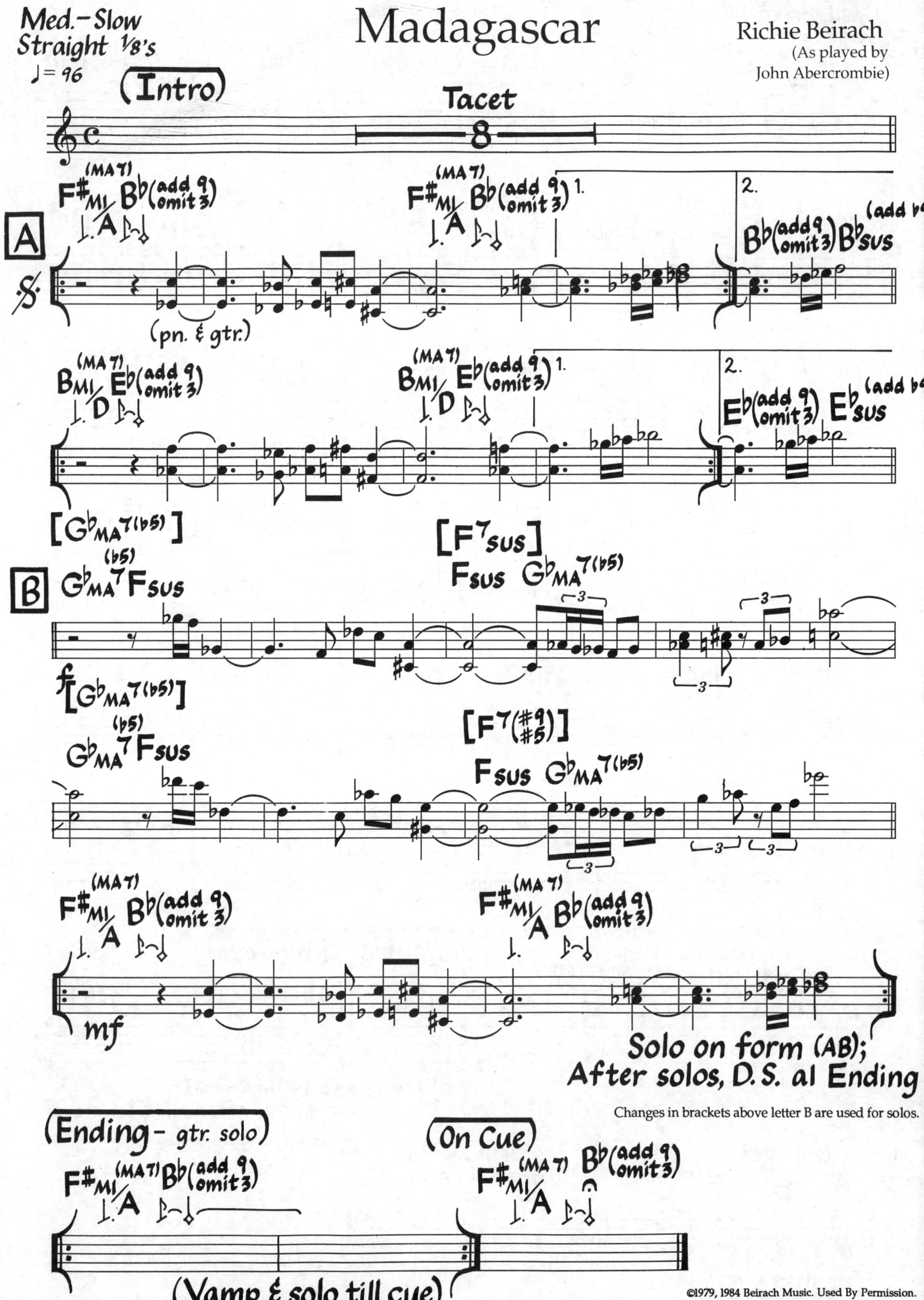

Make Me A Memory
(Sad Samba)

Grover Washington, Jr.

Medium Bossa ♩=120

Guitar sounds one octave lower than written. Kicks do not hold for solos.
Gmi7 may be played on the 'and of 2' instead of the 'and of 3' during solos at letter B.
Play head twice before solos.

©1980 G.W. Jr. Music. Used By Permission.

Solo on AAAABB
After solos, D.S., play head, vamp on letter B, solo and fade.

Matinee Idol

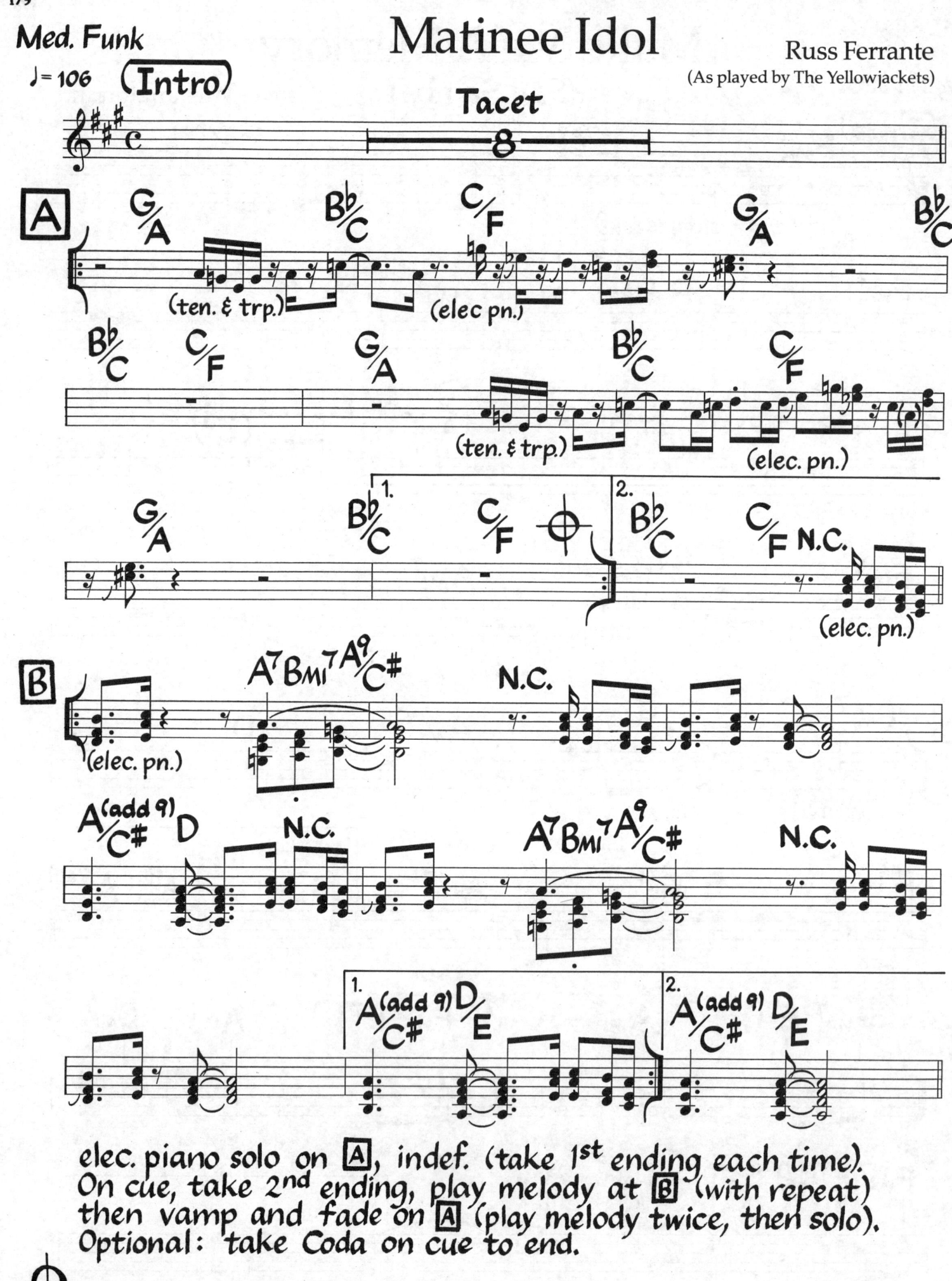

Med. Funk
♩ = 106 (Intro)

Russ Ferrante
(As played by The Yellowjackets)

elec. piano solo on A, indef. (take 1st ending each time).
On cue, take 2nd ending, play melody at B (with repeat)
then vamp and fade on A (play melody twice, then solo).
Optional: take Coda on cue to end.

©1981 Teeth Music & Barracuda Music (BMI). Used By Permission.

Medium-Slow Funky Rock ♩=85

Mercy, Mercy, Mercy

Josef Zawinul

(As played by Cannonball Adderley)

The Midnight Sun

Music by Lionel Hampton & Sonny Burke
Lyric by Johnny Mercer

Med. Ballad

Chords in parentheses are optional.

©1947, renewed 1975 by Regent Music Corp. & Crystal Music Publishers, Inc. All Rights Reserved. Printed By Permission.

The Midnight Sun Will Never Set

Quincy Jones
Henri Salvador

Medium Ballad

Med.-Slow Funk ♪ = 83

Modadji

Dave Grusin

Letter C gets progressively louder and funkier.

Monk's Mood

Med. Ballad — Thelonious Monk

A: Gmi7 | C7(#11)(b9) Dma9 (Dma9) | Emi7 A13(#11)(b5) | EbMA7 | D Db C7 B7 |

(counter-melody)

1. F#7(b9) F7 | Emi7(add11) F#9sus | Emi7(add11) C7(#11)(b9) :||
2. Bb7(b5) A13(b5) | EbMA7(#11) ||

B: C/D B/D | C/D G#mi7 | G#mi7 C#13(b9) | F#6 |

Bmi7(b5) Bb9 A7sus | A#°7 Bmi7(b5) G13(#11) | Gmi7(add11) Fmi7(add11)/C | Emi7(add11) C7(#11)(b9) |

C: Gmi7 C7(#11)(b9) Dma9 (Dma9) | Emi7(b5) A13(#11) | EbMA7 | D Db |

C7 B7 | F#7(b9) F7 | Bb7(b5) A13(b5) | EbMA7(#11) ||

Anticipated chords at letter B are played on the beat for solos. Melody is upper line at letter B.

©1946 (Renewed) by Embassy Music Corp. (BMI). International Copyright Secured. All Rights Reserved. Used By Permission.

Monkey's Uncle

Mitchell Foreman

Solos on form (ABCD)
After solos, D.C. al Coda

Vamp, solo & fade

First 24 bars of letter A are written as 12 bars repeated in the keyboard and bass parts.

KENNY BARRON

Photo by Tom Copi ©1988

Moonlight In Vermont

Music by Karl Suessdorf
Lyric by John Blackburn

Med. Ballad

Mornin'

Al Jarreau
David Foster
Jay Graydon

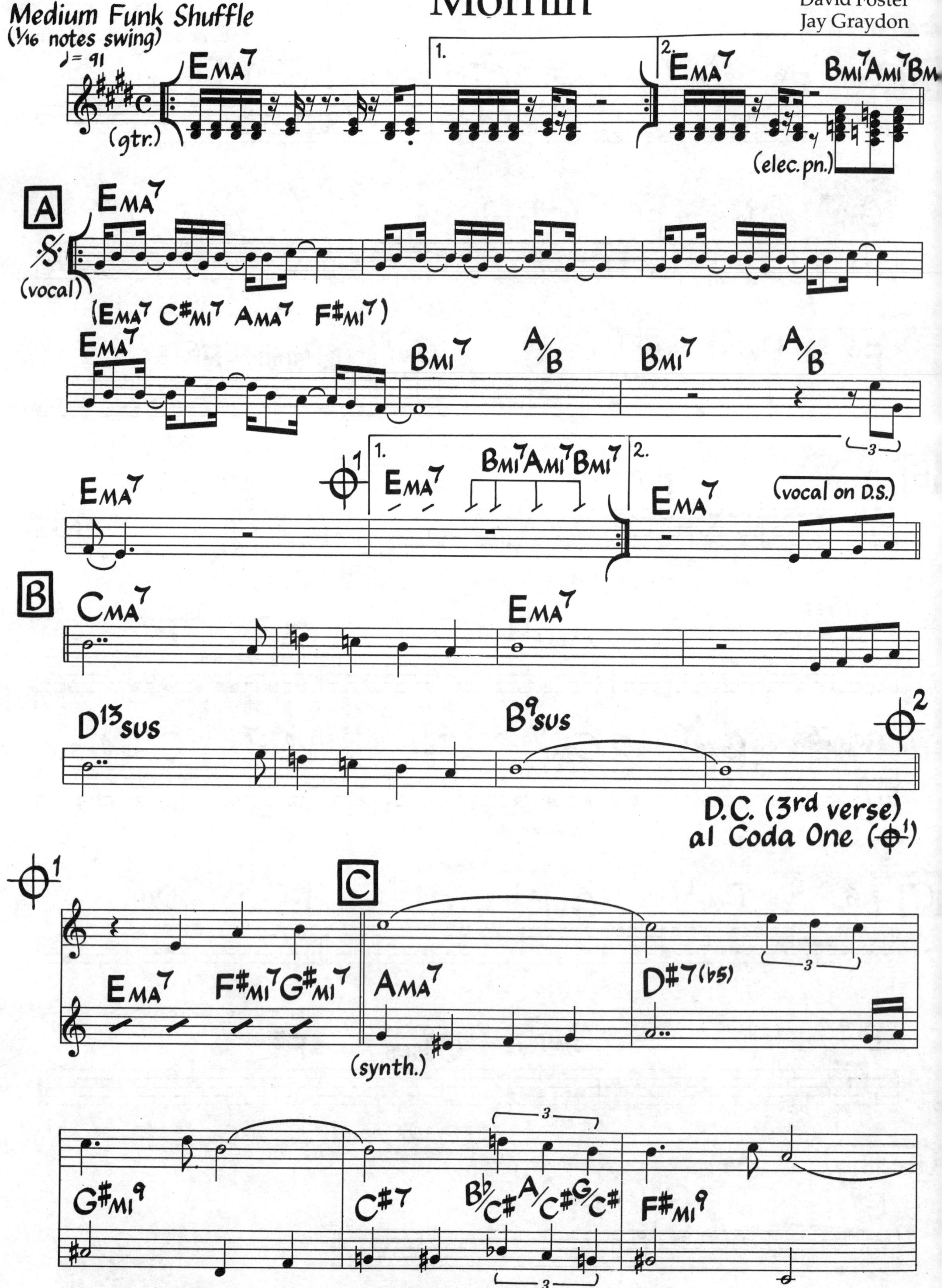

D#MI7(b5) G#7(#9 b5)
C#MA9
D#MI7
BbMI7
3
Eb13
Eb7(#5)
AbMA9
FMI7
BbMI7
CMI7
DbMA7
Db/Eb Eb7 Db/Eb Eb7
(cresc.)
EMA7
EMA7
BMI7 AMI7 BMI7
ff
D.S. (synth. solo for 8) al 2nd ending
al Coda Two (Φ2).
FMA7
DMI7 BbMA7 GMI7
CMI7
Bb/C
Vamp, scat & fade
(After 1st x, voice scats.)

Morning Dance

Jay Beckenstein
(As played by Spyro Gyra)

Med. Samba/Funk

Solo on form (AAB)
After solos, D.S. al Coda

sample ten. fill

(Vamp, solo & fade)

Melody is played with some variation.

FREDDIE HUBBARD

Mr. Clean

Weldon Irvine
(As played by Freddie Hubbard)

Half-Time Funk/Rock
♩ = 82

Tenor sounds one octave lower than written.
Note and chord on beat 4 of bar 5 of letter A may be played on the 'and of 4'.

©1970 Nodlew Music. Used By Permission.

Mr. Gone

Josef Zawinul
(As played by Weather Report)

Medium Swing/Shuffle
♪ = 137

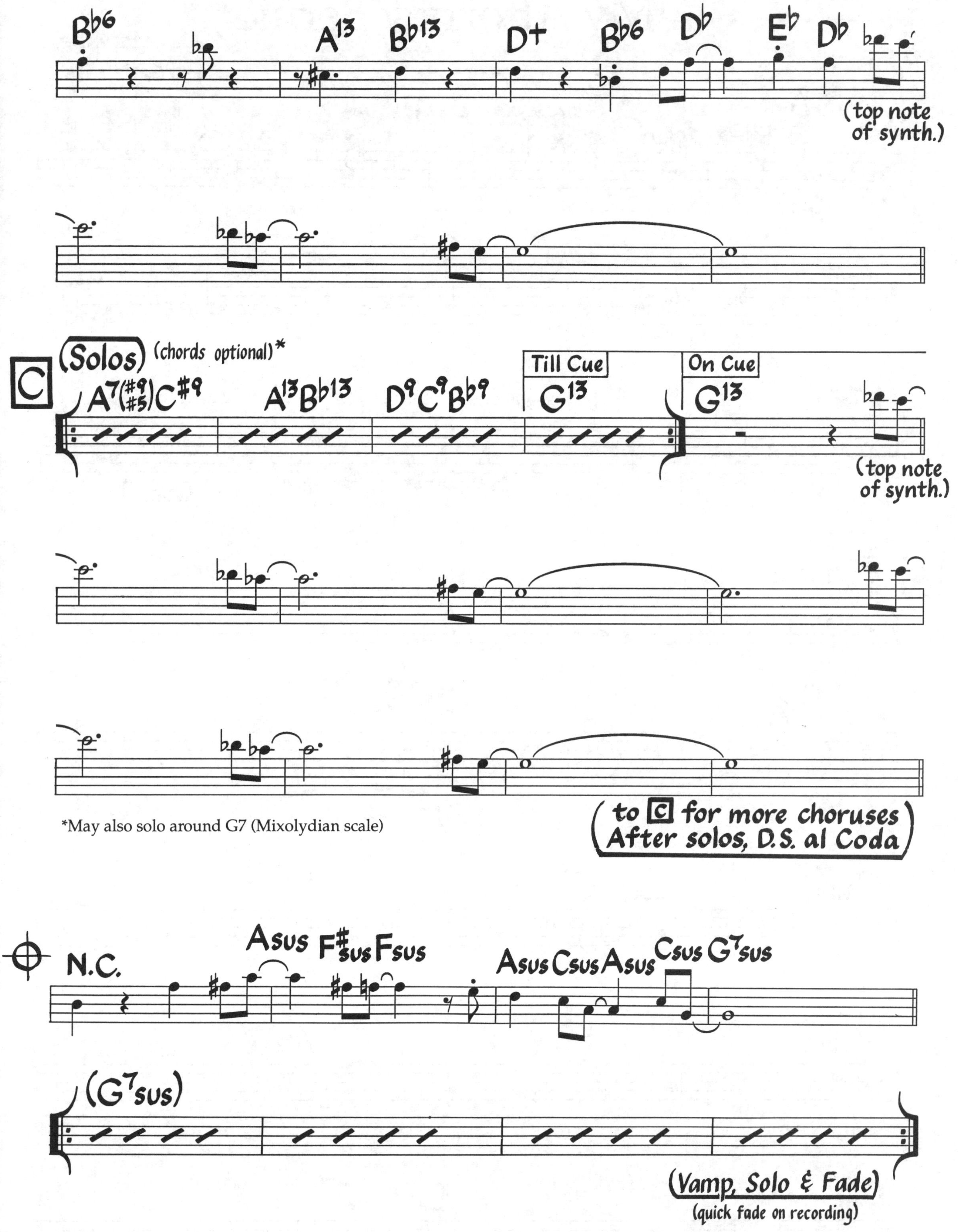

*May also solo around G7 (Mixolydian scale)

My Attorney Bernie

Dave Frishberg

B
EMI7(b5)/A
EMI7(b5)/A
(D#o7)
(pn. & bs.)
(vocal)
GMI7
C9
FMI7
Bb9
EbMA7
AbMA9
DMI7
G7(b9)
Bb9(#11)
A9
C
G9sus
CMA7
E9sus
AMA7
G9sus
CMA7
E9sus
(E7(#5))
AMI
(pn.)
GMI9
C13
F
E7(#9)
3x's
(3rd x take Coda)
F
E7(b9)
A bass
(vocal)
(pn.)

My Shining Hour

Music by Harold Arlen
Lyric by Johnny Mercer

Med.-Up Swing

A | D^{MA7} | (B^{MI7}) | (E^{9}) E^{MI9} | E^{MI9} A^{7} |

| D^{MA7} | (B^{MI7}) | E^{MI7} | C#${}^{MI7(b5)}$ F#^{7} |

| B^{MI} | (G#${}^{MI7(b5)}$) | C#${}^{MI7(b5)}$ | F#^{7} |

| B^{MI7} | B^{MI7} E^{7} | E^{MI7} | A^{7} |

B | A^{MI7} | D^{7} | G^{MA9} | |

| G^{MI9} | C^{13} | (F#${}^{7(#5)}$ B${}^{7(#9)}$ E^{7}) D^{6}/F# F^{o7} | E^{MI7} A^{7} |

| D^{MA7} | (G^{13}) % | (C${}^{9(#11)}$ B^{7}) D^{MA7} E^{MI7} | F#${}^{MI7(b5)}$ B^{7} |

| E^{MI7} | A^{7} | D^{6} | (E^{MI7} A^{7}) |

©1943, 1987 Harwin Music Co., ©Renewed 1971 Harwin Music Co. International Copyright Secured. All Rights Reserved: Used By Permission.

Nature Boy

Med. Ballad*

Eden Ahbez

7th bar of letters A & B were originally 2 bars each. Melody is straight eights, though rather freely interpreted rhythmically.

©1948 Eden Ahbez. Used By Permission.

*may be played rubato, in time, or as a bossa nova.

WAYNE SHORTER

Photo by Tom Copi ©1988

Nefertiti

Wayne Shorter
(As played by Miles Davis)

Medium Swing ♩= 108

Never Givin' Up

Al Jarreau
Tom Canning

Med. Funk/Samba
♩ = 102

(Intro) Tacet

©1983 Al Jarreau Music & Desperate Music. Used By Permission.

(Continued on next page)

A/D G13 F#mi7
(gtr.)
D/E E/D F#mi/B G/F
Dmi9 F/G
(vocal)
D
Cma7 Ami7 Fma7 Fmi7 Gmi7
f
Cma7 Ami7 Fma7 Fmi7 Gmi7
Cma7 Ami7 Fma7 Fmi7 G#o7
1.
Ami C/G F#mi7(b5) G13sus G13(b9)
2.
Ami C/G F#mi7(b5) Bb13sus Bb13(b9)
E
Ebma7 Cmi7
1., 2.
Abma7 Abmi7 Bbmi7
(bkgr. vocal)
3.
Abma7 Abmi7 Bo7
(bkgr. vocal)
Cmi Eb/Bb Ami7(b5) Bb13sus Bb13(b9)
(vocal)
Vamp & fade on E

Never Make Your Move Too Soon

Music by Nesbert "Stix" Hooper
Lyric by Will Jennings
(As played by The Crusaders)

Med. Rock ♩ = 114

Sing (or play) 2 verses, then solo on [A];
After solos, D.S. (3rd verse) al Coda

(molto rit.)

Ending may be played instrumentally (without vocal).
Melody is freely interpreted and varies with each verse.

©1978 Status Cymbal Music & Irving Music. Used By Permission.

Nigerian Marketplace

Oscar Peterson

Use chords in brackets for solos at letter B.
Solos evolve into a funky boogaloo feel.

Solo on form (AABBC)
after solos, D.S. al Fine

Nightlake

Richie Beirach
(As played by John Abercrombie)

Med. Swing 6/4
♩ = 124

Chord in parenthesis is alternate change.

Head is played twice before and after solos

©1979 Beirach Music. Used By Permission.

No Me Esqueca

Joe Henderson

B (Solos)
Bmi7
Dmi7
(G13)
Cma7
Cmi7 F7
B♭ma7
B♭mi7 E♭7
(Ami7 D7)
A♭ma7
(A♭7(♯11 ♯9))
Gma7
F♯7(♯9 ♯5)
After solos, continue to C
C
Bmi7
(alto, w/ten. & trb. 8va b.)
Dmi7
(alto)
(trb. ten.)
Cma7
(ten. & trb. 8va b.)
break
B♭ma7
break
A♭ma7
break
Gma7
F♯7(♯9 ♯5)
1.
2.
F♯7(♯9 ♯5)
Play head (A) twice, then D.C. al fine

Fast Samba/Funk

𝅗𝅥 = 152

Not Ethiopia

Michael Brecker
(As played by The Brecker Bros.)

Horn parts at letters A & C are all played one octave lower than written.

Nothing Personal

Don Grolnic
(As played by Michael Brecke

Bright Swing
♩= 240

Head is played twice before and after solos. Chords in parentheses are for solos (optional)

Off Minor

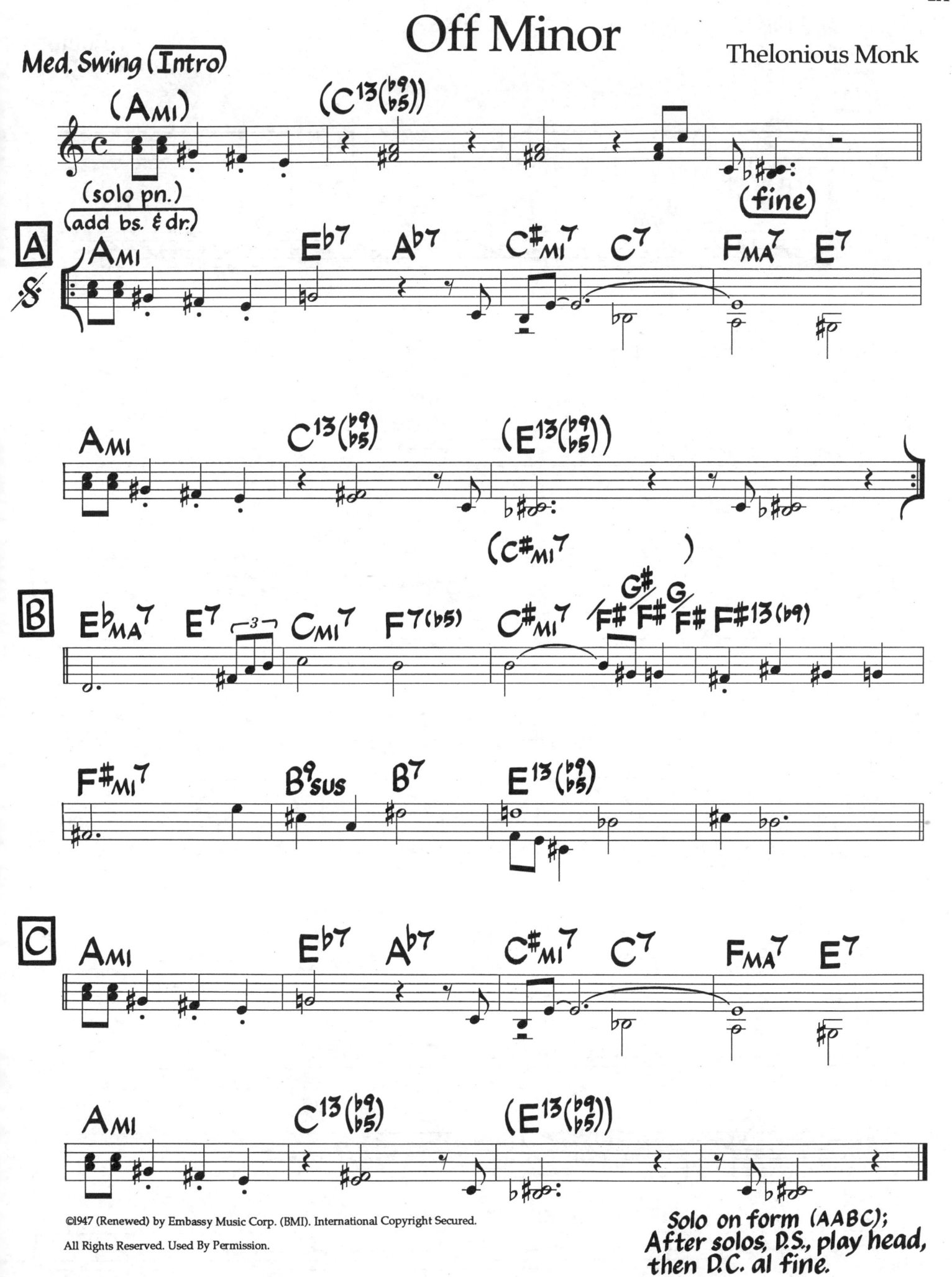

Thelonious Monk

Medium-Up Swing
♩= 224

Oleo

Sonny Rollins
(As played by Miles Davis)

Solo on form (AABC)
("Rhythm Changes")

Once I Loved

Med.-Slow Bossa Nova

Music by Antonio Carlos Jobim
English Lyric by Ray Gilbert

©1965 Ipanema Music. Used By Permission.

One Family

Russell Ferrante
(As played by The Yellowjackets)

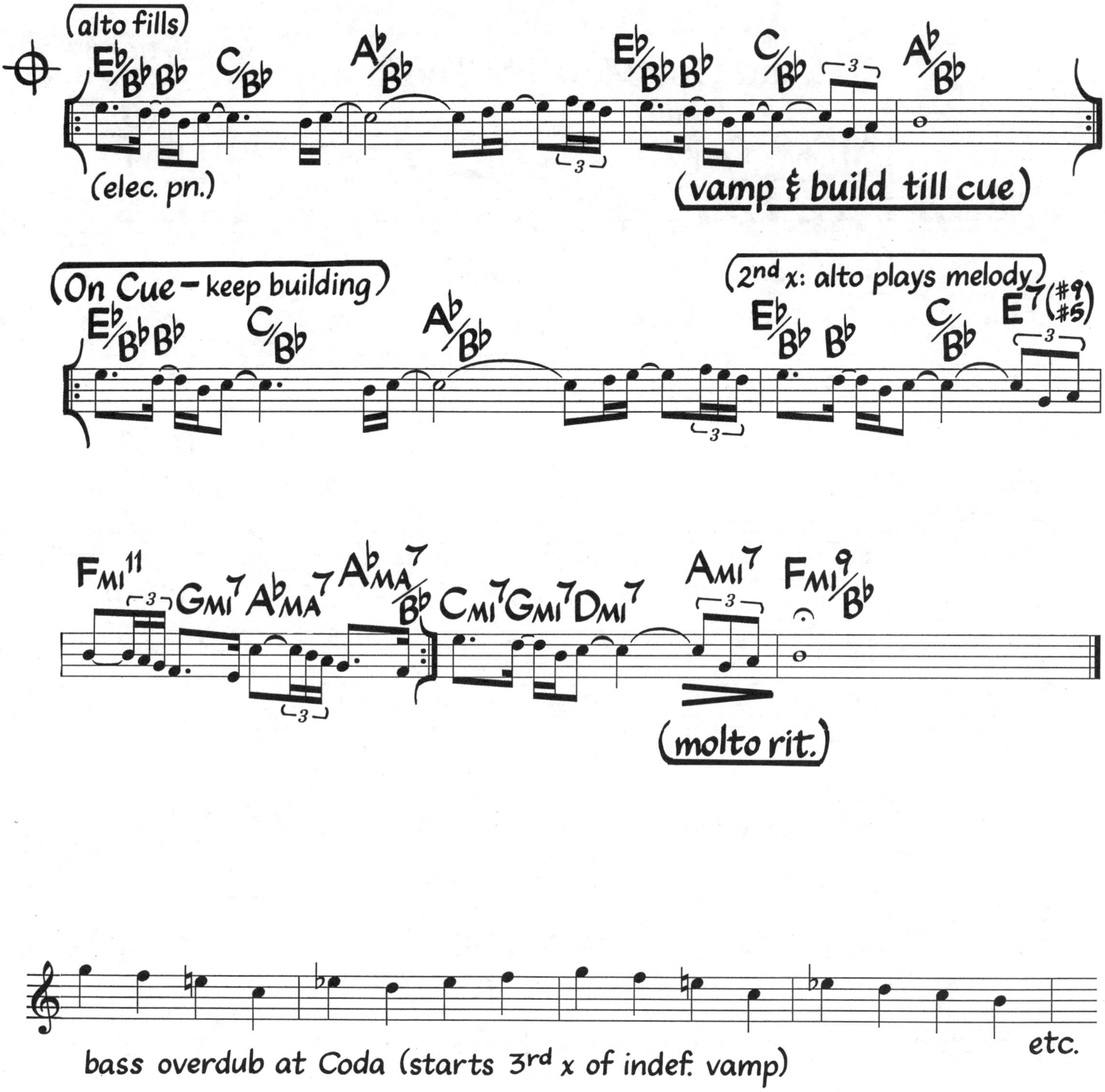
(alto fills)
(elec. pn.)
(vamp & build till cue)
(On Cue – keep building)
(2nd x: alto plays melody)
(molto rit.)
bass overdub at Coda (starts 3rd x of indef. vamp)
etc.

One For My Baby
(And One More For The Road)

Music by Harold Arlen
Lyric by Johnny Mercer

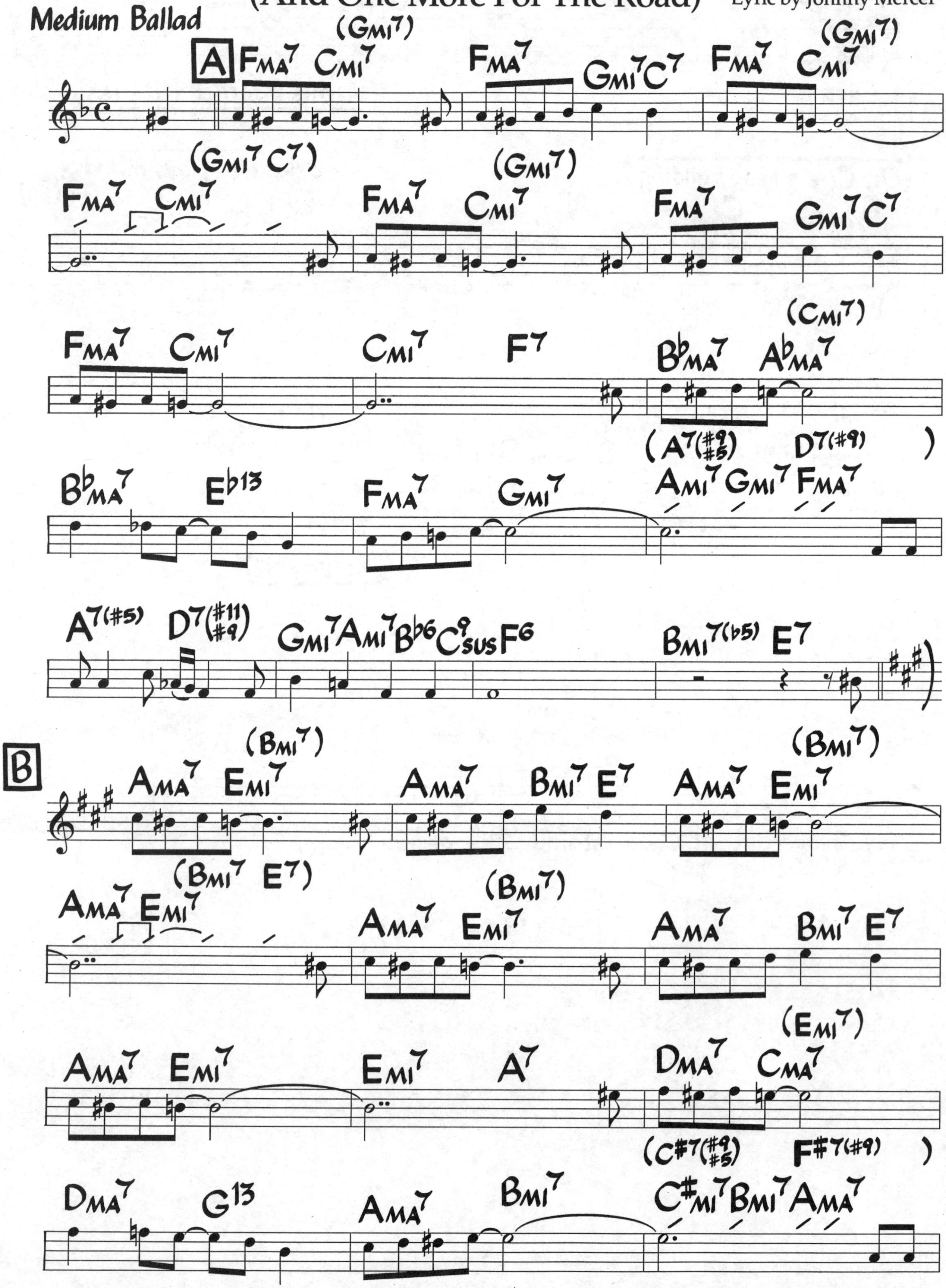

At letter C, Am11 may be substituted for D9sus. Alternate changes (in parentheses) are played on beat 3 (or beats 3 & 4) of the bar.

Out Of This World

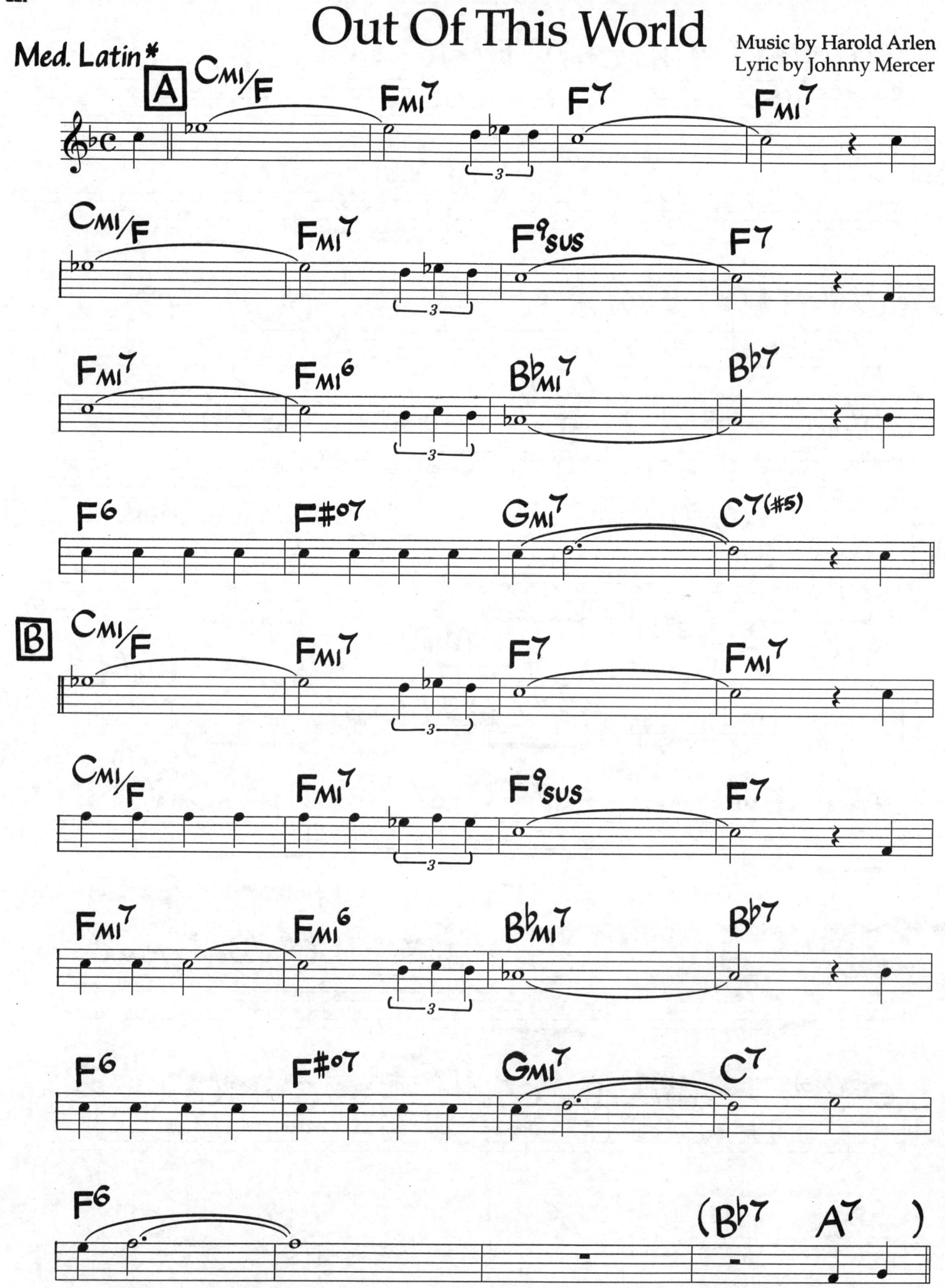

Music by Harold Arlen
Lyric by Johnny Mercer

Med. Latin*

*may also be played as Med. Swing; or letter C and solos may swing.

©1945, 1947, 1987 Edwin H. Morris & Co., A Division of MPL Communications, Inc. © Renewed 1974, 1975 Edwin H. Morris & Co., A Division of MPL Comminications, Inc. International Copyright Secured. All Rights Reserved. Used By Permission.

Last 2 bars of letter C may be omitted.

Oz

Medium-Up 3/4
(Straight 1/8's)
♩ = 208

Andy Narell

EMI9
C#MI7(b5)
F#7(#9 #5)
B9SUS
F13(b5)
C
EMI
AMI9
F#7(#9)
B7(#5)
EMI
EMI
AMI9
C13
B13
Bb13
F9(b5)
CMA7/D
C#9(#5)
Bsus/C
Bbsus/Gb
Asus/B
F9(b5)
EMI
EMI (gtr. fill)
14
Solo on form (AABC);
After solos, D.S. al Coda.
Solos swing
CMA7/D
C#9(#5)
CMA7
B9(#5)
EMI9
EMI7(b5)/A
cresc.
DMI9
G13
CMA7
F13
(Freely)
Bsus
Bbsus/B
Asus/B
B7(b9 #5)
Dbass
Ebass
(EMI11)
f

Papa Lips

Bob Mintzer

Medium Latin (Calypso)

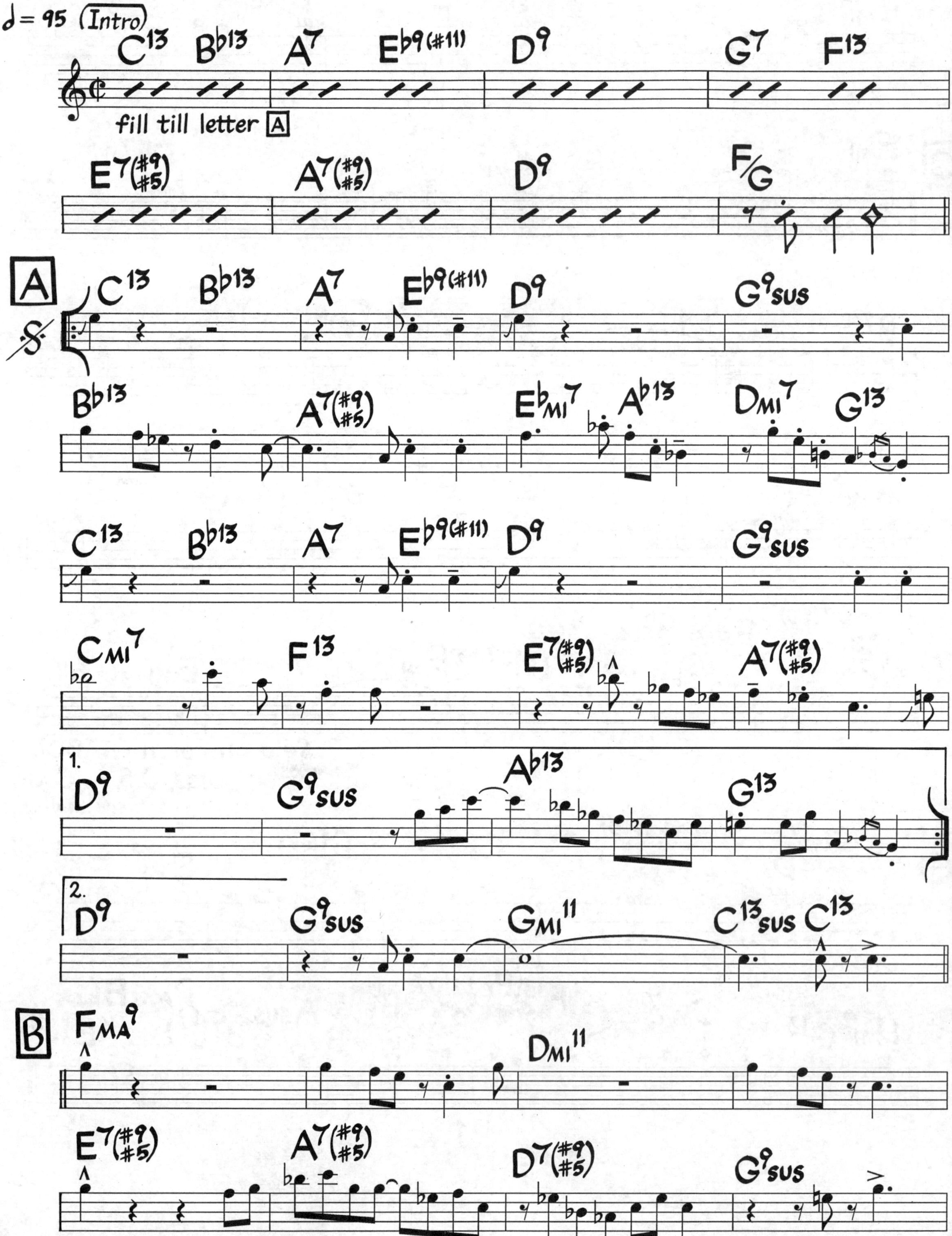

Solo on form (AABC)
After solos, D.S. al Coda

This is a shortened arrangement of the recorded version. On the recording, the solo section consists of the 1st 8 bars of letter A, followed by all of letter C.

Partido Alto

Jose Bertrami
(As played by Airto)

Med. Latin/Funk
♩ = 172

228

THELONIOUS MONK AND DIZZY GILLESPIE

Pent Up House

Sonny Rollins

Medium-Up Swing ♩=200

Head is played twice before and after solos.
Tenor sounds one octave lower than written.

After solos, D.S. (with pick-ups) al Coda

©1965 Prestige Music. Used By Permission.

Plaza Real

Wayne Shorter
(As played by Weather Report)

E
8va
mf (whistling)
8va
loco (sop.)
F
(4x's)
1.-5.
6.
G
mp (melodica)
(melody on bottom)
Alternate melody at C

Polkadots & Moonbeams

Music by Jimmy Van Heusen
Lyric by Johnny Burke

Med. Ballad

Alternate changes, bars 3-4 & 11-12 of [A] and bars 11-12 of [B]:

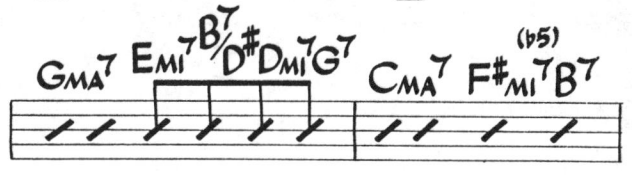

JACO PASTORIUS

Portrait Of Tracy

Jaco Pastorius

Promenade

Denny Zeitlin

(Solos) Med. Ballad ♩= 69
E
AMA7 | E/G# | GMA13 | F#MI11 | EMI11 A9 | DMA9
FMA9(#11) | E♭MA9(#11) | AMA7 | E/G# | GMI7(♭5) C7(#9 #5) | FMA7
B13 B7(#9 #5) | EMA9 A13(#11) | C#(add 11)/G# | CMA7(#5)/G
(Swing (in 2))
F
F#7(alt.) | ./. | B13sus | B7(♭9 ♭5) | EMI11 | B/D# EMI11/D
C#MI11(♭5) | F#13(♭9) (F#7(#9 #5)) | BMI11 | E7(♭9 #5)
AMI11(♭5) | E♭9(#11) D13(♭9) | Gsus | Gsus B9/F#
G
FMI11 E♭MI11 | DMI11 G7(♭9 ♭5) | CMI11 G/B CMI11/B♭
AMI11(♭5) D7(♭9 #5) | GMI11 C7(♭9 ♭5) | FMI11(♭5) BMI7 E7
(in 4)
H
AMA7 | E/G# | GMA13 | F#MI11 | EMI11 A9 | DMA9
FMA9(#11) | E♭MA9(#11) | AMA7 | E/G# | GMI7(♭5) C7(#9 #5) | FMA7
C#13(#11) | F#MI11 B13 | E9sus A9 | D6/9 (BMI7 E7)
Solo on EFGH; After solos, D.C. al fine.

Put It Where You Want It

Med. Funk/Rock
♩ = 126

Joe Sample
(As played by The Crusaders)

©1972 Four Knights Music. Used By Permission.

P.Y.T. (Pretty Young Thing)

Quincy Jones
James Ingram

(As sung by Michael Jackson)

JOHN COLTRANE

Photo by Jim Marshall ©1988

Quintessence

Quincy Jones

Rapture

Harold Land

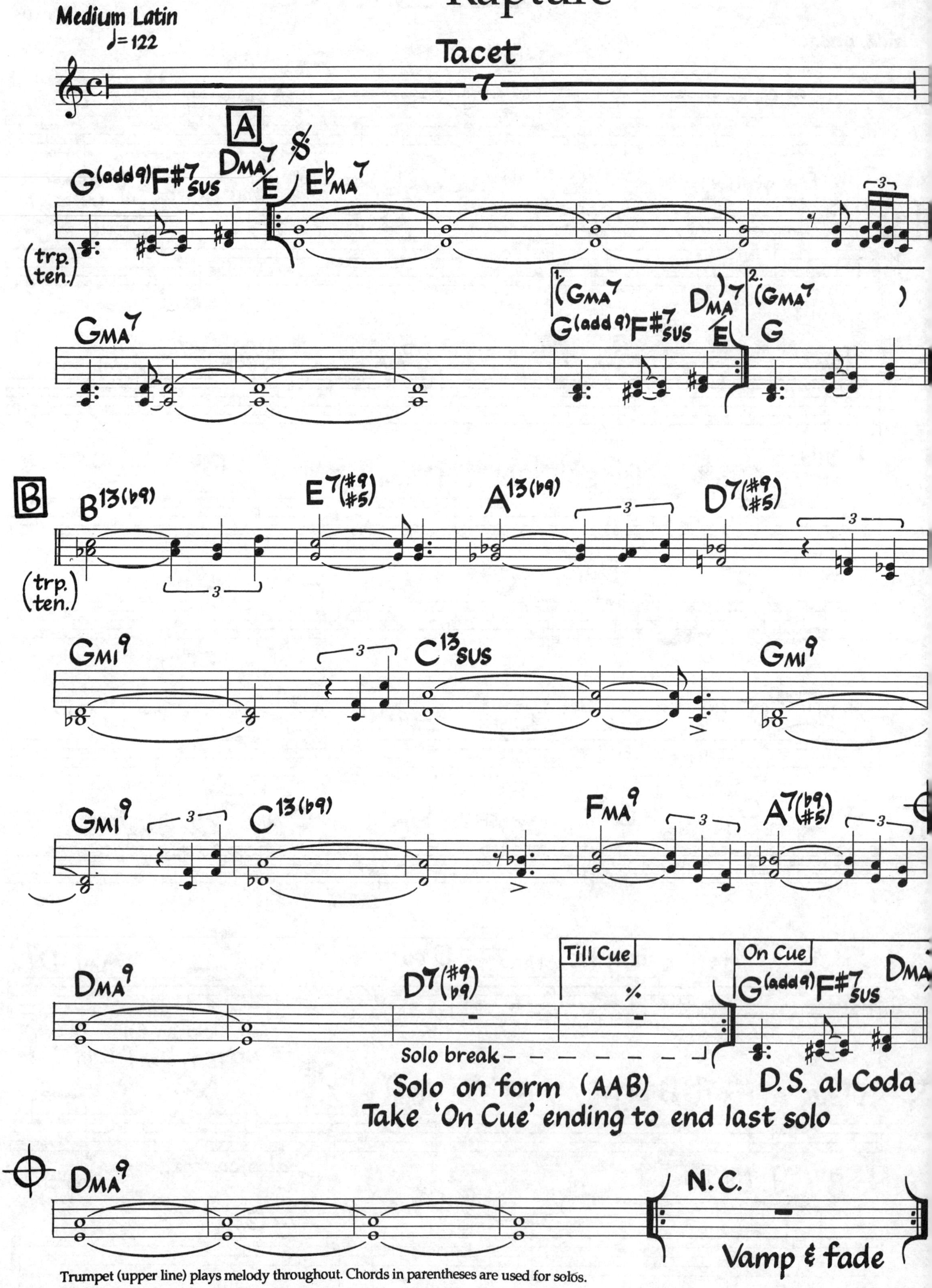

Trumpet (upper line) plays melody throughout. Chords in parentheses are used for solos.

Re: Person I Knew

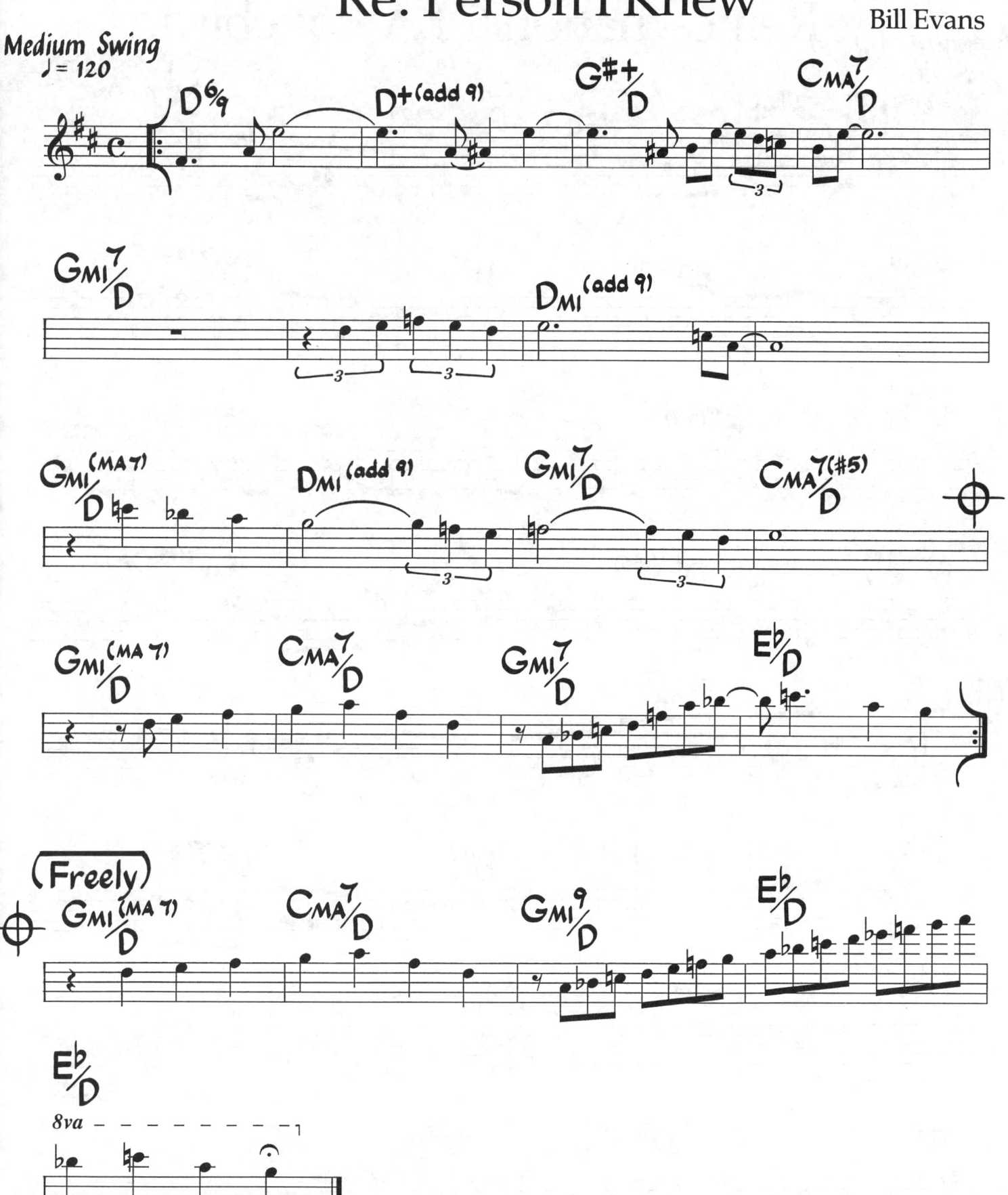

Bill Evans

Reincarnation Of A Lovebird

Charles Mingus

(♩= 𝅗𝅥) (Orig. Tempo)
F#MA7 B9(#11)
D
BMI7 E7 AMA7 D7
C#MI7(b5) C7 BMI7 E7(b9) Bb7 D#7
E
G#MI EMA7 Bb7 D#7(#5)
G#MI E9(#11) Bb7 D#7(#5)
G#MI E7(#9) C#MI7 F13
Bb7(#9 #5) D#7(#5) G#MI A#MI7(b5) D#7
C#MI7 FMA7 Bb7 D#7(#9 #5)
G#MI7 (A#MI7(b5) D#7)
last x: molto rit.
(fine)

CHARLES MINGUS

Remember Rockefeller At Attica

Charles Mingus

Rio

Victor Feldman

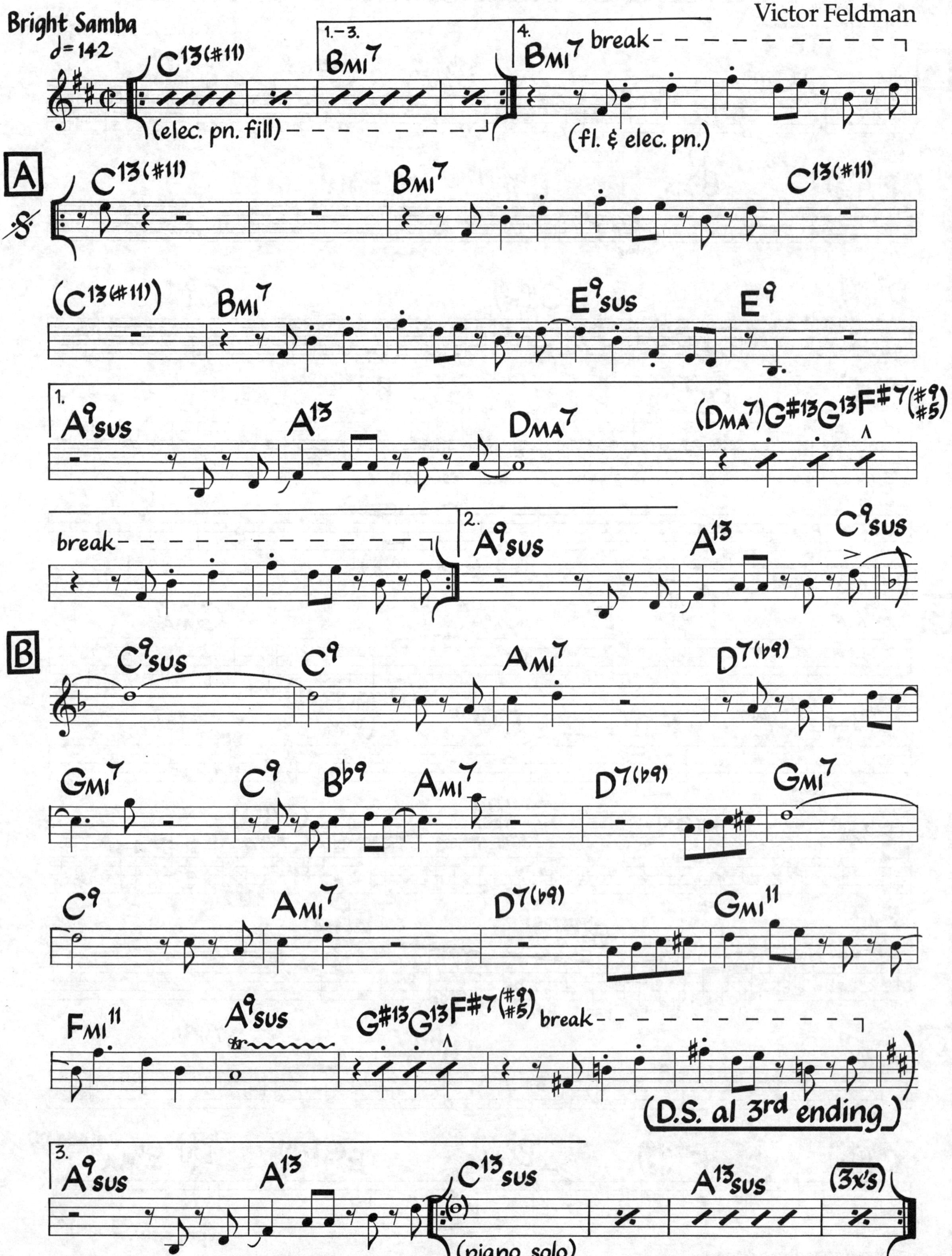

C13sus
A13sus
F#7(#9 #5)
(Solos) (solo continues)
(end solo)
C
C13(#11)
BMI7
C13(#11)
BMI7
E9sus
E9
1.
A9sus
A13
DMA7
F#7(#9 #5)
2.
A9sus
A13
D
C9sus
C9
AMI7
D7(b9)
GMI7
C9 (Bb9)
AMI7
D7(b9)
GMI7
C9
AMI7
D7(b9)
GMI11
FMI11
A9sus
F#7(#9 #5)
E
C13(#11)
BMI7
C13(#11)
BMI7
E9sus
E9
A9sus
A13
Till Cue
DMA7
F#7(#9 #5)
Solo on CCDE; take 'On Cue' ending at end of last solo.
On Cue
C13sus
1.–3.
A13sus
4.
BMI7 break
(solo continues)
(fl. & elec. pn.)
(D.S. al Coda)
A13sus
G#13 G13 F#7(#9 #5) break
C13sus

River People

Jaco Pastorius
(As played by Weather Report)

Robbin's Nest

"Illinois" Batiste Jacquet
Sir Charles Thompson

THELONIOUS MONK

Photo by Jim Marshall ©1988

Ruby, My Dear

Thelonious Monk

Med.-Up Funk ♩= 122

Rush Hour

Russell Ferrante
Robben Ford
(As played by The Yellowjackets)

Safari

Michael Brecker
(As played by Steps Ahead)

Medium Straight 1/8's
♩= 100

Safari (Keyboard)

Medium Straight ⅛'s
♩=100

Letters C and F build dynamically.

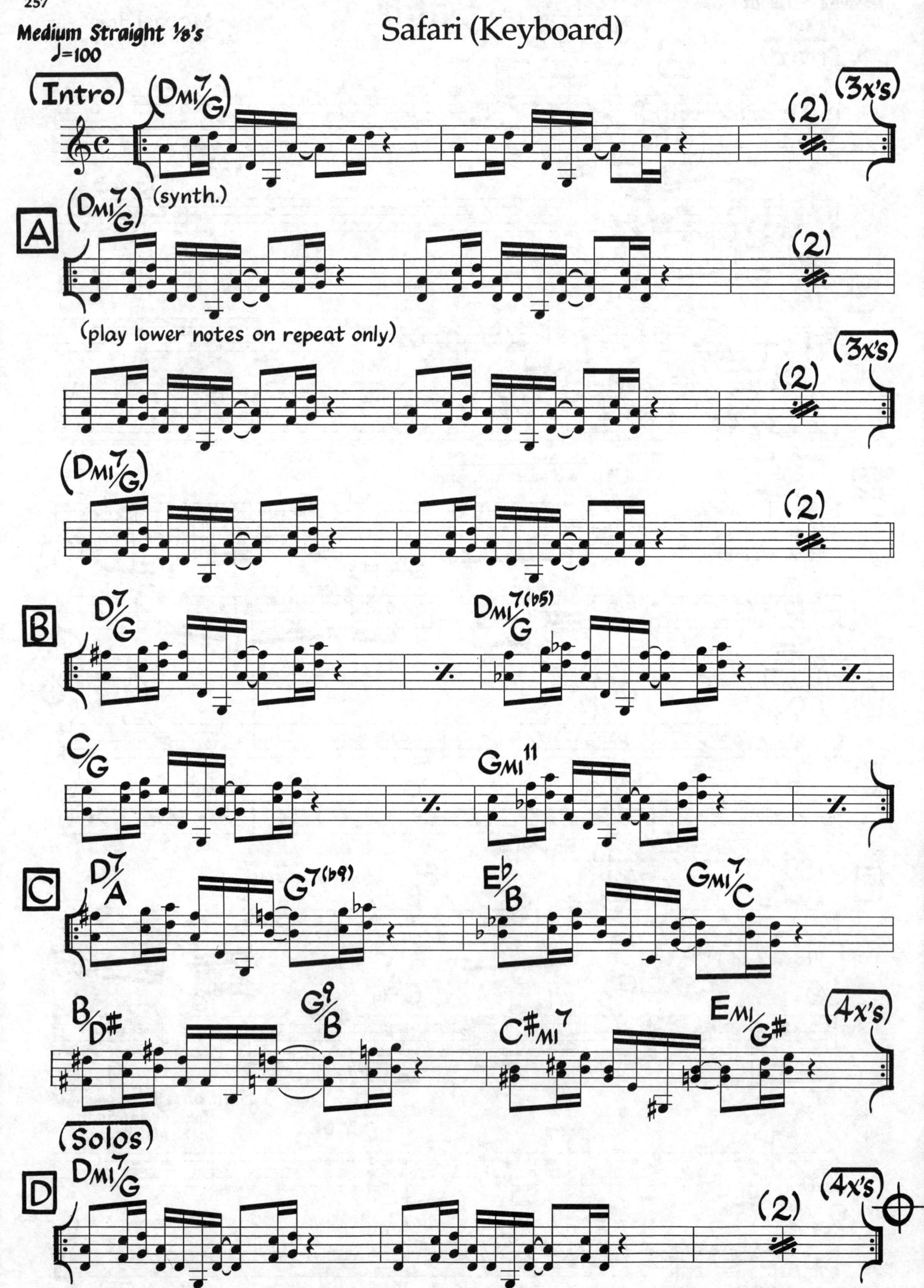

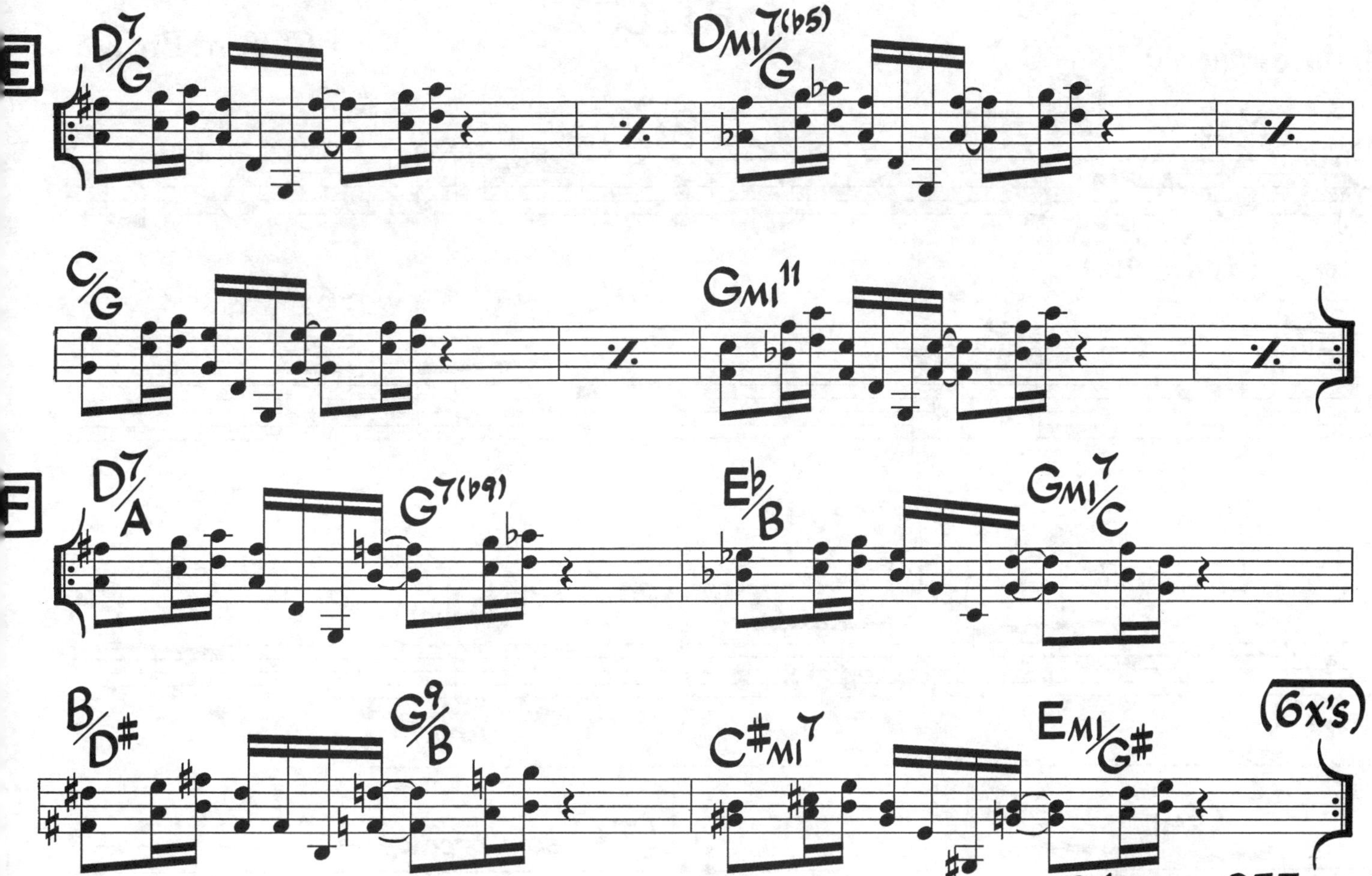

Solos on DEF
(with repeats as marked)
Take Coda during last solo to end.

Synth. line (chime) played
3rd & 4th x's at C and
5th & 6th x's at F:

Sandu

Clifford Brown

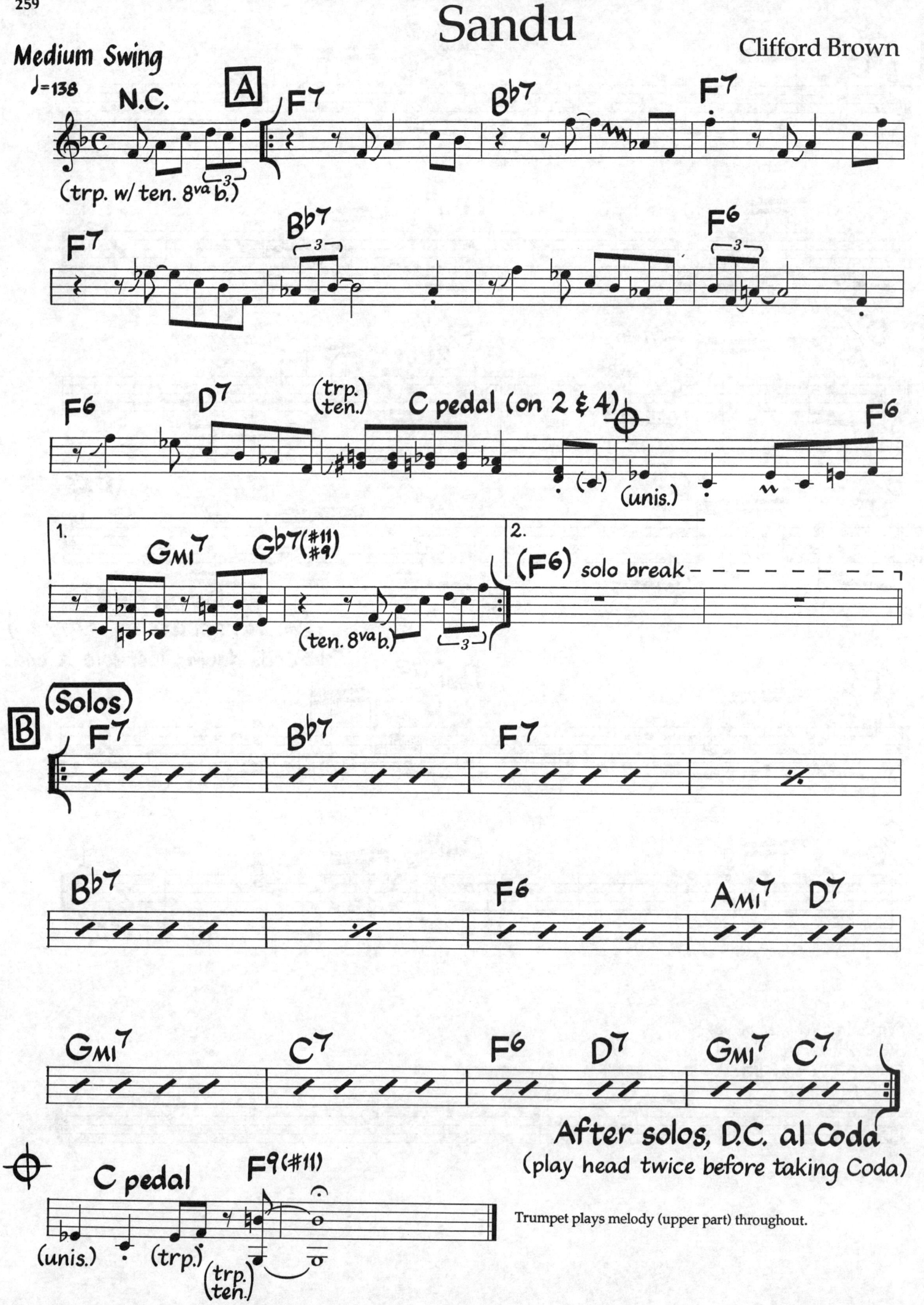

Satin Doll

Duke Ellington
Billy Strayhorn
Johnny Mercer

Solo on form (ABC)
After solos, play head (ABC)
then D.C. al Coda.

Bmi7(b5) may be played as Bmi7.

©1953, 1958 Tempo Music & Duke Ellington Music. Used By Permission.

Save Your Love For Me

Buddy Johnson

(As played by Cannonball Adderley & Nancy Wilson)

Med. Ballad

Recording is one chorus only (Coda taken first time). Melody as written uses straight eighths, but is freely interpreted.

McCOY TYNER

Photo by Jim Marshall ©1988

Search For Peace

McCoy Tyner

Solo on form (AABC);
After solos, D.C. al Coda (no repeat)

Chords in parentheses not used during solos.

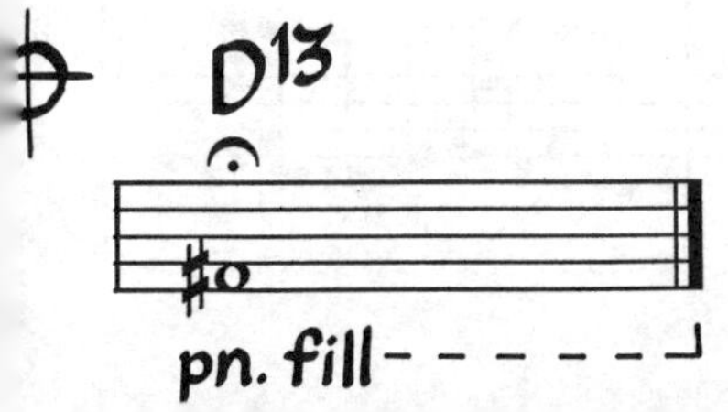

Self Portrait In Three Colors

Charles Mingus

No solos on recording (3x's only).

Shaker Song

Music by Jay Beckenstein
Lyric by David Lasley
and Allee Willis
(As sung by Manhattan Transfer)

Med. Samba (Intro)

268

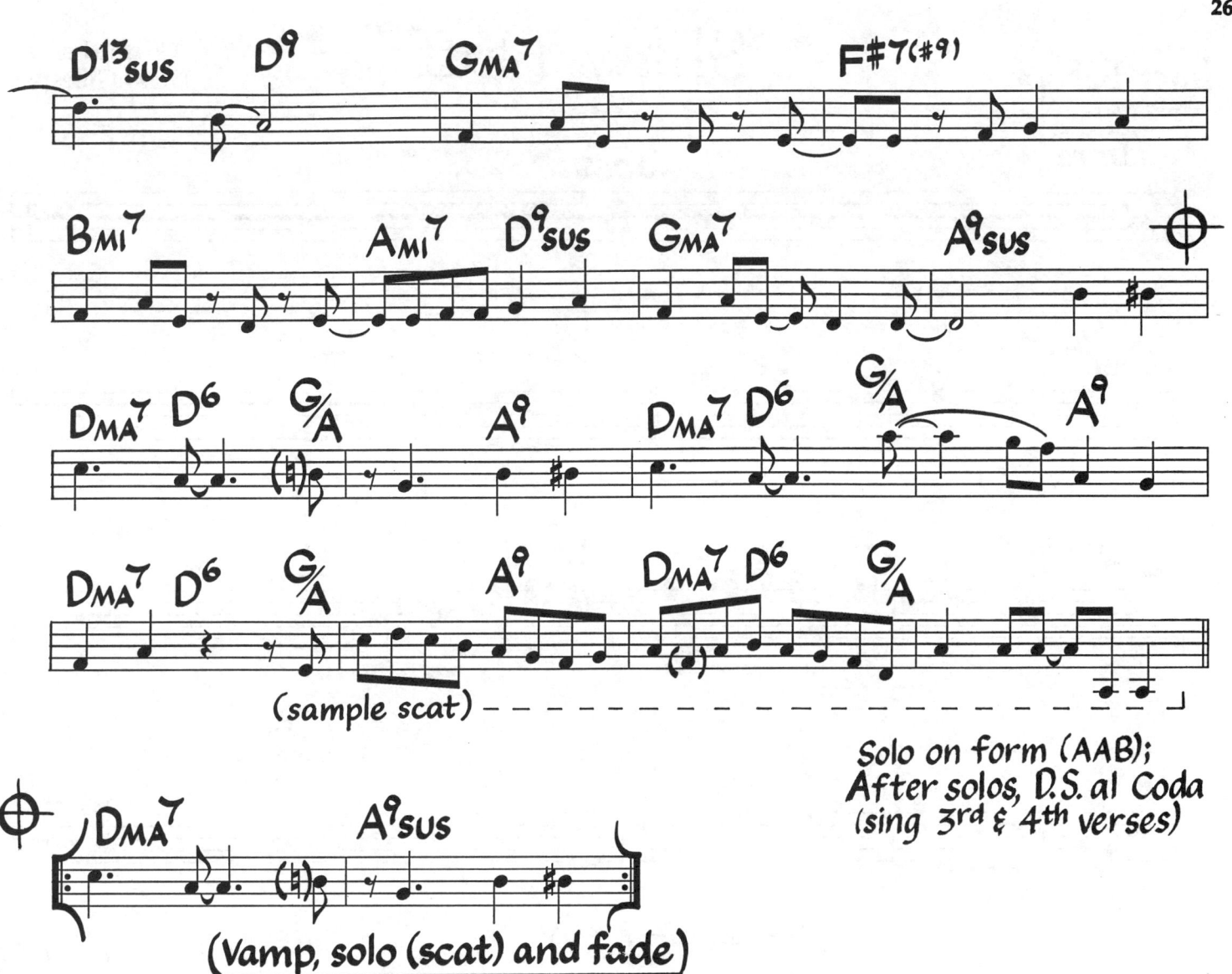

Shaw 'Nuff

Charlie Parker
Dizzy Gillespie

Solo on form (ABC);
After solos, D.S., play head,
then D.C. al fine.

Simple Samba

Jim Hall

D
FMA7
EMI7(b5)
A7
DMI7
G7
CMI7
F7(pn. w/ 8va)
(gtr.)
BMI7(b5)
BbMI7
AMI7
D7(b9)
(pn.)
GMI9(b5)
C7(b9 #5)
F6/9
dr. fill
E
(gtr.)(FMI9)
(FMI9)
Bb bass
(EbMI9)
(EbMI9)
Ab bass
Solo on ABCD; after solos, D.C. al Coda
F#9(b5)
(gtr.)
N.C.
3
F

Skylark

Music by Hoagy Carmichael
Lyric by Johnny Mercer

Med. Ballad

Chords in parentheses are optional.

©1941, 1942 George Simon, Inc. ©Renewed 1969, 1970 Frank Music Corp. This Arrangement ©1988 Frank Music Corp. International Copyright Secured.
All Rights Reserved. Used By Permission.

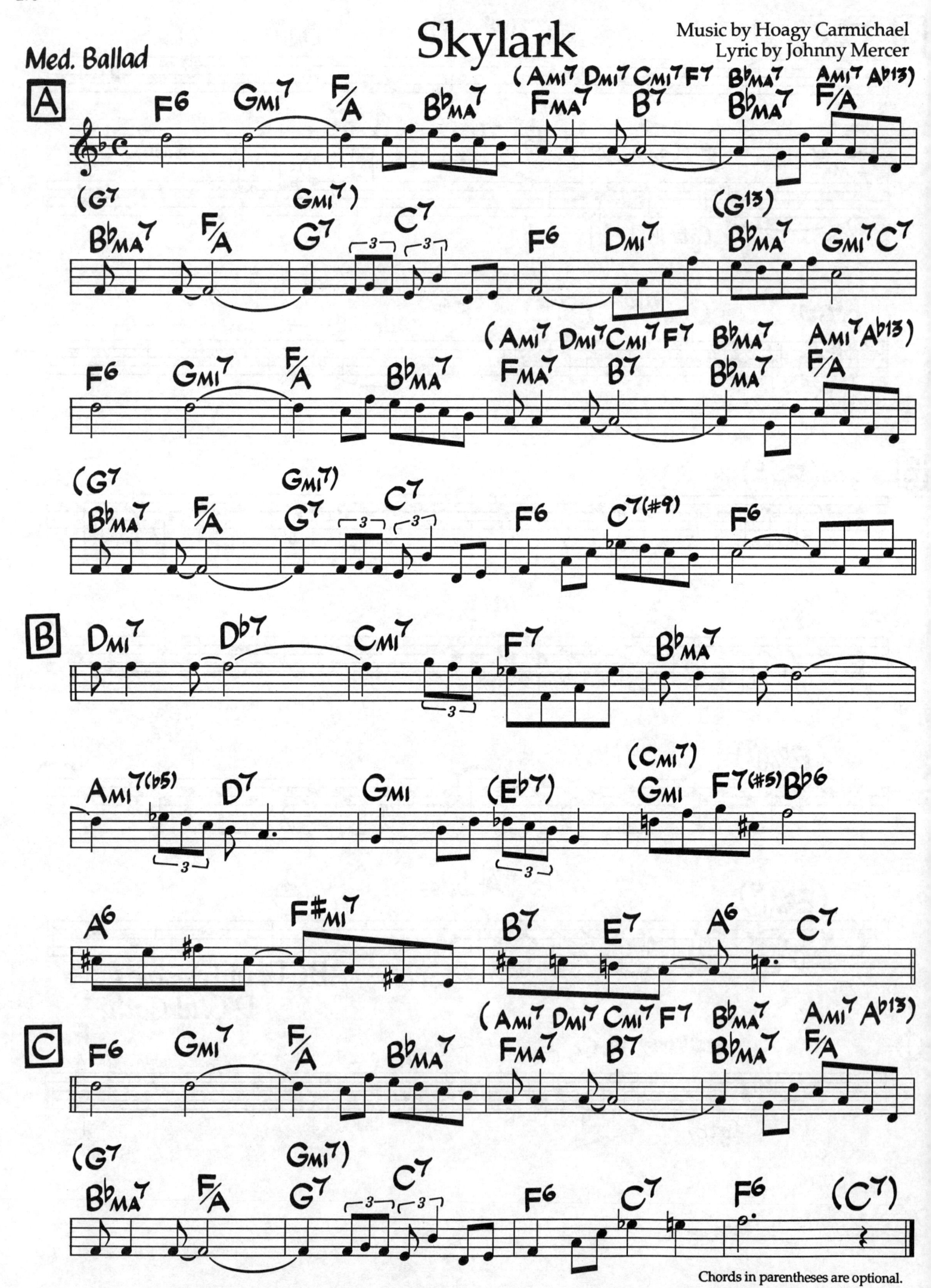

A Sleepin' Bee

Music by Harold Arlen
Lyric by Harold Arlen & Truman Capote

Med. Swing

Small Day Tomorrow

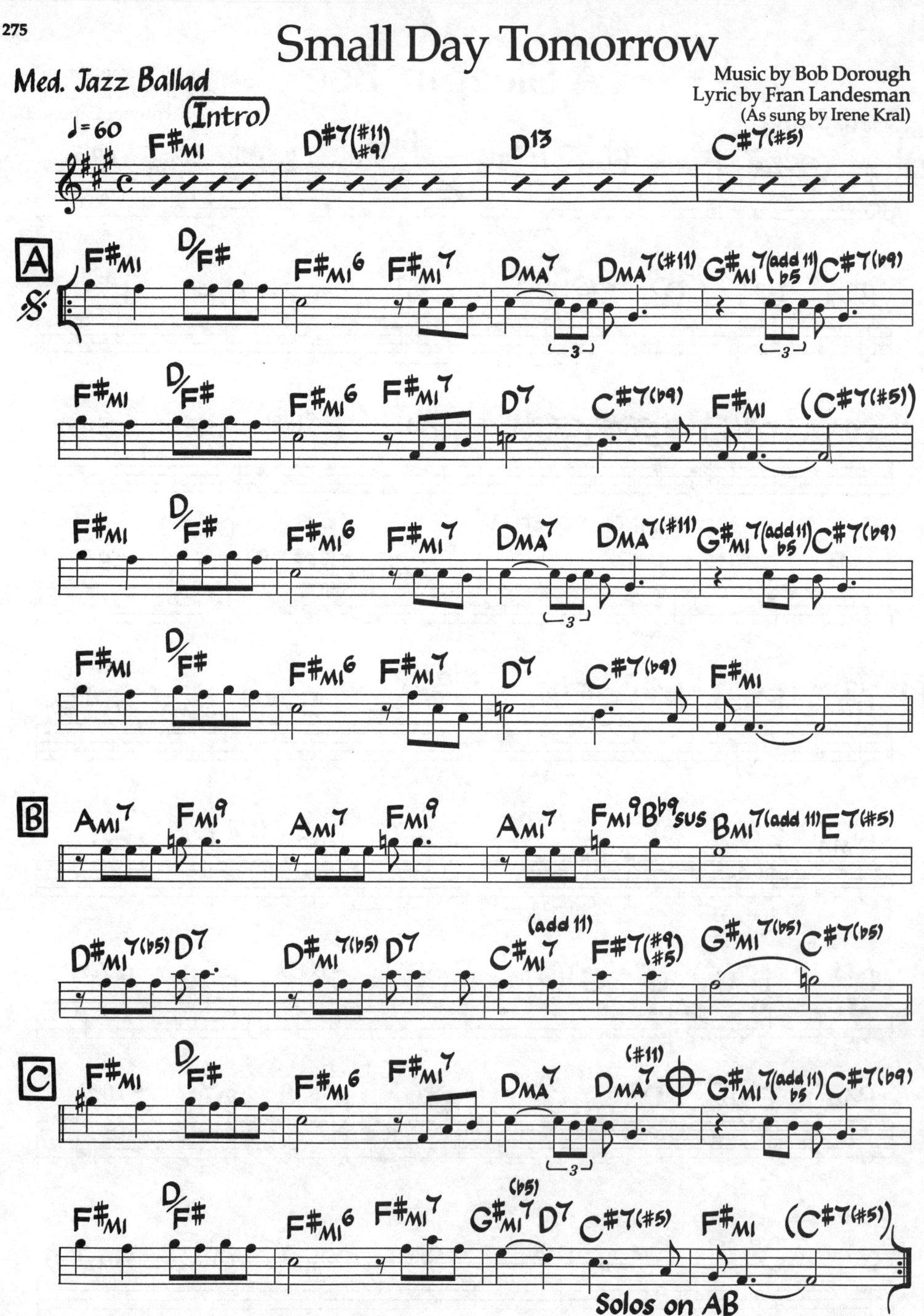

Med. Jazz Ballad

Music by Bob Dorough
Lyric by Fran Landesman
(As sung by Irene Kral)

Solos on AB
After solos, D.S. al Coda

TRO - ©1972 Cromwell Music, Inc., New York, NY. International Copyright Secured. Made In U.S.A. All Rights Reserved Including Public Performance For Profit. Used By Permission.

Solar

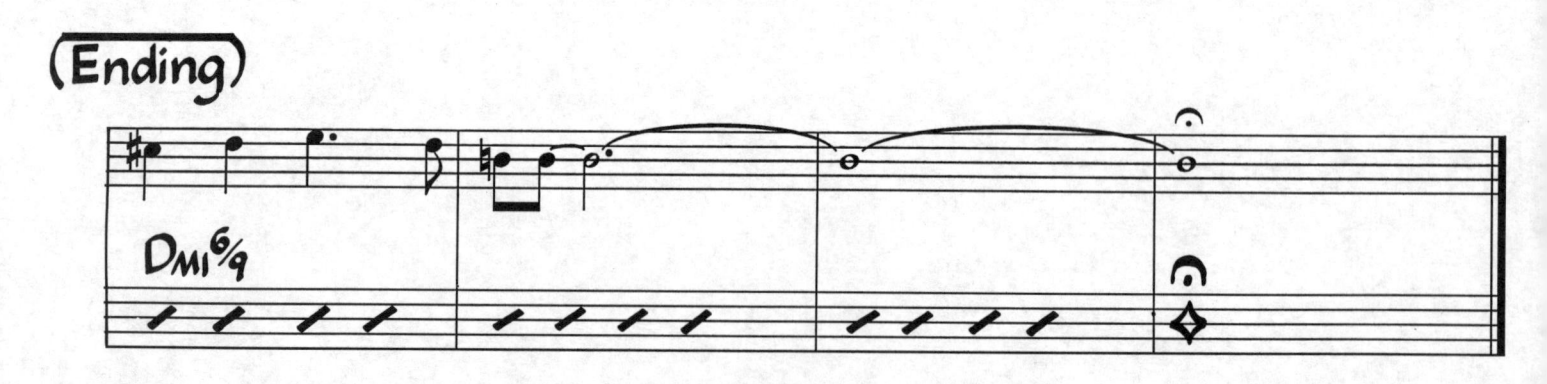

Miles Davis

Medium Swing ♩=165

Head is played twice before and after solos. Melody is freely interpreted.

©1963 Prestige Music. Used By Permission.

Someday My Prince Will Come

Music by Frank Churchill
Lyric by Larry Morey

WES MONTGOMERY

Photo by Tom Copi ©1988

Song For Lorraine

Jay Beckenstein
(As played by Spyro Gyra)

Sonja's Sanfona

Jimmy Haslip
Bill Gable
(As played by The Yellowjackets)

G/F# may be played as F#mi. Keyboard plays chords from E natural minor scale during fade-out.

Soul Sauce
(Wachi Wara)

Dizzy Gillespie
Chano Pozo
(As played by Cal Tjader)

Speak No Evil

Wayne Shorter

Medium Swing ♩=138

Kicks and anticipated chords hold for solos.
The tied G's are started quietly & crescendoed each time.
Ebma7 and Cmi11 chords may also be anticipated for solos.

Solo on form (AABC)
After solos, D.C. al Coda

Vamp & fade

©1965 Miyako Music. Used By Permission.

Spiral

Med. Straight 1/8's
♩= 148

Kenny Barron
(As played by Sphere)

D
(Solos)
EMI11
CMA7(#11)
AMI7(add 11) B7(#9 #5) CMA7(#11) B7(#9 #5)
EMI11
CMA7(#11)
E
G7SUS(b9)
B/G
G7SUS(b9)
E13SUS
C#13
Bb13SUS
F#/E
F
EMI11
CMA7(#11)
AMI7(add 11) B7(#9 #5) CMA7(#11) B7(#9 #5)
Till Cue
EMI11
CMA7(#11)
To D for more choruses;
Take 'On cue' ending to end each solo.
On Cue
Tacet
8
To D for more solos;
After solos, D.S. al Coda.
EMI9 CMA7(#11)
EMI9 CMA7(#11)
EMI11
3

SONNY ROLLINS

Photo by Jim Marshall ©1988

St. Thomas

Medium Swinging Latin

Sonny Rollins

Solos may swing.

After solos, D.C. al fine.
Head is played twice before & after solos.

Sticky Wicket

Al Jarreau
Jay Graydon
Greg Phillinganges

©1983 Al Jarreau Music, Garden Rake Music, Warner Bros. Music & Poopy's Music. Used By Permission.

E7
(2nd x only)
Bb7
A7(#5)
Ab13
(DMI7)
(vocal)
(synth.)
C
DMI7
(vocal)
(F)
G7
DMI7
DMI7
1.
N.C.
DMI7
(gtr.)
2.
F
F#
G7
(Solos)
D
E7
indef.
(On Cue)
E
Bb7
A7(#5)
Ab13
G7
Ab13 A7(#5)
Bb7
A7(#5)
Ab13
G7
Ab13 A7(#5)
Bb7
A7(#5)
Ab13
(DMI7)
(synth.)
D.S., vamp & fade on letter C
(take 2nd ending each time)

Street Life

Music by Joe Sample
Lyric by Will Jennings
(As played by The Crusaders)

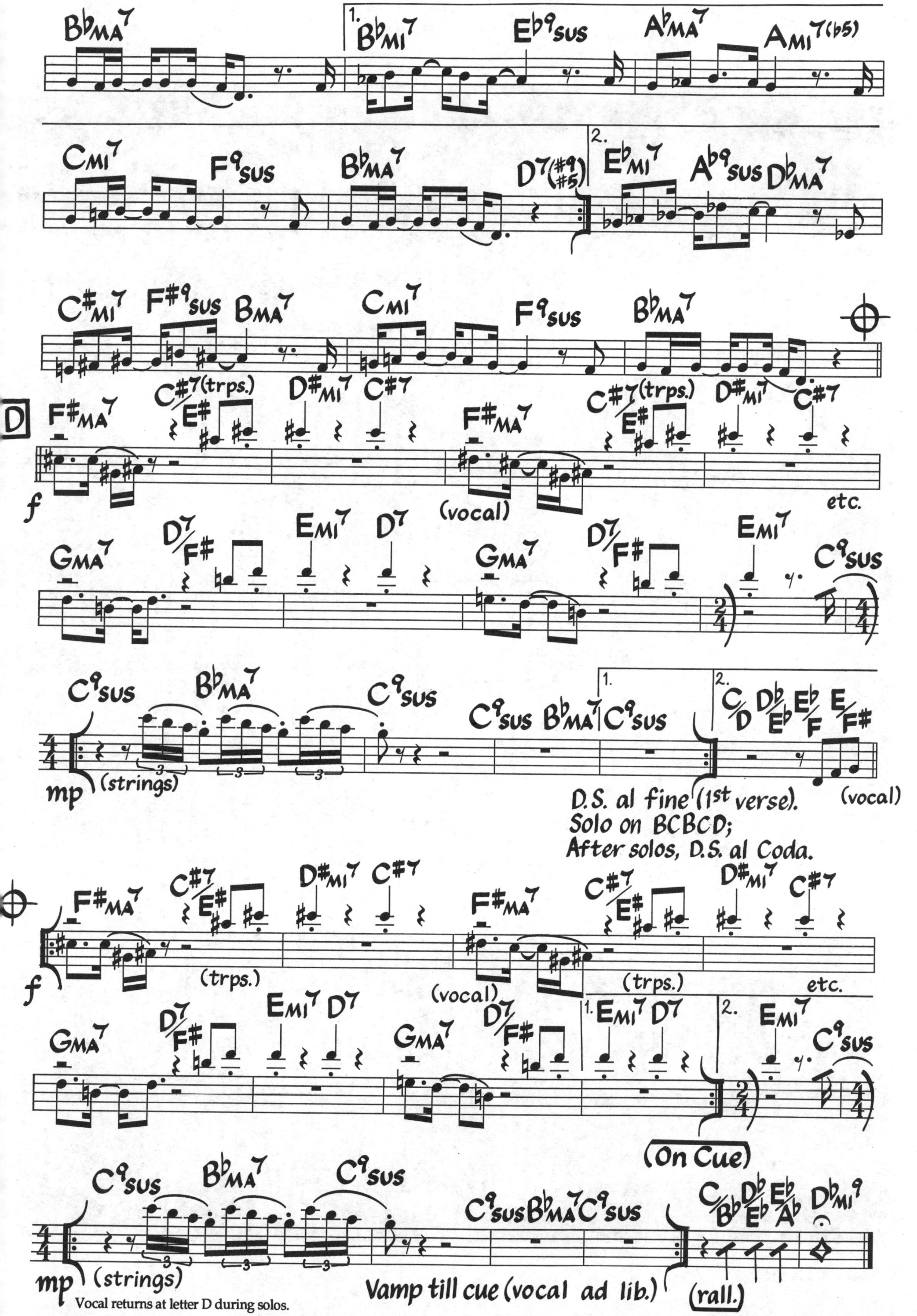

Vocal returns at letter D during solos.

McCOY TYNER

Sudden Samba

Neil Larsen

Break at end of letter B is used at end of each solo only.
Emi7 chords at letter B are not always anticipated during solos.

Solo on form (AB); After solos, D.S. al fine (no repeat)

©1978 Neil Larsen Music. Used By Permission.

Sunrunner

Bob James

C
(Solos)
DMA9
(8)
DMA7 G/D EMI/D A
DMA7 G/D EMI/D A/D
DMA7 G/D EMI/D A
DMA7 G/D EMI/D A/D
D
GMI9 B♭MA7/C C/F C/D
BMI9 D/E E/A E/F#
BMI9 DMA7/E E/A E/F#
BMI9 DMA7/E E/A AMI9 CMA7/D D/G
GMI9 B♭MA7/C C/F G A
After solos, D.S. al Coda
DMA9
Vamp & solo till cue
(On Cue) D pedal
(melody doubled 8va)
(synth.)

Take The "A" Train

Music by Billy Strayhorn
Lyric by Lee Gaines

Med. Swing
(Intro) (D/A Bb7(#5)/Ab D/A Bb7(#5)/Ab D/A Bb7(#5)/Ab D/A Bb7(#5)/Ab)
(pn.)

A D6   E9(#11)
(melody)

Emi7   A7   D6   (Emi7   A7)

D6   E9(#11)

Emi7   A7   D6   D7

B Gma7

E9   Emi9   A9   A7(b9)

©1941, renewed 1968 Tempo Music. Used By Permission.

Solo on form (ABC);
After solos, D.S. al Coda.

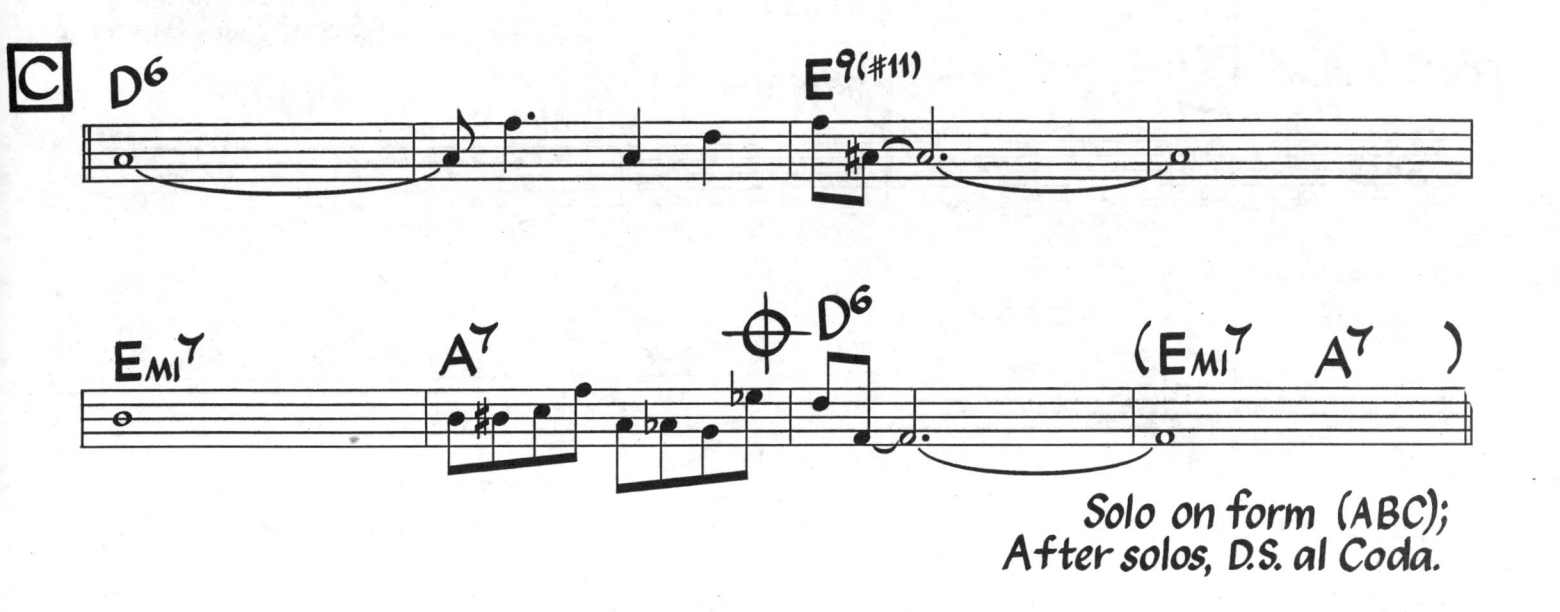

Instrumental background line during solos for bars 1-4 and 9-12 of letter A and bars 1-4 of letter C as required:

Tenderly

Music by Walter Gross
Lyric by Jack Lawrence

May be played in 3/4 (subtract one beat from the first note in each bar).

©1946, 1947, 1987 Edwin H. Morris & Co, a Division of MPL Communications, Inc. ©Renewed 1974, 1975 Edwin H. Morris & Co., A Division of MPL Communications, Inc. International Copyright Secured. All Rights Reserved. Used By Permission.

Theme For Ernie

Fred Lacey
(As played by John Coltrane)

Melody is freely interpreted.

There Will Never Be Another You

Music by Harry Warren
Lyric by Mack Gordon

These Foolish Things

Music by Jack Strachey
& Harry Link
Lyric by Holt Marvell

Alternate changes for soloing on bars 4 & 12 of letter A and bar 4 of letter C: | DMI9 G9 C#MI9 F#9 |

©1936 by Boosey & Co. Ltd., London, assigned to Bourne Co. Copyright Renewed. International Copyright Secured. All Rights Reserved. Used By Permission. Rights for Germany, Austria, Switzerland & CSSR assigned to Melodie Der Welt, J. Michel KG, Musikverlag. Rights for Japan assigned to Kogakusha Music Pub. Co., Ltd. - Used by permission of JASRAC License #8670719.

GEORGE BENSON

This Masquerade

Leon Russell
(As sung by George Benson)

Med.- Slow Latin/Rock

Med. Funk Ballad
♩= 94

The Three Marias

Wayne Shorter

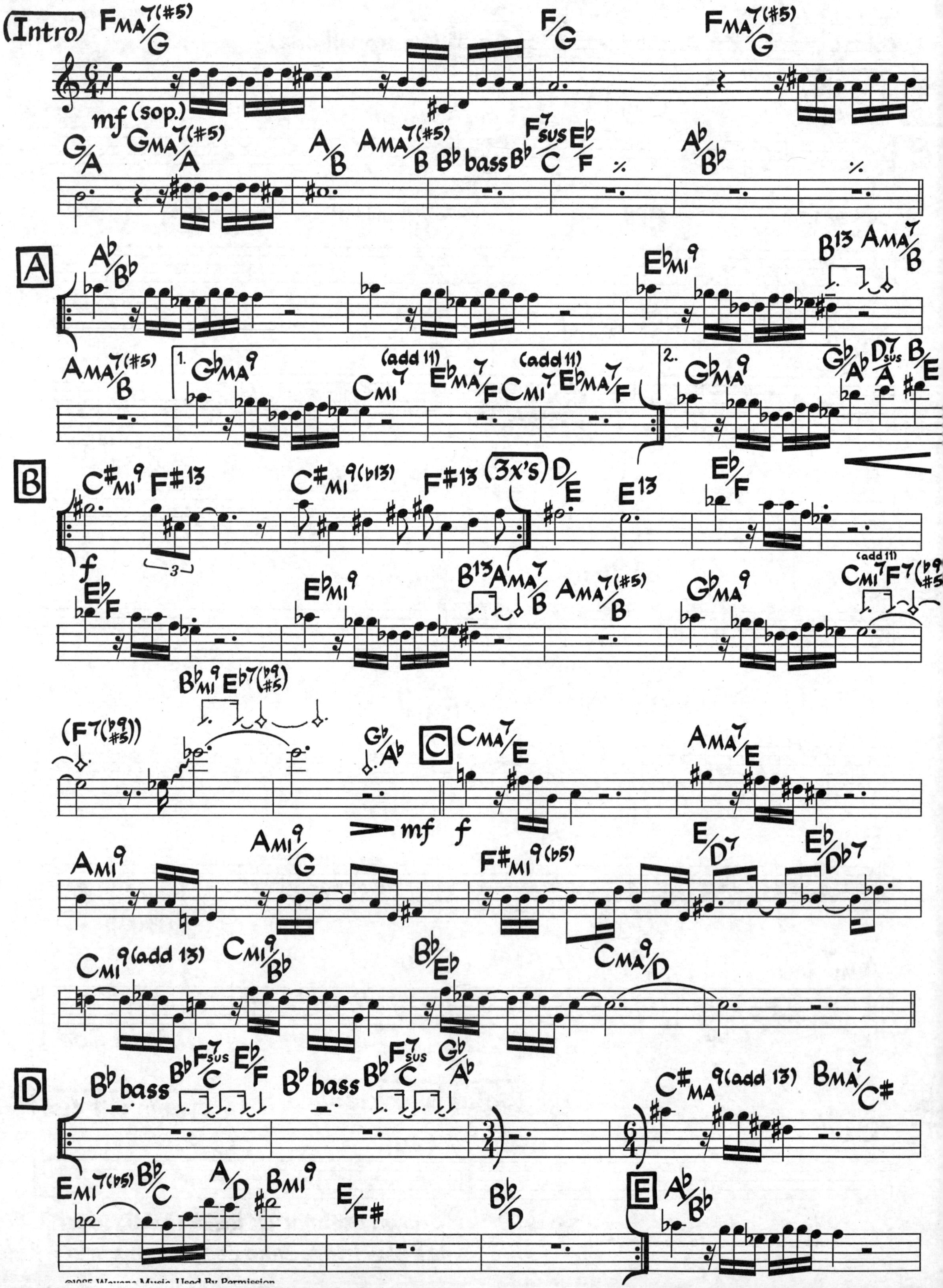

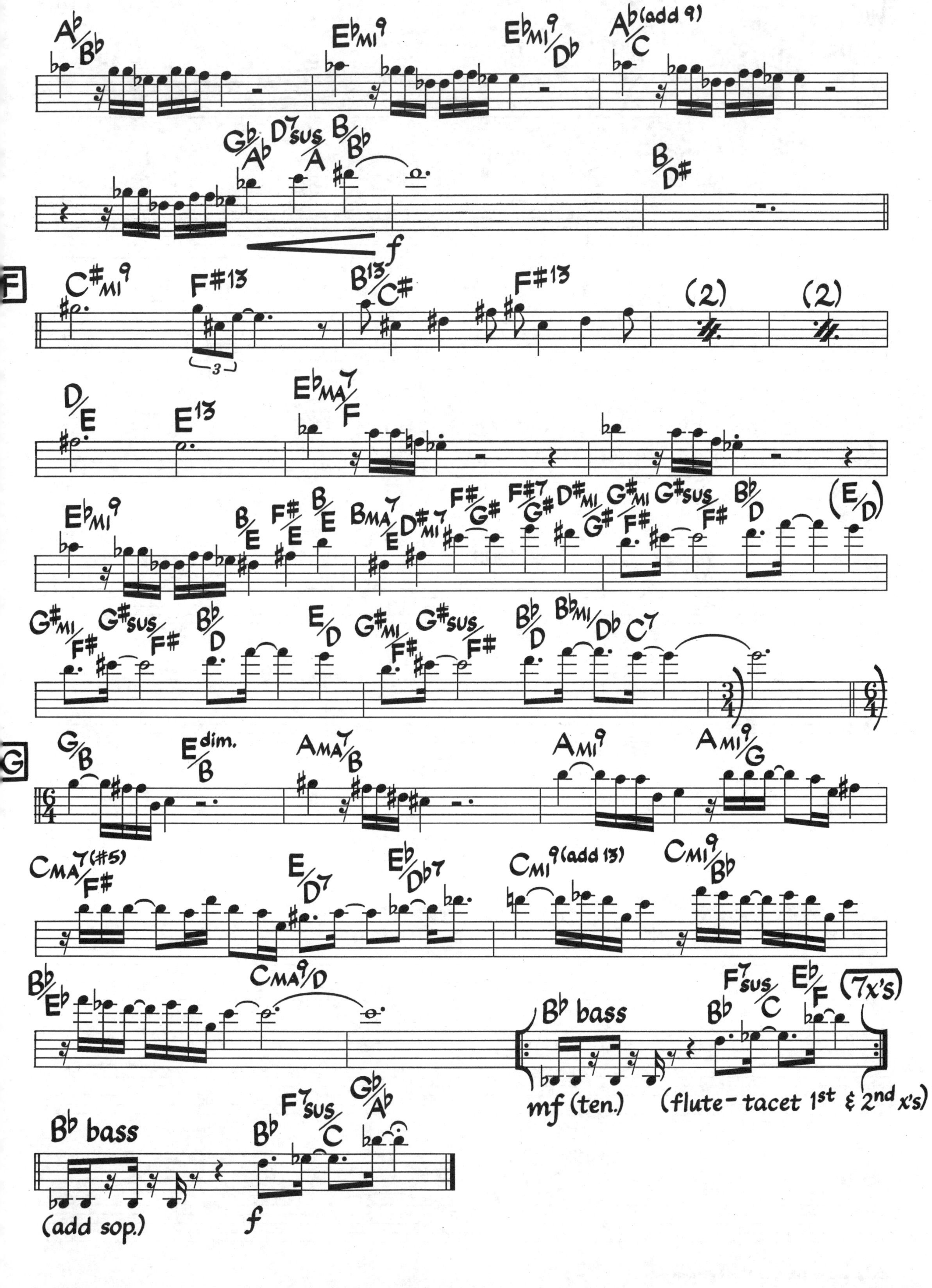
F
G
B♭ bass
mf (ten.)
(7x's)
(flute-tacet 1st & 2nd x's)
B♭ bass
(add sop.)

Three Views Of A Secret

Jaco Pastorius

Medium Jazz Waltz
♩= 112

Harmonica sounds one octave higher than written. Melody is rather freely interpreted (except at letter A).

Time Remembers One Time Once

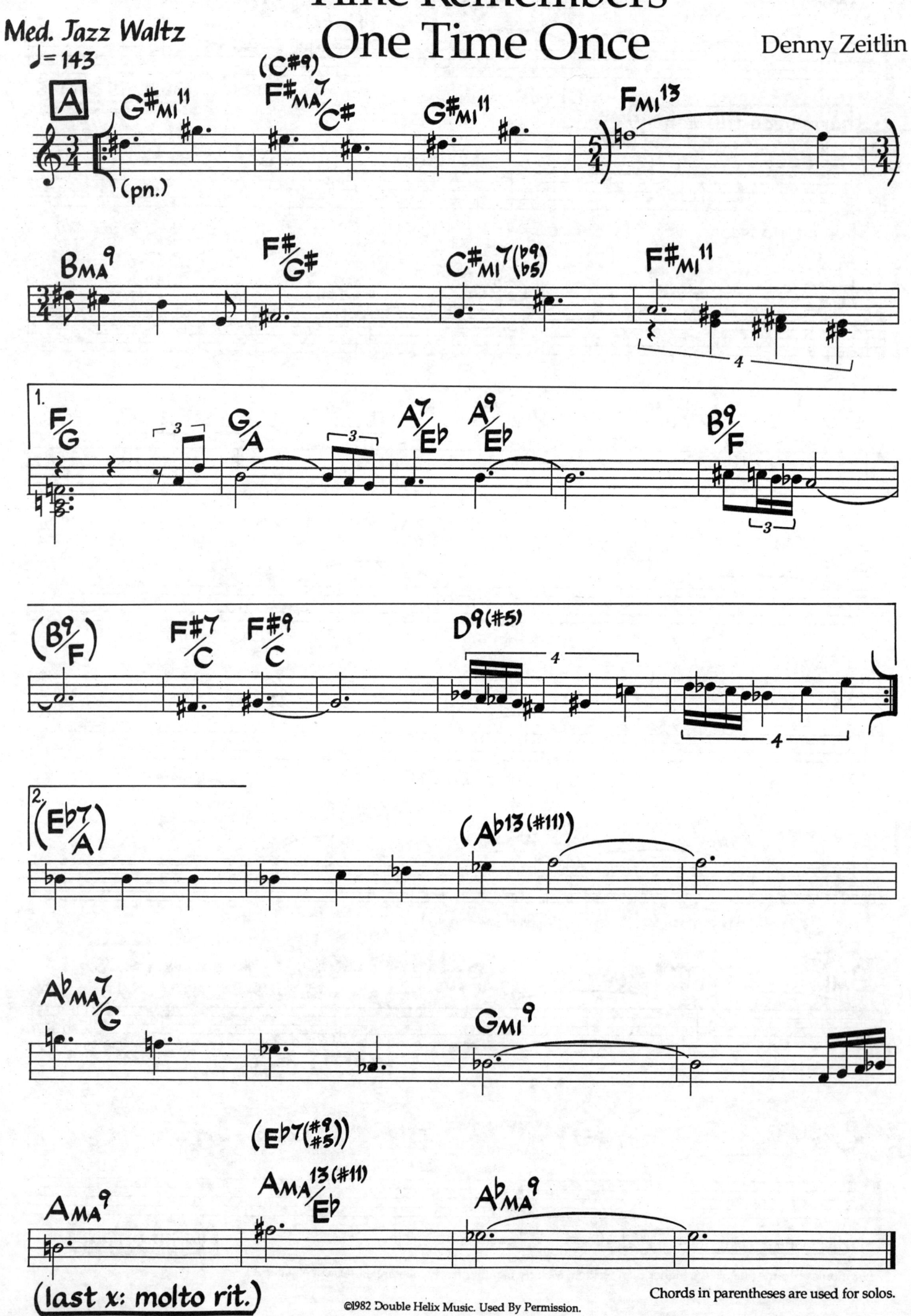

Denny Zeitlin

Med. Jazz Waltz ♩ = 143

(last x: molto rit.)

©1982 Double Helix Music. Used By Permission.

Chords in parentheses are used for solos.

Triste

Antonio Carlos Jobim

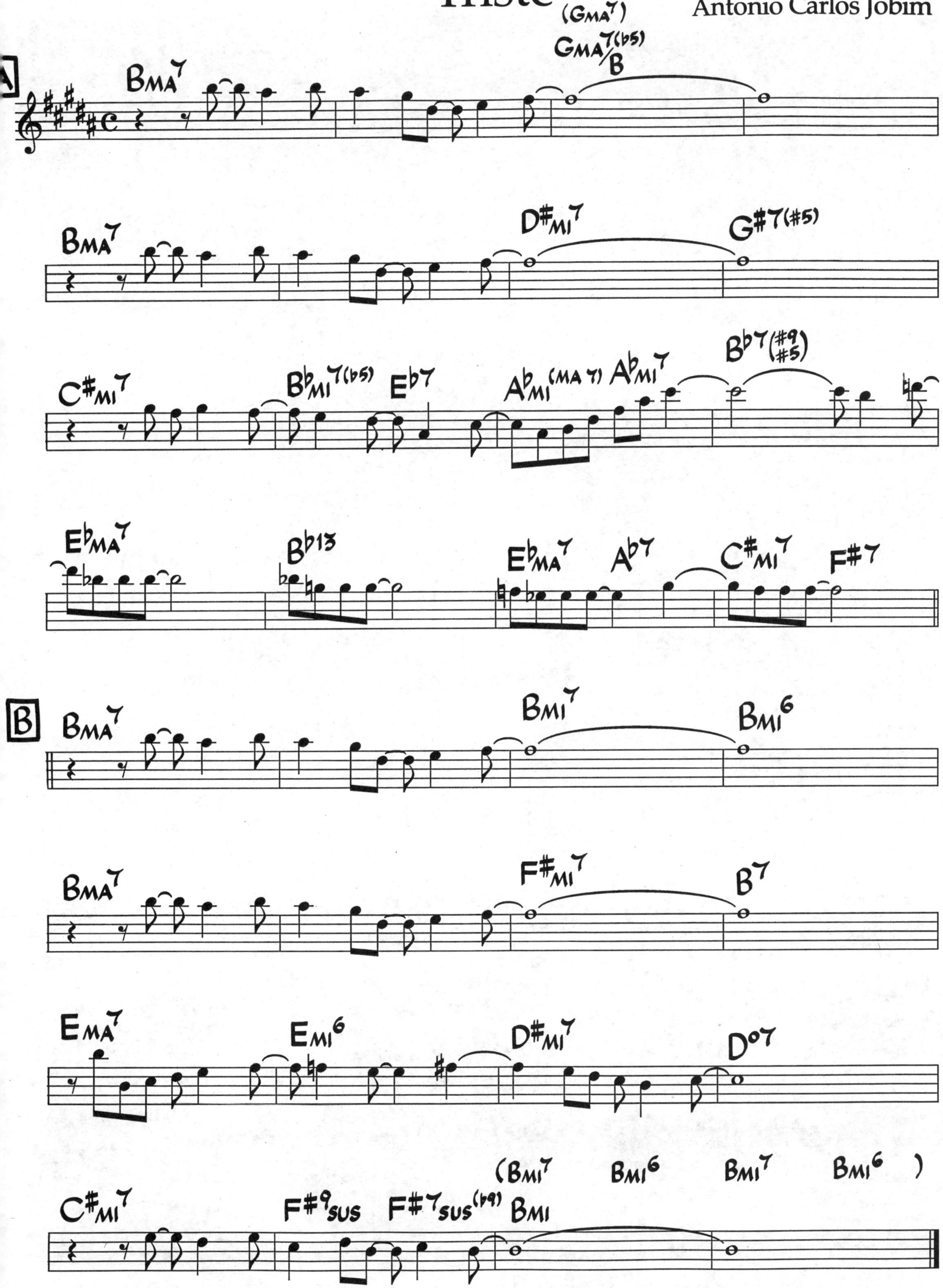

HERBIE HANCOCK, MILES DAVIS & RON CARTER

Tune Up

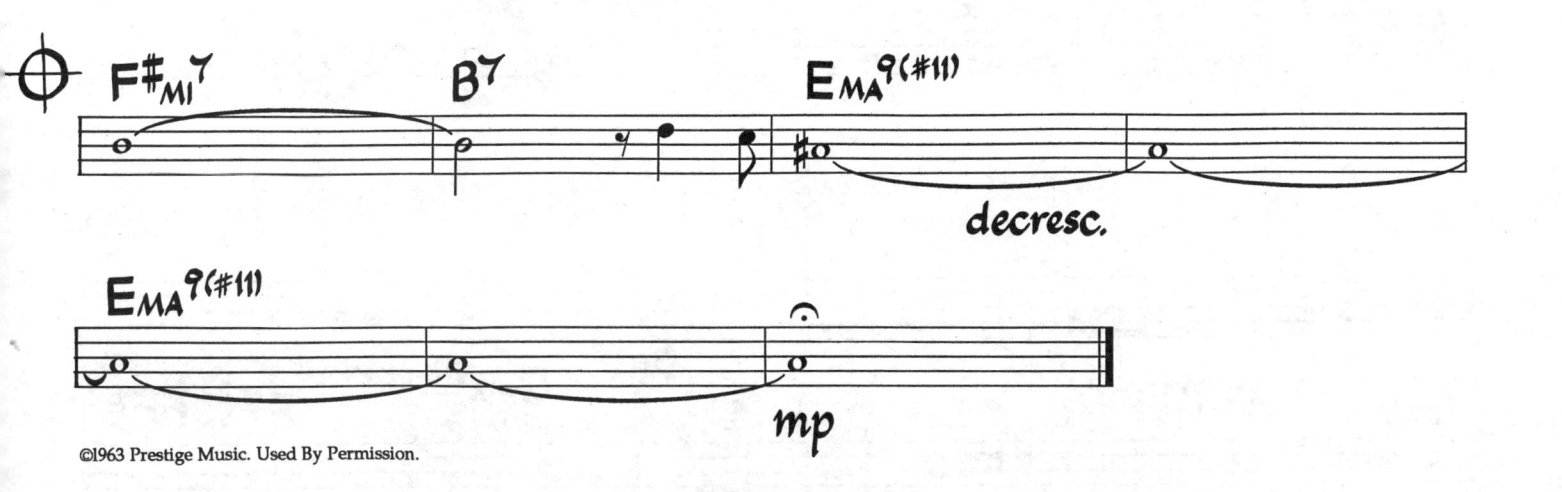

Miles Davis

Fast Swing ♩=280
(Intro) — Tacet

Turn Your Love Around

Jay Graydon
Steve Lukather
Bill Champlin
(As sung by George Benson)

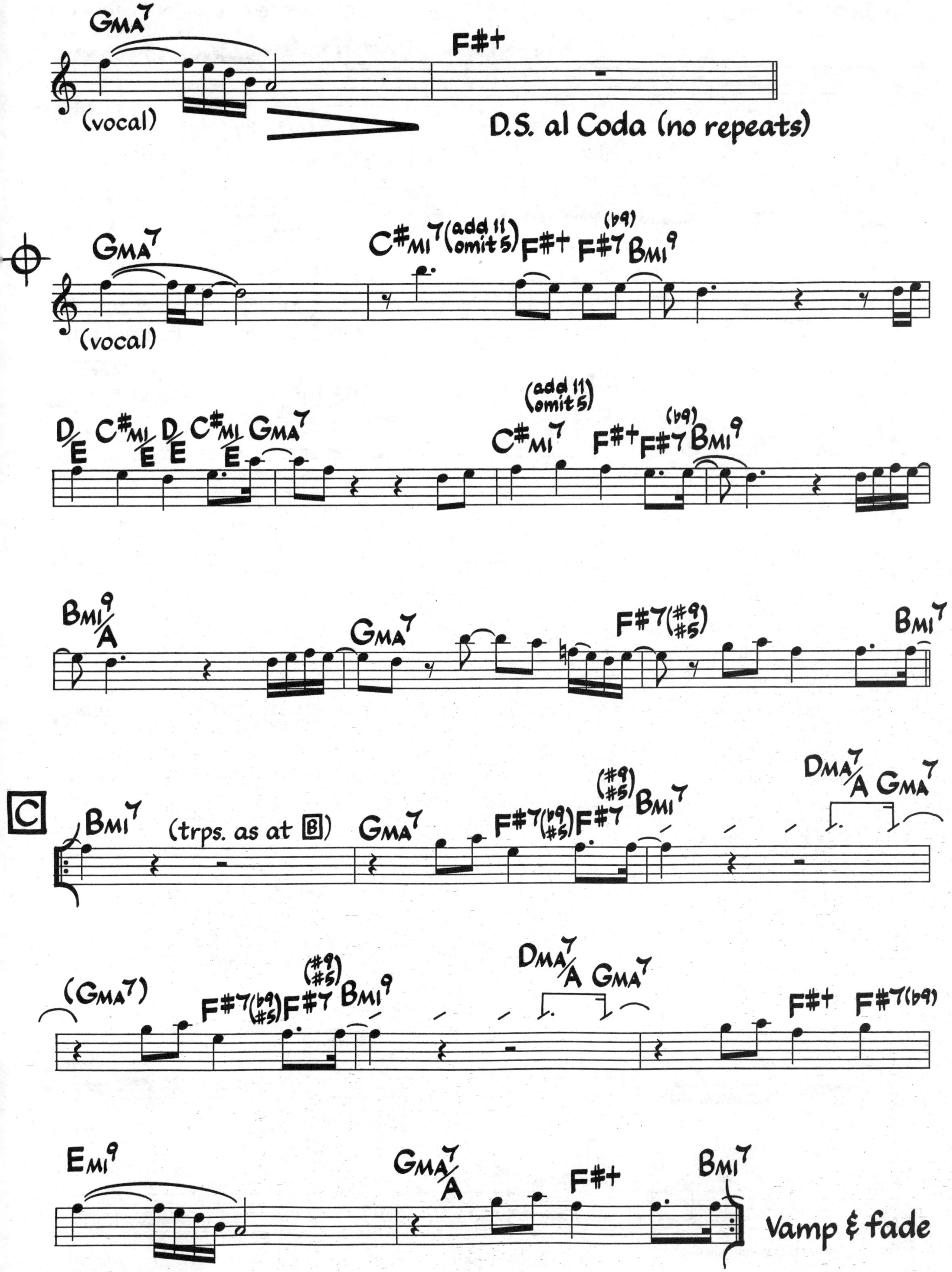

GMA7
F#+
(vocal)
D.S. al Coda (no repeats)
GMA7
C#MI7(add 11 omit 5)
F#+
F#7(b9)
BMI9
(vocal)
D/E
C#MI/E
D/E
C#MI/E
GMA7
C#MI7(add 11 omit 5)
F#+
F#7(b9)
BMI9
BMI9/A
GMA7
F#7(#9 #5)
BMI7
C
BMI7
(trps. as at B)
GMA7
F#7(b9 #5)
F#7(#9 #5)
BMI7
DMA7/A
GMA7
(GMA7)
F#7(b9 #5)
F#7(#9 #5)
BMI9
DMA7/A
GMA7
F#+
F#7(b9)
EMI9
GMA7/A
F#+
BMI7
Vamp & fade

Twisted

Med. Swing
♩ = 165 (Intro)

Music by Wardell Gray
Lyric by Annie Ross

D7
G7
DMA7
F#MI7
B7
EMI7
A7
D6
B7
EMI7
A7
D
D7
G7
D7
D7
G7
DMA7
F#MI7
FMI7
EMI7
A7
D6
F°7
EMI7
A7
D6
D.S. al Coda
(play A twice)
A7
D6 (Ad lib.)
D7

Unit Seven

Sam Jones
(As played by Wes Montgomery)

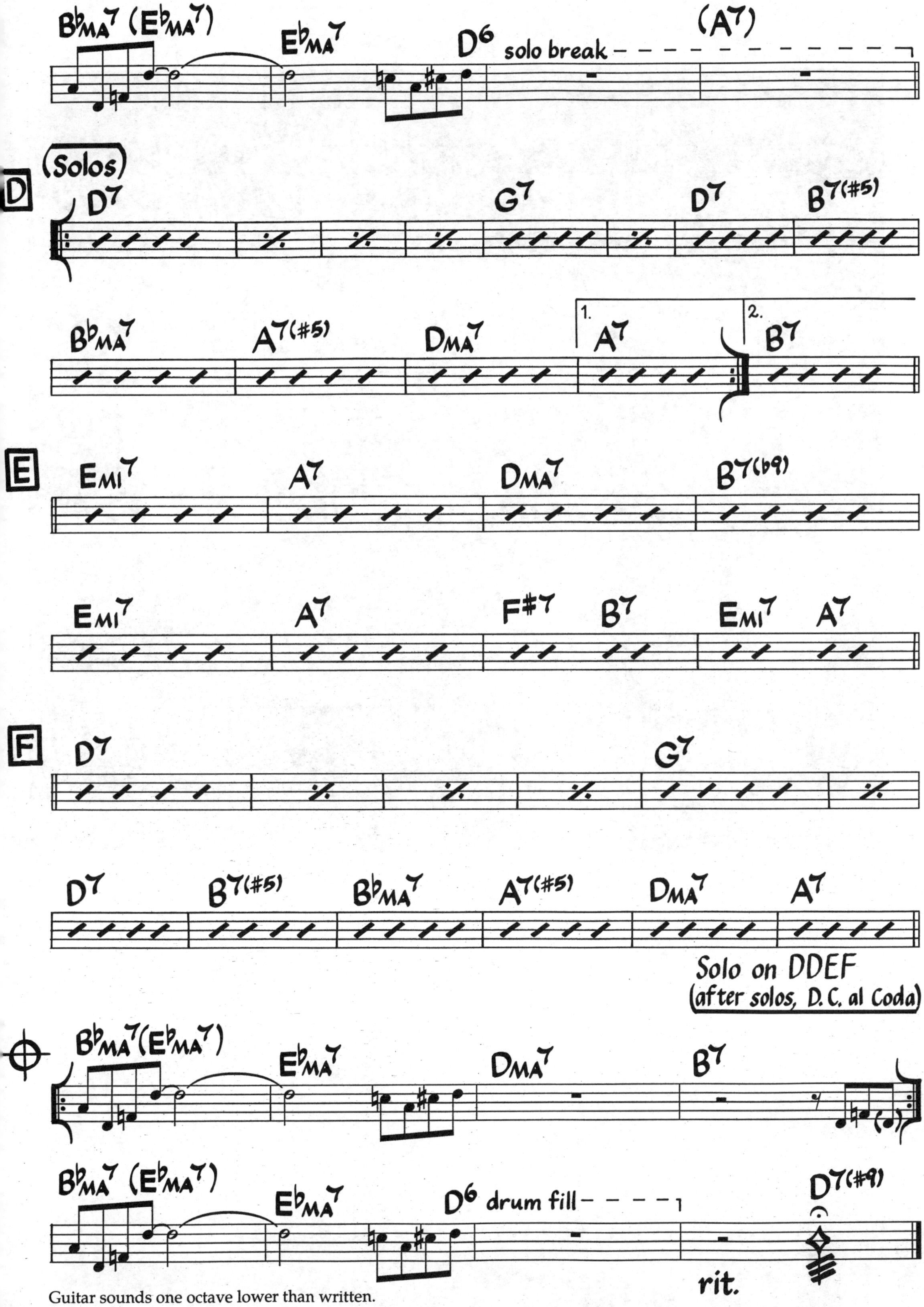

Guitar sounds one octave lower than written.

WAYNE SHORTER AND MILES DAVIS

Up Jumped Spring

Freddie Hubbard

Medium-Up Jazz Waltz
♩= 183

Kicks are not played during solos.
Fmi7 in bars 10 & 12 of letters A and C may be played as F7(+9).

©1962, 1973 Gomace Music. Used By Permission.

Velas
(Velas Içadas)

Ivan Lins
Vitor Martins
(As played by Quincy Jones)

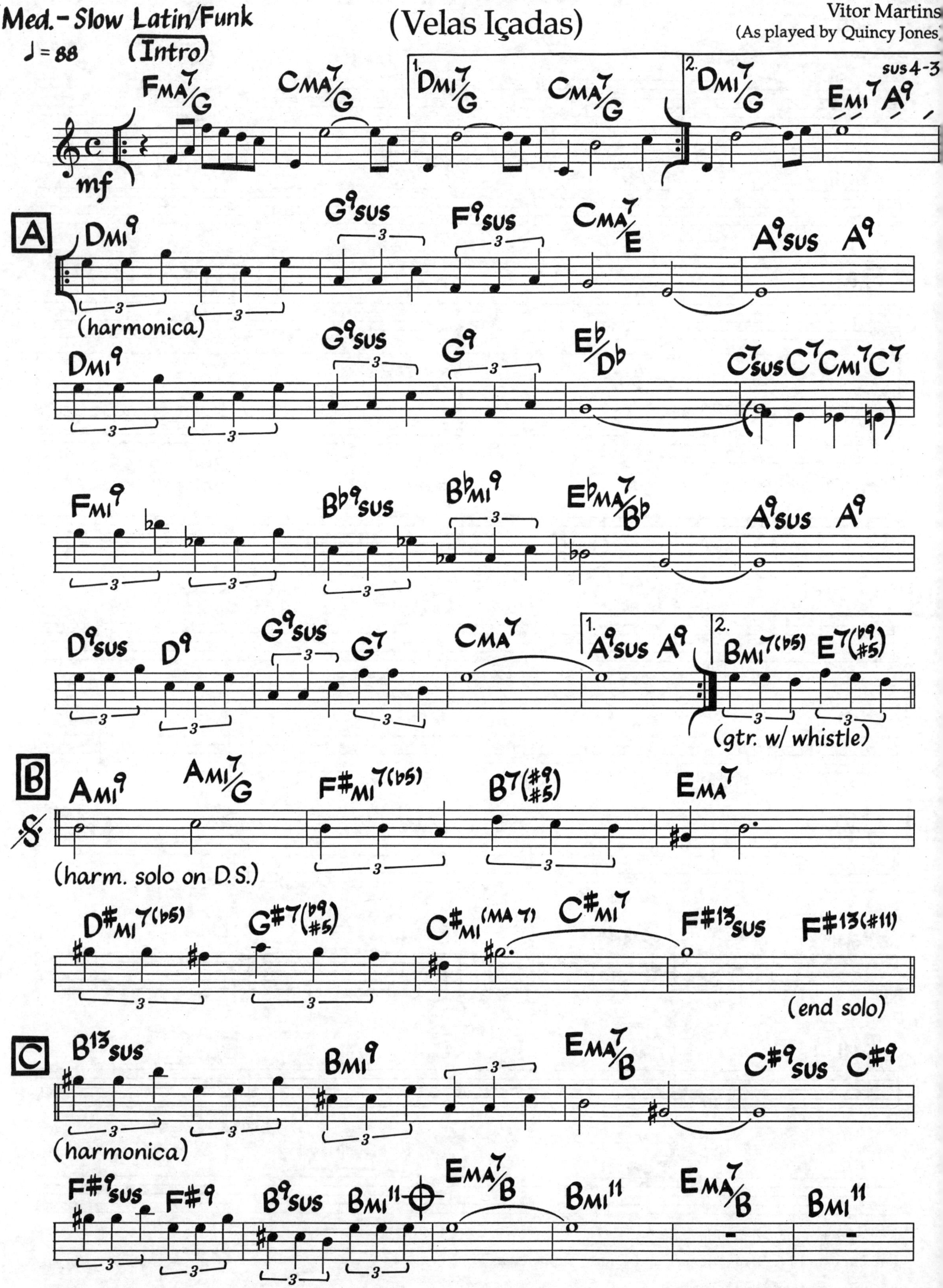

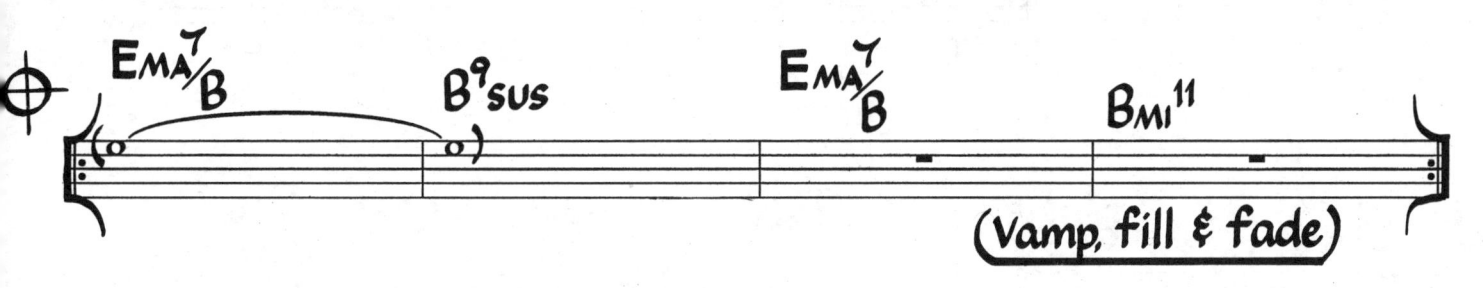

Melodic rhythm is freely interpreted. Intro is from Bobbi Norris LP and is played on bass (15vab.).
On Quincy Jones version, guitar improvises over intro chords.

Very Early

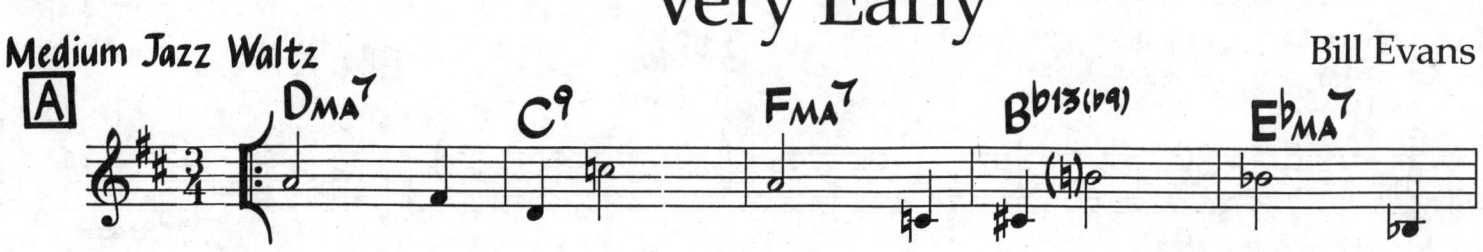

Bill Evans

Medium Jazz Waltz

Voyage

Kenny Barron
(As played by Stan Getz)

Bright Swing ♩=232

Chords in parentheses are used for solos.

©1986 Wazuri Publishing Co. International Copyright Secured. Made In U.S.A. All Rights Reserved. Used By Permission.

Waltz For Debby

Medium Jazz Waltz

Bill Evans

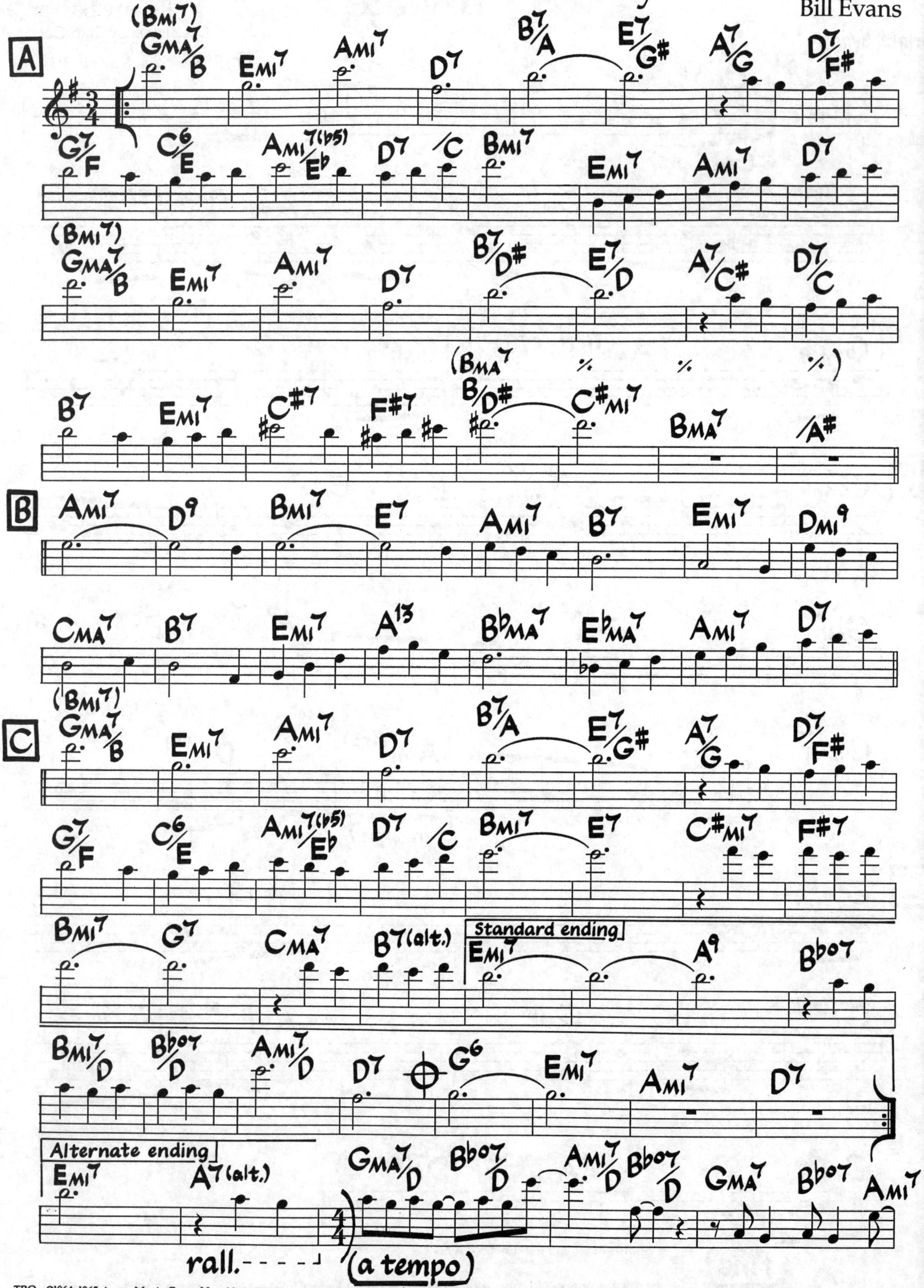

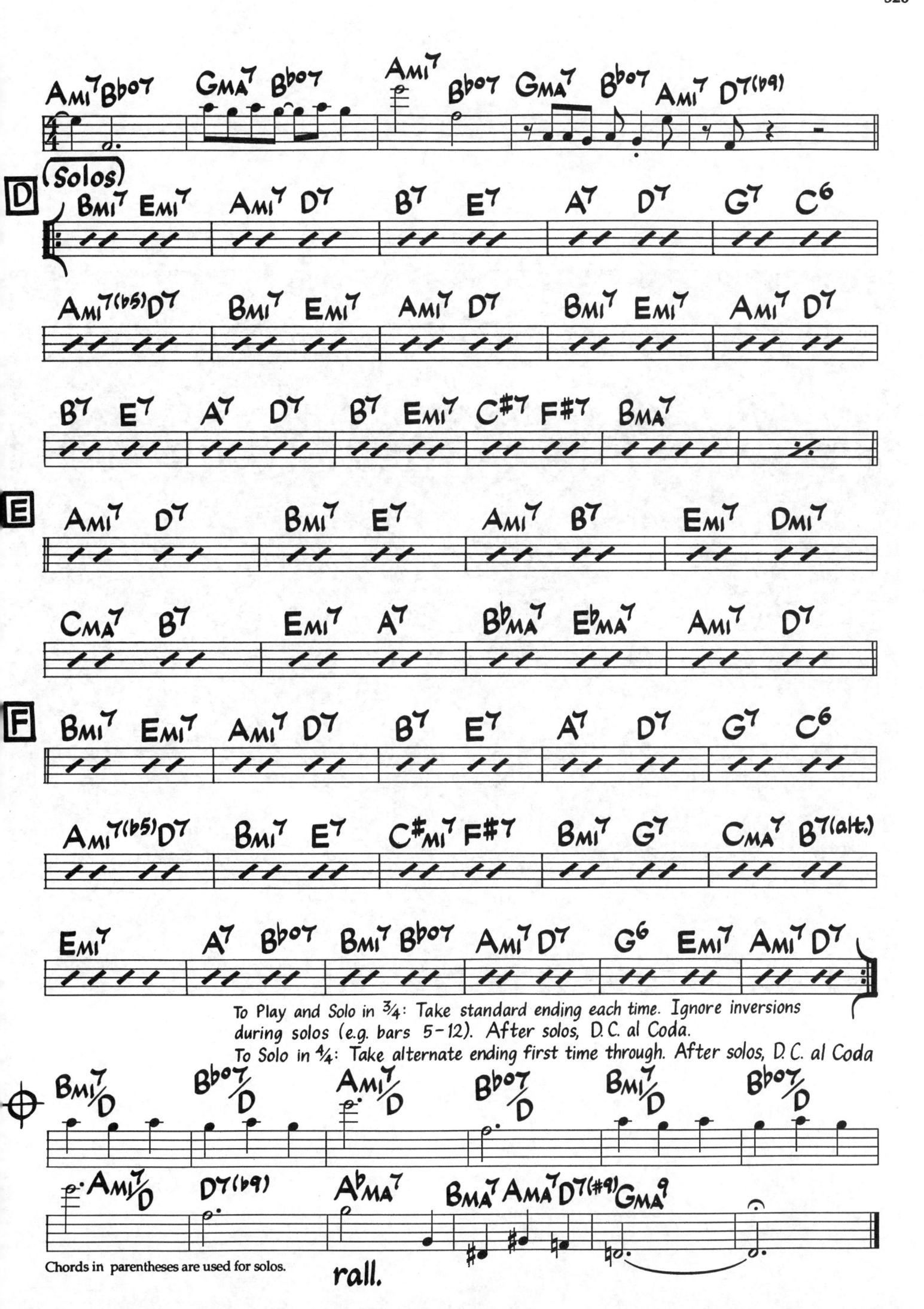

To Play and Solo in 3/4: Take standard ending each time. Ignore inversions during solos (e.g. bars 5–12). After solos, D.C. al Coda.
To Solo in 4/4: Take alternate ending first time through. After solos, D.C. al Coda

Chords in parentheses are used for solos.   rall.

JIM HALL

Waltz New

Jim Hall

Medium-Up Straight 1/8's

Melody is played without chords. Based on the chords of "Someday My Prince Will Come".
Guitar sounds one octave lower than written.

©1978 Janhall Music. Used By Permission

Waterwings

Don Grusin
(As played by Lee Ritenour)

Medium-Up Latin/Funk ♩ = 140

©1980 Bad Dog Music. Used By Permission.

F#MA13(b5)
C13(b5)
D
BMI9
E7(alt.) [Bb13/E]
(Ab13(b5))
1st x: gtr. plays bottom line (switching where marked)
2nd x: add flute on upper line (no switching)
(Ab13(b5) AMA7)
AMA7
Eb13(#11)
G#MI11
D9SUS
C#9SUS
1st x:
E13(b5)
F7(#9 #5)
F#MA7
1st x:
C13(b5)
(Pn. Solo)
E
C#9SUS
C#13(b9)
F/F#
F#MA7
E9SUS
G#/A
AMA7
(Vamp till cue)
(On Cue)
F
G9SUS
AMA7
(4x's)
(pn. solo continues)
Bass solos on letter B (indef.)
then D.S. al Coda (observe both repeats)
F#MA7
D#MI11
D.C., vamp and solo on
letter A, end on cue

Wave

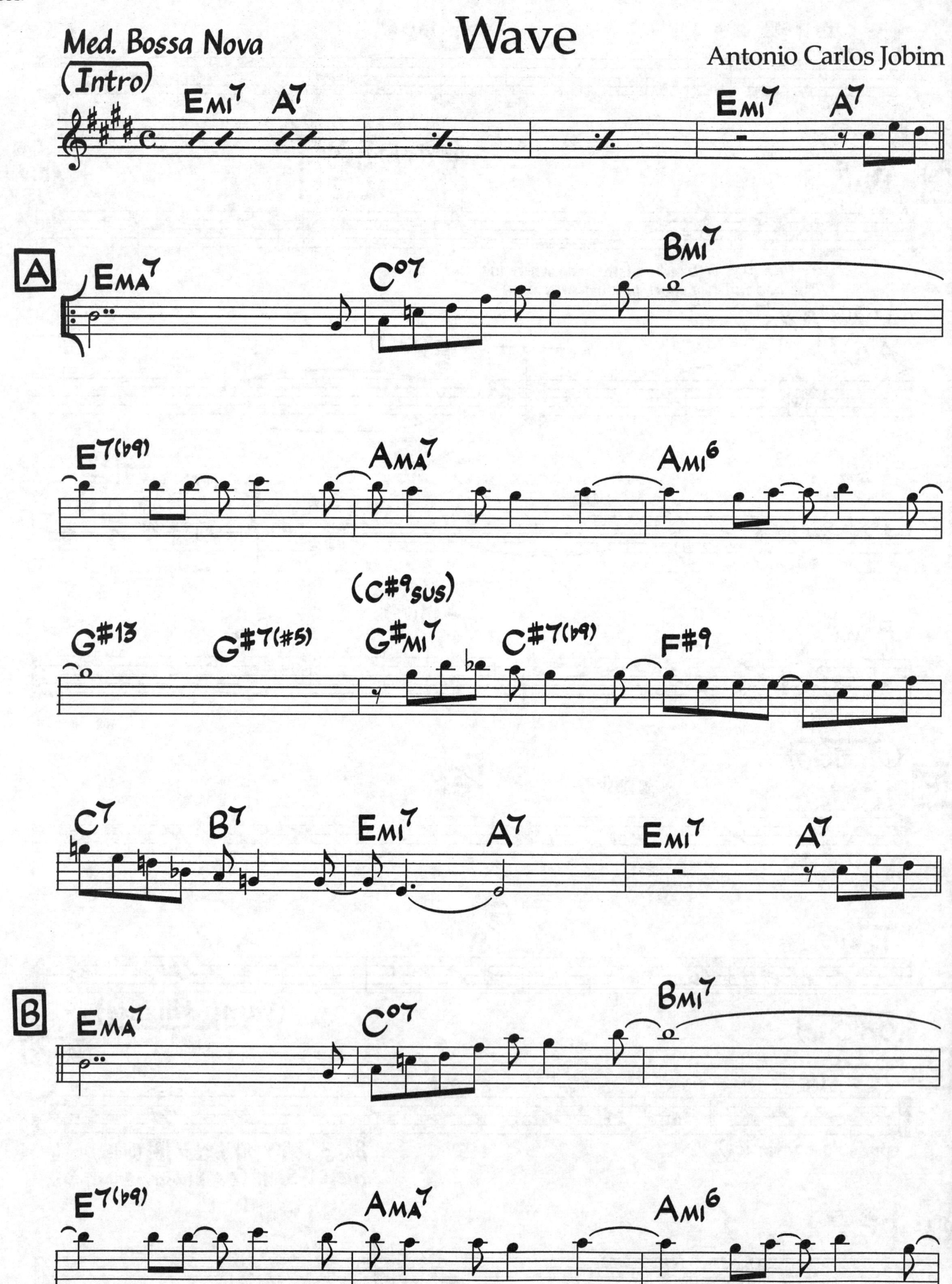

Med. Bossa Nova
Antonio Carlos Jobim

(Intro)

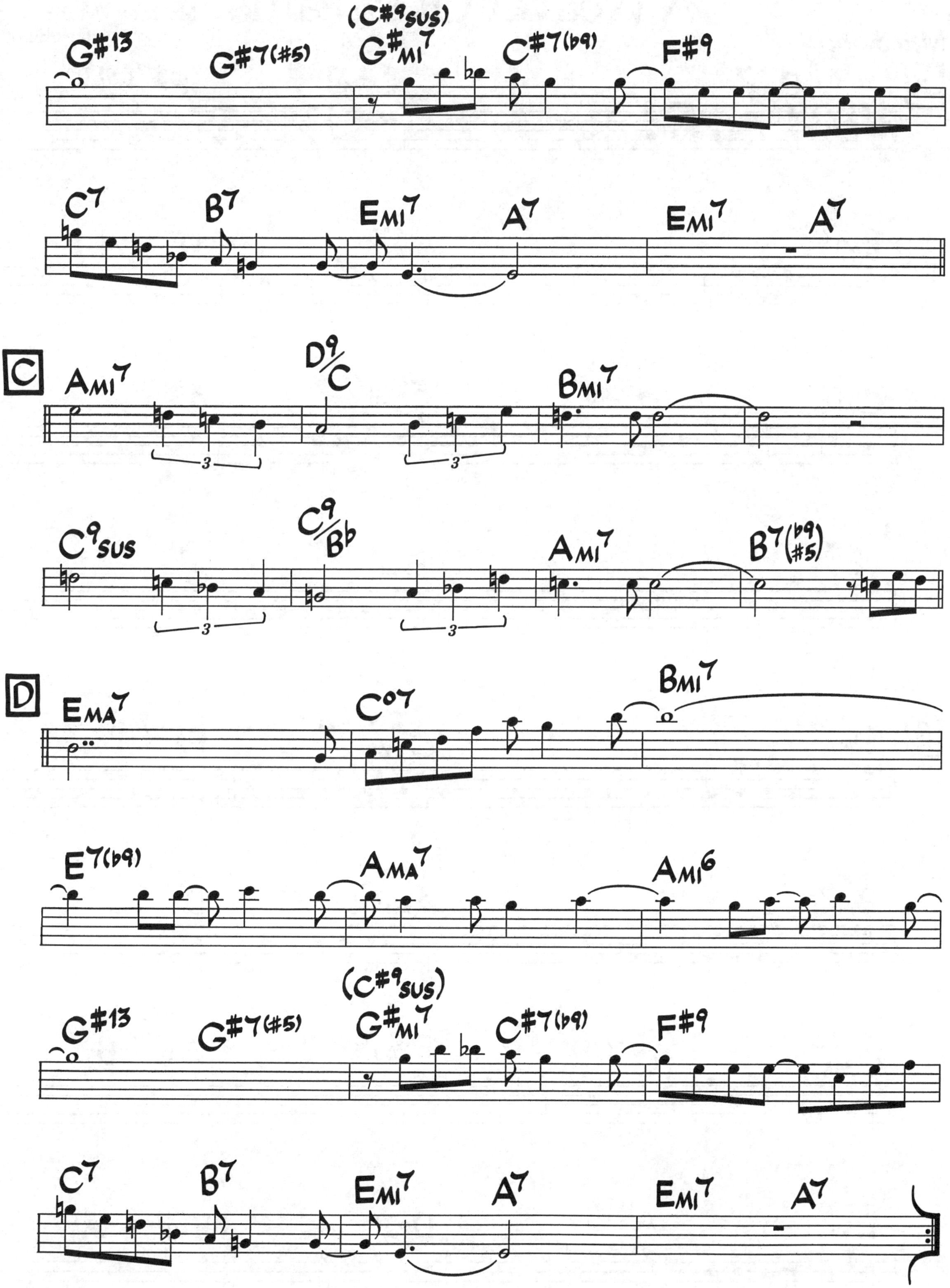
G#13 G#7(#5) (C#9sus) G#MI7 C#7(b9) F#9
C7 B7 EMI7 A7 EMI7 A7
C AMI7 D9/C BMI7
C9sus C9/Bb AMI7 B7(b9 #5)
D EMA7 C°7 BMI7
E7(b9) AMA7 AMI6
G#13 G#7(#5) (C#9sus) G#MI7 C#7(b9) F#9
C7 B7 EMI7 A7 EMI7 A7

A Weaver Of Dreams

Music by Victor Young
Lyric by Jack Elliott

Med. Swing *

*also played as a ballad

©1951 Edward Krassner Music Co., Inc. © Renewed 1979 Edwin H. Morris & Co., A Division of MPL Communications, Inc.
International Copyright Secured. All Rights Reserved. Used By Permission.

We'll Be Together Again

Music by Carl Fischer
Lyric by Frankie Laine

Two changes in a bar get two beats apiece.

Well You Needn't

Thelonious Monk

Medium (-Up) Swing

West Coast Blues

John L. "Wes" Montgomery

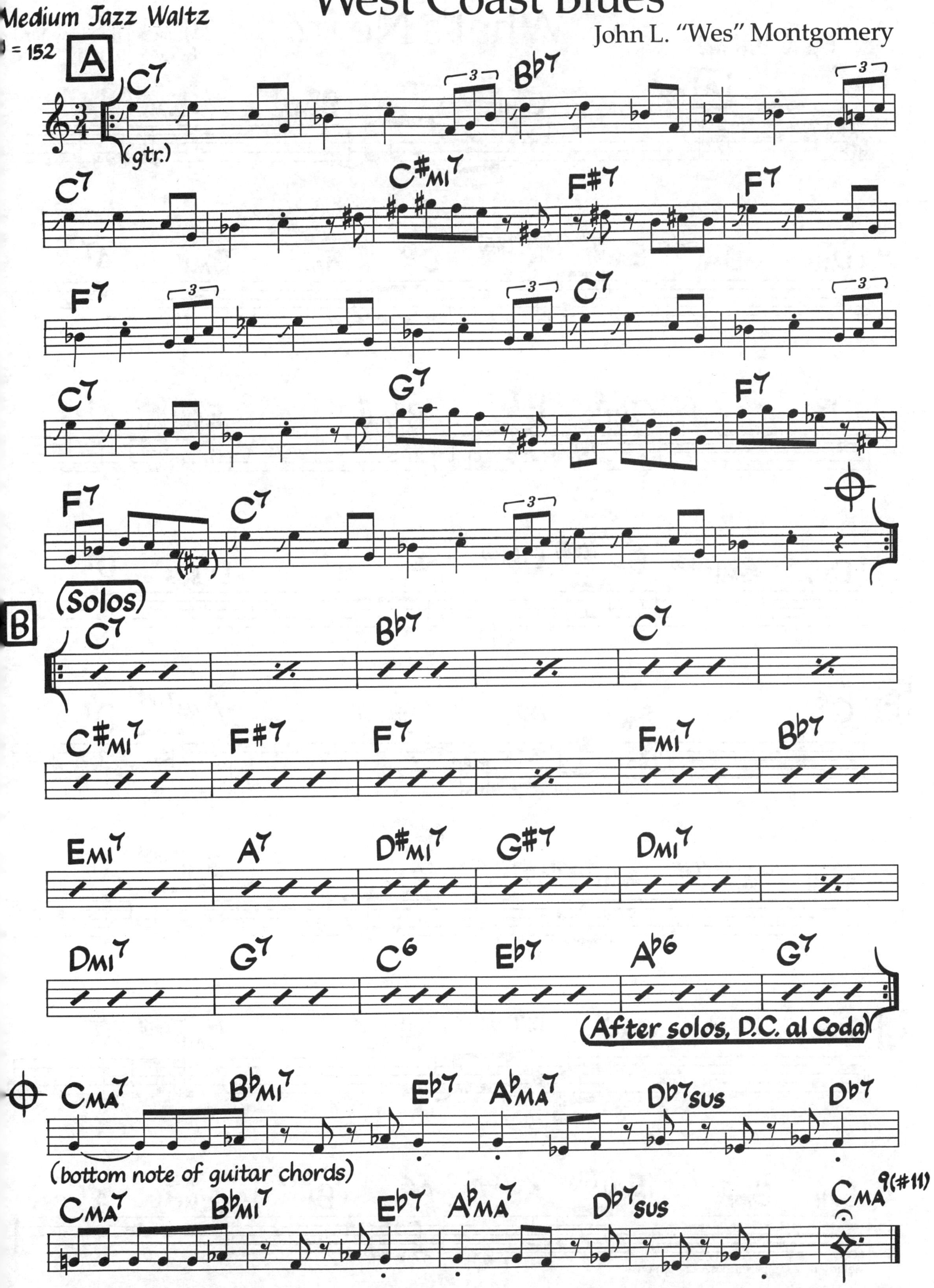

Guitar sounds one octave lower than written.

What's New?

Music by Bob Haggard
Lyric by Johnny Burke

Med. Ballad

Where Is Love?

Lionel Bart
(As sung by Irene Kral)

Medium Ballad

Who Can I Turn To?

Leslie Bricusse
Anthony Newley

Med. Ballad*

*also played as Medium Swing.

Play B natural instead of Bb in bar 13 of letter A when alternate changes are used.

©1964 Concord Music Ltd., London England. TRO - Musical Comedy Productions, Inc., New York, controls all publication rights for the U.S.A. and Canada. International Copyright Secured. Made In U.S.A. All Rights Reserved Including Public Perofrmance For Profit. Used By Permission.
Rights assigned to Essex Musikvertrieb Gmbh, Koln for Germany, Austria, Switzerland, Hungary, Bulgaria, Rumania, Czechoslovia, Yugoslavia, Poland, Greece, Turkey, Saudi Arabia, Iraq and Jordan.

Wildflower

Wayne Shorter

Medium Jazz 6/4
♩ = 160

Trumpet plays melody (upper line).
©1965 Miyako Music. Used By Permission.

Willow Weep For Me

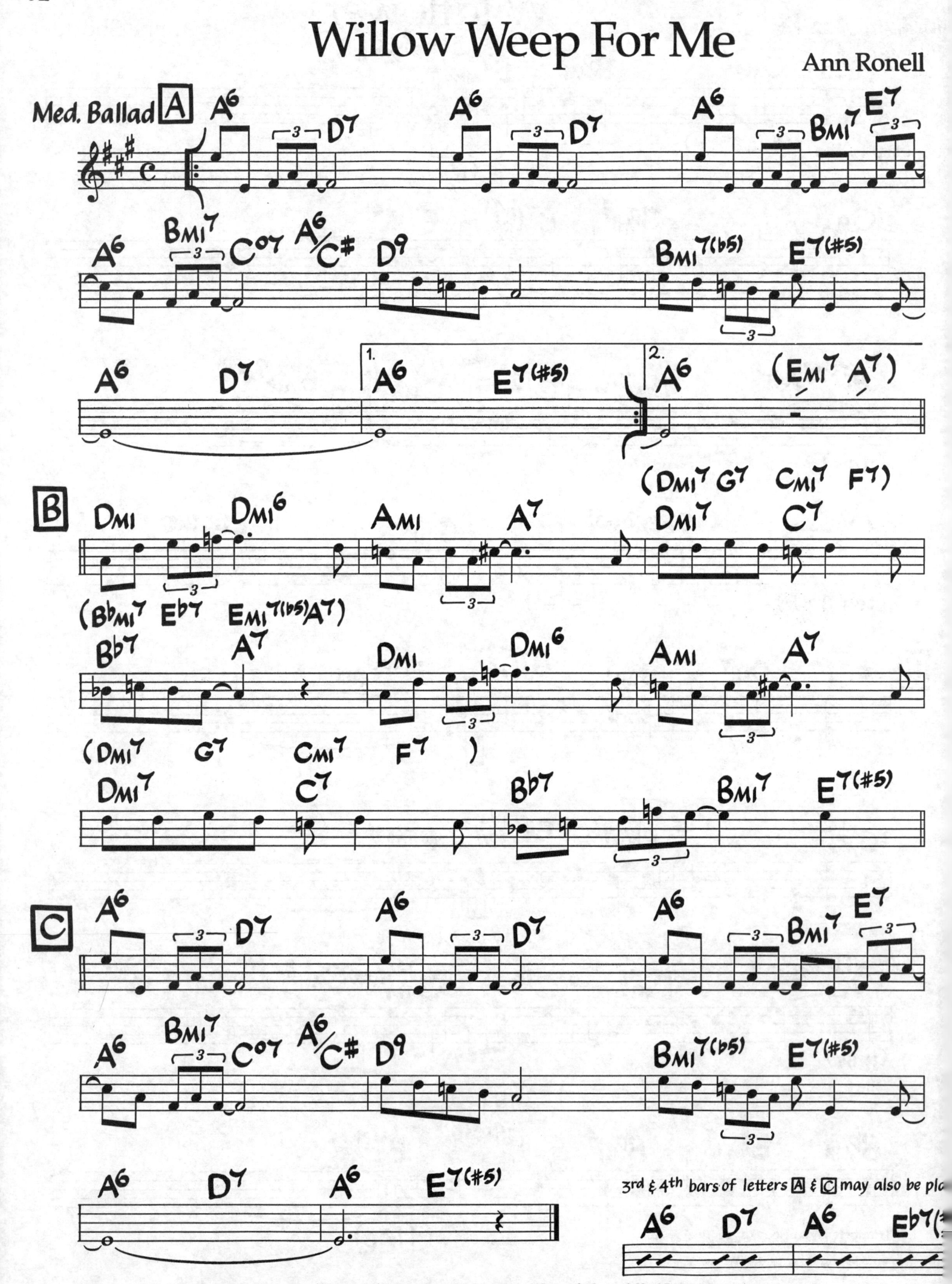

Ann Ronell

Witchcraft

Music by Cy Coleman
Lyric by Carolyn Leigh

Med. Swing

Head is played in 2 (letter B may be in 4); solos in 4.

Yes And No

Wayne Shorter

*piano often plays G7(+5) here (especially during head). Tenor sounds one octave lower than written.

©1964, 1984 Miyako Music. Used By Permission.

Young Rabbits

Wayne Henderson
(As played by The Crusaders)

©1970 American League Music, Silver Carvings Music, Administered by American League Music. Used By Permission.

Solo on form (AABC)
After solos, D.C. al Coda

Vamp out on Gmi9

Your Mind Is On Vacation

Mose Allison

(After solos, D.S.
(3rd verse) al Coda)

Melody is freely interpreted and varies with each verse.

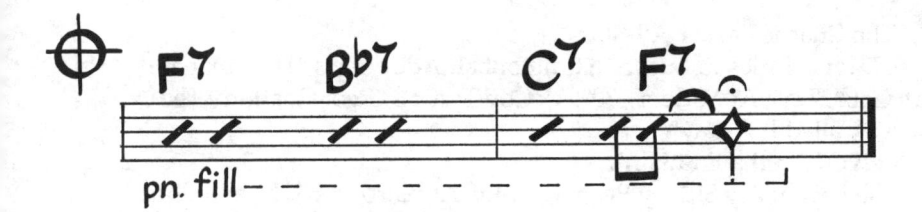

pn. fill

APPENDIX - SOURCES

A wide selection of published music, manuscripts, records, and other sources was used in creating the charts in this book. Below is an alphabetical listing of tunes with the major sources used for each.

Sources on paper fall into four categories:
1) Published sheet music - usually a full piano/vocal arrangement, though only melody and chord symbols in some instances.
2) Published transcription - a literal transcription from a specific recorded version.
3) Publisher's lead sheet - an in-house document created by staff transcribers or an outside transcription service with or without the composer's input; it usually reflects a single recorded version.
4) Composer's lead sheet - an original lead sheet in the composer's own hand.

The recorded sources for each tune are listed in order of contribution - records listed first contributed more to the final chart than those records which follow. Often other recordings were listened to but are not listed if they added no new information to the charts.

A number of other sources used are not listed here. These include fake books (legal and illegal), feedback from the composers, and suggestions from local musicians who proofread the book.

1. AFFIRMATION - George Benson's "Breezin'".
2. AIREGIN - Published sheet music. Miles Davis' "Tallest Trees"; Manhattan Transfer's "Vocalese".
3. ALL OF ME - Published sheet music. Frank Sinatra's "Swing Easy"; Chick Corea's "Echoes Of An Era"; Benny Goodman's "The King"; Billie Holiday (from the Smithsonian collection of Classic Jazz).
4. ALL OR NOTHING AT ALL - Published sheet music. John Coltrane's "Ballads"; Sarah Vaughn's "Sarah Plus 2"; Billie Holiday's "All Or Nothing At All".
5. ALL THE THINGS YOU ARE - Published sheet music. Charlie Parker & Dizzy Gillespie's "In The Beginning"; Keith Jarrett's "Standards - Volume 1"; Sarah Vaughn's "Send In The Clowns"; Bill Evans' "Intuition".
6. ALWAYS THERE - Published sheet music; Publisher's lead sheet. Jeff Lorber's "It's A Fact".
7. ANA MARIA - Composer's lead sheet. Wayne Shorter's "Native Dancer".
8. ANGEL EYES - Published sheet music. Frank Sinatra's "Sinatra Sings For Only The Lonely"; "Jim Hall Live"; Jackie & Roy's "Angel Eyes"; Gene Ammons' "Angel Eyes".
9. ANTHROPOLOGY - Dizzy Gillespie's "Dizziest"; "The Charlie Parker All-Stars".
10. AUTUMN LEAVES - Published sheet music. Miles Davis' "Miles In Europe"; Cannonball Adderley's "The Japanese Concerts"; Bill Evans' "Portrait In Jazz"; Stan Getz' "Live At Midem -'80"; McCoy Tyner's "Reevaluation - The Impulse Years"; Frank Sinatra's "The Night We Called It A Day".
11. BABY, I LOVE YOU - Publisher's lead sheet. "The Best Of Aretha Franklin".
12. BASIN STREET BLUES - Published sheet music. "The Legendary Sidney Bechet"; Louis Armstrong's "Chicago Concert"; Ella Fitzgerald's "The Best Of Ella".
13. BEAUTIFUL LOVE - Published sheet music. Bill Evans' "Spring Leaves"; Bill Evans' "The Best Of Bill Evans".
14. BERNIE'S TUNE - Published sheet music. "The Genius Of Gerry Mulligan"; Sue Raney & Bob Florance's "Ridin' High"; Clare Fischer's "Crazy Bird".
15. BIRD FOOD - Published sheet music. Ornette Coleman's "Change Of The Century"; Denny Zeitlin's "TimeRemembers One Time Once".
16. BLACK ICE - Jeff Lorber's "Soft Space"
17. BLACK NARCISSUS - Joe Henderson's "Foresight".
18. BLAME IT ON MY YOUTH - Published sheet music. Carmen McRae's "Second To None"; Gary Burton's "Easy As Pie".
19. BLIZZARD OF LIES - Published sheet music. "The Dave Frishberg Songbook - Volume 2".
20. BLUE DANIEL - "The Cannonball Adderley Quintet Live At The Lighthouse".
21. BLUE BOSSA - Joe Henderson's "Page One"; "Joe Henderson In Japan".
22. BLUES CONNOTATION - Published sheet music. Ornette Coleman's "This Is Our Music".
23. BLUES ON THE CORNER - Published transcription. McCoy Tyner's "The Real McCoy".
24. BOOGIE DOWN - Published sheet music. Al Jarreau's "Jarreau".
25. BOTH SIDES OF THE COIN - "Steps Ahead" (First American release).
26. BOUNCIN' WITH BUD - Bud Powell's "Alternate Takes" (two versions); Bud Powell's "Bouncin' With Bud"; Art Blakey's "Blakey In Paris"; Charles McPhearson's "Live In Tokyo".
27. BREAKFAST WINE - Composer's lead sheet. Bobby Shew's "Breakfast Wine".
28. BREAKIN' AWAY - Publisher's lead sheet. Al Jarreau's "Breakin' Away".
29. BUT BEAUTIFUL - Published sheet music. Bill Evans' Since We Met"; Art Pepper's "Live At The Village Vanguard - Volume 2"; Bobbe Norris' "Velas Icadas (Hoisted Sails)".
30. CHAIN OF FOOLS - Publisher's lead sheet. "The Best Of Aretha Franklin".
31. CHANGE OF MIND - Composer's lead sheet. "Peter Erskine".
32. CHEGA DE SAUDADE - Published sheet music. Antonio Carlos Jobim's "The Composer Of 'Desafinado' Plays"; Dizzy Gillespie's "Dizzy On The French Riviera"; Sue Raney & Bob Florence's "Ridin' High".
33. CHELSEA BRIDGE - Published sheet music. Duke Ellington's "Concert In The Virgin Islands"; Joe Henderson's "Foresight"; "Ella Fitzgerald Sings The Duke Ellington Songbook - Volume 2"; Sarah Vaughn's "The Duke Ellington Songbook - Volume 2".
34. COME SUNDAY - Published sheet music. Duke Ellington's "Carnegie Hall Concerts"; "Presenting Joe Williams And The Thad Jones/Mel Lewis Orchestra"; "Oscar Peterson With Nelson Riddle"; Cannonball Adderley's "The Japanese Concerts".

35. COMPARED TO WHAT - Les McCann's "Swiss Movement"; Roberta Flack's "First Take".
36. CREEK - Airto's "Free".
37. CRYSTAL LOVE - Makoto Ozone's "Crystal Love".
38. CUBANO CHANT - Ray Bryant's "Alone At Montreaux"; Ray Bryant's "It Was A Very Good Year".
39. DARN THAT DREAM - Published sheet music. Dexter Gordon's "After Hours"; Bill Evans & Jim Hall's "Undercurrant"; "Billie Holiday" (MGM Golden Archive Series); "The Chet Baker Big Band"; "George Shearing & The Montgomery Bros."; Dexter Gordon's "The Bethlehem Years".
40. DEARLY BELOVED - Published sheet music. Sonny Rollin's "The Freedom Suite Plus"; Wes Montgomery's "Yesterdays"; "Al Haig Plays The Music Of Jerome Kern".
41. DELEVANS - Jeff Lorber's "It's A Fact".
42. DESAFINADO - Published sheet music. Stan Getz' "The Girl From Ipanema - The Bossa Nova Years"; "Lambert, Hendricks And Bavan At BAsin Street East"; Antonio Carlos Jobim's "The Composer Of 'Desafinado' Plays"; Antonio Carlos Jobim's "Terra Brasilis"; Dizzy Gillespie's "Dizzy On The French Riviera".
43. DESIRE - Publisher's lead sheet. Tom Scott's "Desire".
44. DIG - Published sheet music. Miles Davis' "Dig".
45. DINDI - Publisher's lead sheet. "The Wonderful World Of Antonio Carlos Jobim"; Jackie & Roy's "Star Sounds"; Sarah Vaughn's "Copacabana".
46. DO NOTHING 'TIL YOU HEAR FROM ME - Published sheet music. Billie Holiday's "All Or Nothing At All"; Ben Webster's "Ballads"; "Duke Ellington's Greatest Hits"; Ernestine Anderson's "Live From Concord To London"; "Mose Allison Sings".
47. DON'T GET AROUND MUCH ANYMORE - Published sheet music. Ben Webster's "The King Of The Tenors"; "Duke Ellington's Greatest Hits"; "Johnny Hodges At The Sports Palace"; Kenny Burrell's "Ellington Is Forever"; Ernestine Anderson's "Live From Concord To London".
48. DON'T GO TO STRANGERS - Published sheet music. Mark Murphy's "Satisfaction Guaranteed"; Etta Jones' "Don't Go To Strangers".
49. DOORS - Composer's lead sheet. Mike Nock's "Ondas".
50. EARLY AUTUMN - Published sheet music. "Ella Fitzgerald Sings The Johnny Mercer Songbook"; Woody Herman's "Keeper Of The Flame".
51. EASY - Publisher's lead sheet. Al Jarreau's "Breakin' Away".
52. EIGHTY ONE - Published sheet music. Miles Davis' "E.S.P."
53. ELM - Composer's lead sheet. Richie Beirach's "Elm".
54. ENDANGERED SPECIES - Composer's lead sheet. Wayne Shorter's "Atlantis".
55. E.S.P. - Composer's lead sheet; published sheet music. Miles Davis' "E.S.P.".
56. EVERYTHING HAPPENS TO ME - Published sheet music. Billie Holiday's "Stormy Blues"; Bill Evans' "Trio '65"; "Matt Dennis Plays And Sings Matt Dennis"; Charlie Parker "The Verve Years - 1948-50".
57. FALL - Composer's lead sheet. Miles Davis'"Nefertiti".
58. FARMER'S MARKET - Publisher's lead sheet. Art Farmer's "Farmer's Market"; "The Wardell Gray Memorial Album"; "Lambert, Hendricks & Ross".
59. FAVELA - Publisher's lead sheet. Antonio Carlos Jobim's "The Composer Of 'Desafinado Plays"; Stan Getz & Luis Bonfa's "Jazz Samba - Encore"; "The Wonderful World Of Antonio Carlos Jobim"; "Vince Guaraldi & Bola Sete Live At El Matador"; "Ella Fitzgerald Sings The Antonio Carlos Jobim Songbook".
60. FEEL LIKE MAKIN' LOVE - Published sheet music. "The Best Of Roberta Flack".
61. FIRE - Joe Henderson's "The Elements".
62. FIRST LIGHT - Freddie Hubbard's "First Light".
63. FOOLKILLER - Mose Allison's "The Word From Mose".
64. FOOTPRINTS - Composer's lead sheet. Wayne Shorter's "Adam's Apple"; Miles Davis' "Miles Smiles"; Pat Martino's "Footprints".
65. FOUR - Published sheet music. Miles Davis' "Blue Haze"; Lambert, Hendricks & Ross' "The Swingers".
66. FOUR BROTHERS - Published sheet music. Woody Herman's "The Three Herds"; Ron McCroby's "The Other Whistler".
67. FOUR ON SIX - Wes Montgomery's "Smokin' At The Half Note".
68. FRIENDS AND STRANGERS - Publisher's lead sheet. Dave Grusin's "Mountain Dance"; Dave Grusin & The GRP All-Stars "Live In Japan".
69. FUNKALLERO - Published sheet music. "The Bill Evans Album".
70. GAVIOTA - Composer's lead sheet. Clare Fischer's "Machaca".
71. GEE BABY, AIN'T I GOOD TO YOU - Published sheet music. Billie Holiday's "The Unforgettable Lady Day"; "Joe Williams Presents Joe Williams And The Thad Jones/Mel Lewis Orchestra".
72. GEMINI - Published sheet music. "The Cannonball Adderley Sextet In New York"; Jimmy Heath's "Fast Company".
73. GLORIA'S STEP - Bill Evans' "The Village Vanguard Sessions"; Bill Evans' "From The 70's".
74. GOIN' HOME - Composer's lead sheet. The Yellowjackets' "Mirage A Trois".
75. GONE WITH THE WIND - Published sheet music. "The Complete Blue Note & Pacific Jazz Jazz Recordings Of Clifford Brown"; Bill Evans' "California, Here I Come"; Ella Fitzgerald's "Ella In Berlin".
76. GOOD MORNING HEARTACHE - Published sheet music. "The Magnificent Tommy Flanagan"; Billie Holiday's "All Or Nothing At All"; Charles McPhearson's "Siker Ya Bibi".
77. THE GOODBYE LOOK - Published sheet music. Donald Fagen's "Nightfly".
78. GUARUJA - Composer's lead sheet. Randy Brecker & Eliane Elias' "Amanda".

79. HALLUCINATIONS - Published transcription. "The Genius Of Bud Powell"; The Phil Woods Quartet "Live - Volume 1"; "Bobby McFerrin".
80. HAUNTED BALLROOM - Composer's lead sheet. Victor Feldman's "Artful Dodger".
81. HAVONA - Weather Report's "Heavy Weather".
82. HERE'S THAT RAINY DAY - Published sheet music. Ella Fitzgerald's "Ella In Hamburg"; Bill Evans' "Alone"; Gene Ammons' "The Boss Is Back"; "Stan Getz" (Verve boxed set).
83. HIDEAWAY - Dave Sanborn's "Straight To The Heart".
84. I LOVE LUCY - Published sheet music. Richie Cole's "Hollywood Madness"; Richie Cole & Reuben Brown's "Starburst".
85. I MEAN YOU - Published transcription. Thelonious Monk's "Mulligan Meets Monk"; Thelonious Monk's "Big Band Monk"; Thelonious Monk's "The Genius Of Modern Music".
86. I SHOULD CARE - Published sheet music. Bill Evans' "How My Heart Sings"; "Bill Evans At Town Hall"; "Mel Torme"; Hank Mobley's "Another Workout"; Etta Jones' "Love Me With All Your Heart".
87. I THOUGHT ABOUT YOU - Published sheet music. Miles Davis' "Someday My Prince Will Come"; Miles Davis' "Miles In Concert"; Billie Holiday's "Lady Sings The Blues"; Kenny Burrell & Coleman Hawkins' "Moonglow"; Jenny Ferris' "Not So Long Ago".
88. IF I WERE A BELL - Published sheet music. Miles Davis' "Relaxin'"(="Chronicles"); Carmen McRae's "Recorded Live At Bubba's"; Bobby Hutcherson's "Four Seasons"; Ella Fitzgerald's "Ella Sings Broadway".
89. IF YOU NEVER COME TO ME - Published sheet music; Publisher's lead sheet. "The Wonderful World Of Antonio Carlos Jobim"; Frank Sinatra's "Sinatra Sings Antonio Carlos Jobim"; "Ella Fitzgerald Sings The Antonio Carlos Jobim Songbook".
90. I'LL TAKE ROMANCE - Published sheet music. Shelly Manne's "Double Piano Jazz Quartet"; Bud Shank & Bill Mays' "Crystal Comment"; Art Farmer's "Farmer's Market".
91. I'M ALL SMILES - Published sheet music. Hank Jones & Tommy Flanagan's "I'm All Smiles"; Bill Evans' "From Left To Right"; Barbra Streisand's "People".
92. I'M OLD FASHIONED - Published sheet music. John Coltrane's "Blue Train"; Shirley Horn's "A Lazy Afternoon"; "Al Haig Plays The Music Of Jerome Kern".
93. IMAGINATION - Published sheet music. Carmen McRae's "It Takes A Whole Lot Of Human Feeling"; "Rosemary Clooney Sings The Music Of Jimmy Van Heusen"; Maynard Ferguson's "Boy With Lots Of Brass".
94. IN WALKED BUD - Published transcription. Thelonious Monk's "The Genius Of Modern Music"; Thelonious Monk's "Mysterioso"; Thelonious Monk's "Underground".
95. THE ISLAND - Published sheet music. Mark Murphy's "Brazil Song"; Pete Escovedo's "The Island"; Ivan Lins' "Juntos".
96. IT HAPPENS EVERY DAY - Publisher's lead sheet. The Crusaders' "Free As The Wind".   "The Best Of Hubert Laws".
97. JERSEY BOUNCE - Published sheet music. Benny Goodman's "Solid Gold Instrumental Hits"; Benny Goodman's "Live At Carnegie Hall".
98. JOSHUA - Miles Davis' "Seven Steps To Heaven"; Miles Davis' "Miles Davis In Europe".
99. KEEP THAT SAME OLD FEELING - The Crusaders' "Those Southern Knights".
100. KILLING ME SOFTLY WITH HIS SONG - Published sheet music. "The Best Of Roberta Flack".
101. LA SAMBA - Composer's lead sheet. Andy Narell's "Light In Your Eyes".
102. LA VIDA FELIZ - McCoy Tyner's "Le Leyunda de la Hora (The Legend Of The Hour)".
103. LADY BIRD - "Miles Davis & Jimmy Forrest - Live At The Barrel, Volume 2". Alternate Version - Fats Navarro's "The Prime Source" (=Tadd Dameron's selection in the Smithsonian collection of Classic Jazz); Dizzy Gillespie's "The Bop Session"; "Barry Harris Plays Tadd Dameron".
104. LAST FIRST - Composer's lead sheet. Gary Peacock's "Shift In The Wind".
105. LAST TRAIN TO OVERBROOK - Published sheet music; Publisher's lead sheet. James Moody's "Moody" (Prestige Two-fer); James Moody's "Last Train From Overbrook".
106. LAURIE - Published sheet music. Bill Evans' The Paris Concert - Edition Two".
107. LET ME BE THE ONE - "The Best Of Angela Bofill".
108. LET'S GO DANCIN' - Publisher's lead sheet. Victor Feldman's "Secret Of The Andes".
109. LIKE SOMEONE IN LOVE - Published sheet music. "Tommy Flanagan Trio & Sextet"; John Coltrane's "Lush Life"; Sarah Vaughn's "Live In Japan".
110. LINE FOR LYONS - Gerry Mulligan's "Mulligan & Baker At Carnegie Hall"; "The Complete Jazz Live Recording Of the Chet Baker Quartet"; Stan Getz & Chet Baker's "Line For Lyons".
111. LITTLE SUNFLOWER - Freddie Hubbard's "Backlash"; Milt Jackson's "Sunflower"; Freddie Hubbard's "The Love Connection".
112. A LITTLE TEAR - Publisher's lead sheet. Sarah Vaughn's "I Love Brazil".
113. LITTLE WALTZ - Published sheet music. VSOP's "The Quintet"; Ron Carter's "Piccolo".
114. LONG AGO AND FAR AWAY - Published sheet music. Art Pepper's "The Omega Man"; "The Hi-Lo's Under Glass".
115. LOVE CAME ON STEALTHY FINGERS - Composer's lead sheet; Publisher's lead sheet. Bob Dorough's "Devil May Care"; Irene Kral's "Where Is Love?".

116. LOVE DANCE - Publisher's lead sheet. Diane Schuur's "Schuur Thing"; Carol Fredata's "Love Dance"; Ivan Lins' "Daquila Que Eu Sei".
117. LUSH LIFE - Published sheet music. John Coltrane's "Lush Life"; "John Coltrane And Johnny Hartman".
118. MADAGASCAR - Composer's lead sheet. "The John Abercrombie Quartet".
119. MAKE ME A MEMORY (Sad Samba) - Published sheet music. Grover Washington Jr.'s "Winelight".
120. MATINEE IDOL - Composer's lead sheet. "The Yellowjackets".
121. MERCY, MERCY, MERCY - Cannonball Adderley's "Mercy, Mercy, Mercy".
122. THE MIDNIGHT SUN - Published sheet music. "The Best Of Sarah Vaughn"; "The Lionel Hampton Big Band".
123. THE MIDNIGHT SUN WILL NEVER SET - Published sheet music. Benny Carter's "Further Definitions"; Count Basie's "One More Time"; "The Music Of Quincy Jones".
124. MISTY - Published sheet music. "Erroll Garner Plays Misty"; Sarah Vaughn "Recorded Live"; Ella Fitzgerald's "Ella In Berlin".
125. MODADJI - Composer's lead sheet. "Dave Grusin's "One Of A Kind"; Dave Grusin & The GRP All-Stars "Live In Japan"; Hubert Laws' "The San Francisco Concert".
126. MONK'S MOOD - Published transcription. "The Thelonious Monk Orchestra At Town Hall"; Thelonious Monk's "The Genius Of Modern Music".
127. MONKEY'S UNCLE - Composer's lead sheet. Mitchell Foreman's "Train Of Thought".
128. MOONLIGHT IN VERMONT - Published sheet music. Ella Fitzgerald's "Lady Be Good -'57"; Stan Getz'"Reflections".
129. MORNIN' -Published sheet music; Publisher's lead sheet. Al Jarreau's "Jarreau".
130. MORNING DANCE - Published sheet music. Spyro Gyra's "Morning Dance".
131. MR. CLEAN - Freddie Hubbard's "Straight Life".
132. MR. GONE -Published sheet music. Weather Report's "Mr. Gone".
133. MY ATTORNEY BERNIE - Published sheet music. "The Dave Frishberg Songbook - Volume 2".
134. MY ROMANCE - Published sheet music. Bill Evans' "The Village Vanguard Sessions"; Ernestine Anderson's "Live From Concord To London"; Ella Fitzgerald's "Ella Sings The Rodgers & Hart Songbook".
135. MY SHINING HOUR - Published sheet music. John Coltrane's "Coltrane Jazz"; Pepper Adams' "The Master"; Lorez Alexandria Sings Songs Of Johnny Mercer"; Ernestine Anderson's "Never Make Your Move Too Soon"; "Ella Fitzgerald Sings The Harold Arlan Songbook".
136. NATURE BOY - Composer's lead sheet; Published sheet music. Etta Jones' "Hollar"; "The Nat King Cole Story - Volume One"; Ella Fitzgerald & Joe Pass' "Again"; "Stan Getz"(Verve boxed set); Miles Davis' "Blue Moods".
137. NEFERTITI - Composer's lead sheet. Miles Davis' "Nefertiti"; VSOP's The Quintet".
138. NEVER GIVIN' UP - Al Jarreau's "This Time".
139. NEVER MAKE YOUR MOVE TOO SOON - Publisher's lead sheet. The Crusaders' "Royal Jam"; Ernestine Anderson's "Never Make Your Move Too Soon".
140. NIGERIAN MARKETPLACE - Oscar Peterson's "Nigerian Marketplace".
141. NIGHTLAKE - Composer's lead sheet. `John Abercrombie's "Arcade".
142. NO ME ESQUECA - Joe Henderson's "In Pursuit Of Blackness".
143. NOT ETHIOPIA - The Brecker Bros.' "Straphangin'"; Steps Ahead's "Smokin' In The Pit".
144. NOTHING PERSONAL - Composer's lead sheet. "Michael Brecker".
145. OFF MINOR - Published transcription. "The Thelonious Monk Orchestra At Town Hall"; Thelonious Monk's "The Genius Of Modern Music"; Thelonious Monk's "Monk's Music".
146. OLEO - Published sheet music. Neils Henning Orsted Peterson & Joe Pass' "Chops"; Red Garland's "Crossings"; Miles Davis' "Relaxin'"; Miles Davis' "Tallest Trees".
147. ONCE I LOVED - Publisher's lead sheet. Antonio Carlos Jobim's "The Composer Of 'Desafinado' Plays"; Frank Sinatra's "Sinatra Sings Antonio Carlos Jobim"; McCoy Tyner's "Trident".
148. ONE FAMILY - Composer's lead sheet. The Yellowjackets' "Shades".
149. ONE FOR MY BABY - Published sheet music. "Ella Fitzgerald Sings The Harold Arlan Songbook"; Frank Sinatra's "One More For The Road"; Joe Williams' "Something Old, New And Blue"; "Tommy Flanagan Plays The Music Of Harold Arlan".
150. OUT OF THIS WORLD - Published sheet music. "Ella Fitzgerald Sings The Harold Arlan Songbook"; "Tommy Flanagan Plays The Music Of Harold Arlan"; John Coltrane's "Coltrane"; George Shearing's "The Shearing Spell".
151. OZ - Composer's lead sheet. Andy Narell's "Stickman".
152. PAPA LIPS - Composer's lead sheet. Bob Mintzer's "Papa Lips".
153. PARTIDO ALTO - Airto's "Touching You, Touching Me".
154. PENT UP HOUSE - Published sheet music. Sonny Rollins' "Sonny" (Prestige Two-fer).
155. PLAZA REAL - Composer's lead sheet. Weather Report's "Procession".
156. POLKADOTS AND MOONBEAMS - Published sheet music. "The Complete Blue Note Recordings Of Bud Powell"; Bill Evans' "The Second Trio"; Sarah Vaughn's "Recorded Live".
157. PORTRAIT OF TRACY - "Jaco Pastorius".
158. PROMENADE - Composer's lead sheet. Denny Zeitlin's "Tidal Wave".
159. PUT IT WHERE YOU WANT IT - Publisher's lead sheet. "The Best Of The Crusaders".
160. P.Y.T. - Published sheet music. Michael Jackson's "Thriller".

160. QUINTESSENCE - Quincy Jones' "Quintessence".
161. RAPTURE - Harold Land & Blue Mitchell's "Mapenzi".
162. RE:PERSON I KNEW - Published sheet music. "The Bill Evans Album".
163. REINCARNATION OF A LOVEBIRD - Brian Priestly's "Mingus - A Critical Biography". Charles Mingus' "Reincarnation Of A Lovebird"; Charles Mingus' "The Clown".
164. REMEMBER ROCKEFELLER AT ATTICA - Charles Mingus' "Changes - Volume 1".
165. RIO - Publisher's lead sheet. Victor Feldman's "In The Pocket".
166. RIVER PEOPLE - Weather Report's "Mr. Gone".
167. ROBBIN'S NEST - Published transcription. "Illinois Jacquet In Swinging Sweden"; "Illinois Jacquet Flies Again"; Lester Young's "Carnie Blues"; Tommy Flanagan & Hank Jones' "Our Delight"; Oscar Peterson's "Girl Talk".
168. RUBY MY DEAR - Publisher's lead sheet; Published sheet music; Published transcription. "Solo Monk"; "Thelonious Monk And John Coltrane"; "Monk's Music"; Thelonious Monk's "The Genius Of Modern Music".
168. RUSH HOUR - "The Yellowjackets".
169. SAFARI - Steps Ahead's "Modern Times".
170. SANDU - Clifford Brown's "The Quintet - Volume 2".
171. SATIN DOLL - Published sheet music. Duke Ellington's "Duke - '66"; Duke Ellington's "All Star Road Band - Volume 2"; Ella Fitzgerald & Count Basie's "On The Sunny Side Of The Street"; "Ella Fitzgerald Sings The Duke Ellington Songbook"; Ernestine Anderson's "Sunshine".
172. SAVE YOUR LOVE FOR ME - "Cannonball Adderley & Nancy Wilson"; Cannonball Adderley & Nancy Wilson's "Together"; Etta Jones' "Save Your Love For Me".
173. SEARCH FOR PEACE - McCoy Tyner's "The Real McCoy".
174. SELF PORTRAIT IN THREE COLORS - Charles Mingus' "Mingus Ah Um".
175. SHAKER SONG - Publisher's lead sheet. Manhattan Transfer's "Ententions"; "Spyro Gyra".
176. SHAW 'NUFF - The Smithsonian Collection Of Classic Jazz (Side 9 - Charlie Parker & Dizzy Gillespie); Bud Powell's "Swinging With Bud".
177. SIMPLE SAMBA - Published transcription. Jim Hall's "Where Would I Be?'.
178. SKYLARK - Published sheet music."Ella Fitzgerald Sings The Johnny Mercer Songbook"; "Hoagy Sings Carmichael"; "The Greatest Of Carmen McRae"; Art Blakey's "Thermo"; Sonny Criss' "This Is Criss".
179. A SLEEPIN' BEE - Published sheet music. Bill Evans' "Trio 64"; "Tommy Flanagan Plays The Music Of Harold Arlan"; "Cannonball Adderley & Nancy Wilson"; "Bill Evans At The Montreaux Jazz Festival".
180. SMALL DAY TOMORROW - Publisher's lead sheet. Irene Kral's "Kral Space"; Bob Dorough's "Beginning To See The Light".
181. SOLAR - Published sheet music. Miles Davis' "Tune Up"; "Chet Baker In New York"; "The Shelly Manne Trio In Zurich"; Bill Evans' "The Village Vanguard Sessions".
182. SOMEDAY MY PRINCE WILL COME - Published sheet music. Miles Davis' "Someday My Prince Will Come"; Bill Evans' "Spring Leaves".
183. SONG FOR LORRAINE - Publisher's lead sheet. Spyro Gyra's "Morning Dance".
184. THE SONG IS YOU - Published sheet music. Gene Ammons & Dodo Marmorosa's "Jug & Dodo"; "Oscar Peterson Plays The Jerome Kern Songbook"; Joe Pass' "Virtuoso"; "Al Haig Plays The Music Of Jerome Kern".
185. SONJA'S SANFONA - Composer's lead sheet. The Yellowjackets' "Shades".
186. SOUL SAUCE (Wachi Wara) - Cal Tjader's "Soul Sauce"; Cal Tjader's "Good Vibes".
187. SPEAK LOW - Published sheet music. "The Magnificent Tommy Flanagan"; Bill Evans' "Crosscurrents"; Billie Holiday's "All Or Nothing At All"; Ahmed Jamal's "Happy Moods".
188. SPEAK NO EVIL - Composer's lead sheet. Wayne Shorter's "Speak No Evil".
189. SPIRAL - Sphere's "Sphere On Tour".
190. ST. THOMAS - Published sheet music. Sonny Rollins' "Saxophone Colossus"; Cedar Walton's "Eastern Rebellion".
191. STICKY WICKET - Publisher's lead sheet. Al Jarreau's "High Crime".
192. STORMY WEATHER - Published sheet music. Billie Holiday's "First Verve Sessions"; Lena Horne's "Stormy Weather"; "Ella Fitzgerald Sings The Harold Arlan Songbook"; Johnny Hodges' "Blue Pyramid".
193. STREET LIFE - Published transcription. The Crusaders' "Street Life".
194. SUDDEN SAMBA - Neil Larsen's "Jungle Fever".
195. SUNRUNNER - Published sheet music. Bob James' "Touchdown".
196. TAKE THE 'A' TRAIN - Published sheet music. "Duke Ellington & His Orchestra And Johnny Hodges & His Orchestra"; "Ella Fitzgerald Sings The Duke Ellington Songbook"; Duke Ellington's "1941 Classics"; Duke Ellington's "Washington DC Armory Concert"; Ernestine Anderson's "Live From Concord To London"; Mel Torme's "The Duke Ellington & Count Basie Songbook".
197. TENDERLY - Published sheet music. "Everybody Loves Bill Evans"; Duke Ellington's "Ellington Indigos"; Nat King Cole's "Love Is Here To Stay"; George Shearing's "Lullaby Of Birdland".
198. THEME FOR ERNIE - John Coltrane's "Soultrane".
199. THERE WILL NEVER BE ANOTHER YOU - Published sheet music. Art Pepper's "One September Afternoon"; Jackie & Roy's "Free And Easy"; Coleman Hawkins' "Body & Soul"; Nat King Cole's "Love Is Here To Stay"; "The Greatest - Count Basie Plays And Joe Williams Sings".
200. THESE FOOLISH THINGS - Published sheet music. Charles McPhearson's "Live In Tokyo"; Ella Fitzgerald's "Lady be Good - '57"; "Mark Murphy Sings The Nat Cole Songbook - Volume 1"; Nat King Cole "Just One Of Those Things".

201. THIS MASQUERADE - Published transcription. George Benson's "Breezin"" Leon Russel's "Carney".
202. THE THREE MARIAS - Composer's lead sheet. Wayne Shorter's "Atlantis".
203. THREE VIEWS OF A SECRET - Jaco Pastorius' "Word Of Mouth"; Weather Report's "Night Passage".
204. TIME REMEMBERS ONE TIME ONCE - Composer's lead sheet. Denny Zeitlin's "Time Remembers One Time Once".
205. TRISTE - Publisher's lead sheet. Antonio Carlos Jobim's "Wave"; Brazil '66's "Equinox"; "Ella Fitzgerald Sings The Antonio Carlos Jobim Songbook"; Oscar Peterson's "Tristeza".
206. TUNE UP - Published sheet music. Miles Davis' "Tune Up" (="Blue Haze"); "Sonny Rollins" (Blue Note re-issue).
207. TURN YOUR LOVE AROUND - Published sheet music; Publisher's lead sheet. "The George Benson Collection".
208. TWISTED - "The Best Of Lambert, Hendricks & Ross"; "The Wardell Gray Memorial Album - Volume 1".
209. UNIT SEVEN - Wes Montgomery's "Smokin' At The Half Note"; "Cannonball Adderley & Nancy Wilson".
210. UP JUMPED SPRING - Art Blakey's "Three Blind Mice"; Freddie Hubbard's "Backlash".
211. UP WITH THE LARK - Published sheet music. Bill Evans' "The Tokyo Concert".
212. VELAS - Published sheet music; Publisher's lead sheet. Quincy Jones' "The Dude"; Bobbe Norris' "Velas Icadas (Hoisted Sails)"; Mark Murphy's "Nightmood".
213. VERY EARLY - Composer's lead sheet; Publisher's lead sheet; Published sheet music; Published transcription. Bill Evans' "Montreaux II"; Bill Evans' "Spring Leaves".
214. VOYAGE - Publisher's lead sheet. Stan Getz' "Voyage".
215. WALTZ FOR DEBBY - Published transcriptions (Three versions). Cannonball Adderley & Bill Evans' "Know What I Mean?"; Bill Evans' "The Village Vanguard Sessions"; "The Bill Evans Album".
216. WALTZ NEW - Published sheet music; Published transcription. "Jim Hall & Red Mitchell".
217. WATCH WHAT HAPPENS - Published sheet music. Sergio Mendes' "Equinox"; Ella Fitzgerald's "Watch What Happens"; Oscar Peterson's "Tristeza"; Wes Montgomery's "A Day In The Life".
218. WATERWINGS - Composer's lead sheet. Lee Ritenour's "Friendship".
219. WAVE - Publisher's lead sheet. Antonio Carlos Jobim,'s "Wave"; "Ella Fitzgerald Sings The Antonio Carlos Jobim Songbook";
220. THE WAY YOU LOOK TONIGHT - Published sheet music. "The Complete Blue Note & Pacific Jazz Recordings Of Clifford Brown"; Tete Monteliu's "Tete a Tete"; "The Billie Holiday Story - Volume 1"; Sonny Rollins' "Vintage Sessions"; "Ella Fitzgerald Sings The Jerome Kern Songbook".
221. A WEAVER OF DREAMS - "The Cannonball Adderley Quintet In Chicago" (featuring John Coltrane); Carmen McRae's "Ronnie Scott's Presents Carmen Live"; Bobbe Norris' "Velas Icadas (Hoisted Sails)"; Freddie Hubbard's "Ready For Freddie".
222. WE'LL BE TOGETHER AGAIN - Published sheet music. "The Tony Bennett/Bill Evans Album"; Bobbe Norris' "Velas Icadas (Hoisted Sails)".
223. WELL, YOU NEEDN'T - Published sheet music. "Miles Davis - Volume 1"' Miles Davis' "Chronicle"; Thelonious Monk's "Misterioso"; Thelonious Monk's "The Genius Of Modern Music".
224. WEST COAST BLUES - Wes Montgomery's "While We're Young".
225. WHAT'S NEW? - Published sheet music. Billie Holiday's "All Or Nothing At All"; Wes Montgomery & Wynton Kelly's "Smokin' At The Half Note"; John Coltrane's "Ballads"; Frank Sinatra's "Sinatra Sings For Only The Lonely".
226. WHERE IS LOVE? - Published sheet music. Irene Kral's "Where Is Love?".
227. WHO CAN I TURN TO? - Published sheet music. Bill Evans' "Trio 65"; Carmen McRae's "Alfie"; "Bill Evans At Town Hall"; "The Best Of The Gerald Wilson Orchestra".
228. WILDFLOWER - Composer's lead sheet. Wayne Shorter's "Speak No Evil".
229. WILLOW WEEP FOR ME - Published sheet music. Billie Holiday's "Lady Sings The Blues"; "Tommy Flanagan Trio In Stockholm - '57"; "The Immortal Clifford Brown"; Wes Montgomery's "A Day In The Life"; Sarah Vaughn's "Live In Japan".
230. WITCHCRAFT - Published sheet music. Frank Sinatra's "All The Way"; Bill Evans' "Portrait In Jazz"; Oscar Peterson's "A Jazz Portrait Of Frank Sinatra"; Jackie & Roy's "We've Got It".
231. YES AND NO - Composer's lead sheet; Published sheet music. Wayne Shorter's "Ju Ju".
232. YESTERDAYS - Published sheet music. "Clifford Brown With Strings"; "Al Haig Plays The Music Of Jerome Kern"; George Shearing's "The Shearing Spell"; "Ella Fitzgerald Sings The Jerome Kern Songbook".
233. YOUNG RABBITS - The Jazz Crusaders' "Young Rabbits".
234. YOUR MIND IS ON VACATION - Mose Allison's "The Best Of Mose".

The Harold Arlen tunes in this book can also be found in "The Harold Arlen Songbook" which contains complete piano/vocal versions of 76 of his best songs and is available from Hal Leonard Publishing (800- 642-6692).

Sher Music Co. – The finest in Jazz & Latin Publications
THE NEW REAL BOOK SERIES

The Standards Real Book (C, Bb or Eb)

A Beautiful Friendship	Days Of Wine And Roses	I Only Have Eyes For You	Old Folks	Summer Night
A Time For Love	Dreamsville	I'm A Fool To Want You	On A Clear Day	Summertime
Ain't No Sunshine	Easy To Love	Indian Summer	Our Love Is Here To Stay	Teach Me Tonight
Alice In Wonderland	Embraceable You	It Ain't Necessarily So	'Round Midnight	That Sunday, That Summer
All Of You	Falling In Love With Love	It Never Entered My Mind	Secret Love	The Girl From Ipanema
Alone Together	From This Moment On	It's You Or No One	September In The Rain	Then I'll Be Tired Of You
At Last	Give Me The Simple Life	Just One Of Those Things	Serenade In Blue	There's No You
Baltimore Oriole	Have You Met Miss Jones?	Love For Sale	Shiny Stockings	Time On My Hands
Bess, You Is My Woman	Hey There	Lover, Come Back To Me	Since I Fell For You	'Tis Autumn
Bluesette	I Can't Get Started	The Man I Love	So In Love	Where Or When
But Not For Me	I Concentrate On You	Mr. Lucky	So Nice (Summer Samba)	Who Cares?
Close Enough For Love	I Cover The Waterfront	My Funny Valentine	Some Other Time	With A Song In My Heart
Crazy He Calls Me	I Love You	My Heart Stood Still	Stormy Weather	You Go To My Head
Dancing In The Dark	I Loves You Porgy	My Man's Gone Now	The Summer Knows	And Hundreds More!

The New Real Book - Volume 1 (C, Bb or Eb)

Angel Eyes	Eighty One	I Thought About You	My Shining Hour	Shaker Song
Anthropology	E.S.P.	If I Were A Bell	Nature Boy	Skylark
Autumn Leaves	Everything Happens To Me	Imagination	Nefertiti	A Sleepin' Bee
Beautiful Love	Feel Like Makin' Love	The Island	Nothing Personal	Solar
Bernie's Tune	Footprints	Jersey Bounce	Oleo	Speak No Evil
Blue Bossa	Four	Joshua	Once I Loved	St. Thomas
Blue Daniel	Four On Six	Lady Bird	Out Of This World	Street Life
But Beautiful	Gee Baby Ain't I Good	Like Someone In Love	Pent Up House	Tenderly
Chain Of Fools	To You	Little Sunflower	Portrait Of Tracy	These Foolish Things
Chelsea Bridge	Gone With The Wind	Lush Life	Put It Where You Want It	This Masquerade
Compared To What	Here's That Rainy Day	Mercy, Mercy, Mercy	Robbin's Nest	Three Views Of A Secret
Darn That Dream	I Love Lucy	The Midnight Sun	Ruby, My Dear	Waltz For Debby
Desafinado	I Mean You	Monk's Mood	Satin Doll	Willow Weep For Me
Early Autumn	I Should Care	Moonlight In Vermont	Search For Peace	And Many More!

The New Real Book Play-Along CDs (For Volume 1)

CD #1 - Jazz Classics - Lady Bird, Bouncin' With Bud, Up Jumped Spring, Monk's Mood, Doors, Very Early, Eighty One, Voyage **& More!**
CD #2 - Choice Standards - Beautiful Love, Darn That Dream, Moonlight In Vermont, Trieste, My Shining Hour, I Should Care **& More!**
CD #3 - Pop-Fusion - Morning Dance, Nothing Personal, La Samba, Hideaway, This Masquerade, Three Views Of A Secret, Rio **& More!**
World-Class Rhythm Sections, featuring Mark Levine, Larry Dunlap, Sky Evergreen, Bob Magnusson, Keith Jones, Vince Lateano & Tom Hayashi

The New Real Book - Volume 2 (C, Bb or Eb)

Afro-Centric	Django	I'm Glad There Is You	Nica's Dream	Stablemates
After You've Gone	Equinox	Impressions	Once In A While	Stardust
Along Came Betty	Exactly Like You	In Your Own Sweet Way	Perdido	Sweet And Lovely
Bessie's Blues	Falling Grace	It's The Talk Of The Town	Rosetta	That's All
Black Coffee	Five Hundred Miles High	Jordu	Sea Journey	There Is No Greater Love
Blues For Alice	Freedom Jazz Dance	Killer Joe	Senor Blues	'Til There Was You
Body And Soul	Giant Steps	Lullaby Of The Leaves	September Song	Time Remembered
Bolivia	Harlem Nocturne	Manha De Carnaval	Seven Steps To Heaven	Turn Out The Stars
The Boy Next Door	Hi-Fly	The Masquerade Is Over	Silver's Serenade	Unforgettable
Bye Bye Blackbird	Honeysuckle Rose	Memories Of You	So Many Stars	While We're Young
Cherokee	I Hadn't Anyone 'Til You	Moment's Notice	Some Other Blues	Whisper Not
A Child Is Born	I'll Be Around	Mood Indigo	Song For My Father	Will You Still Be Mine?
Cold Duck Time	I'll Get By	My Ship	Sophisticated Lady	You're Everything
Day By Day	Ill Wind	Naima	Spain	And Many More!

The New Real Book - Volume 3 (C, Bb, Eb or Bass clef)

Actual Proof	Dolphin Dance	I Hear A Rhapsody	Maiden Voyage	Speak Like A Child
Ain't That Peculiar	Don't Be That Way	If You Could See Me Now	Moon And Sand	Spring Is Here
Almost Like Being In Love	Don't Blame Me	In A Mellow Tone	Moonglow	Stairway To The Stars
Another Star	Emily	In A Sentimental Mood	My Girl	Star Eyes
Autumn Serenade	Everything I Have Is Yours	Inner Urge	On Green Dolphin Street	Stars Fell On Alabama
Bird Of Beauty	For All We Know	Invitation	Over The Rainbow	Stompin' At The Savoy
Black Nile	Freedomland	The Jitterbug Waltz	Prelude To A Kiss	Sweet Lorraine
Blue Moon	The Gentle Rain	Just Friends	Respect	Taking A Chance On Love
Butterfly	Get Ready	Just You, Just Me	Ruby	This Is New
Caravan	A Ghost Of A Chance	Knock On Wood	The Second Time Around	Too High
Ceora	Heat Wave	The Lamp Is Low	Serenata	(Used To Be A) Cha Cha
Close Your Eyes	How Sweet It Is	Laura	The Shadow Of Your Smile	When Lights Are Low
Creepin'	I Fall In Love Too Easily	Let's Stay Together	So Near, So Far	You Must Believe In Spring
Day Dream	I Got It Bad	Lonely Woman	Solitude	And Many More!

The All Jazz Real Book

Over 540 pages of tunes as recorded by: Miles, Trane, Bill Evans, Cannonball, Scofield, Brecker, Yellowjackets, Bird, Mulgrew Miller, Kenny Werner, MJQ, McCoy Tyner, Kurt Elling, Brad Mehldau, Don Grolnick, Kenny Garrett, Patitucci, Jerry Bergonzi, Stanley Clarke, Tom Harrell, Herbie Hancock, Horace Silver, Stan Getz, Sonny Rollins, and MORE!

Includes a free CD of many of the melodies (featuring Bob Sheppard & Friends.). $44 list price. Available in C, Bb, Eb

The European Real Book

An amazing collection of some of the greatest jazz compositions ever recorded! Available in C, Bb and Eb. $40

- Over 100 of Europe's best jazz writers.
- 100% accurate, composer-approved charts.
- 400 pages of fresh, exciting sounds from virtually every country in Europe.
- Sher Music's superior legibility and signature calligraphy makes reading the music easy.

Listen to FREE MP3 FILES of many of the songs at **www.shermusic.com!**

See **www.shermusic.com** for more information, including a complete list of tunes in all our fake books.
To order, call **(800) 444-7437** or fax **(707) 763-2038**

SHER MUSIC JAZZ PUBLICATIONS

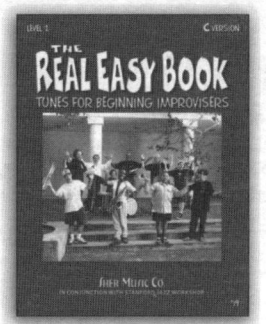

The Real Easy Book Vol. 1
TUNES FOR BEGINNING IMPROVISERS

Published by Sher Music Co. in conjunction with the Stanford Jazz Workshop. $22 list price.

The easiest tunes from Horace Silver, Eddie Harris, Freddie Hubbard, Red Garland, Sonny Rollins, Cedar Walton, Wes Montgomery Cannonball Adderly, etc. Get yourself or your beginning jazz combo sounding good right away with the first fake book ever designed for the beginning improviser.
Available in C, Bb, Eb and Bass Clef.

The Real Easy Book Vol. 2
TUNES FOR INTERMEDIATE IMPROVISERS

Published by Sher Music Co. in conjunction with the Stanford Jazz Workshop. Over 240 pages. $29.

The best intermediate-level tunes by: Charlie Parker, John Coltrane, Miles Davis, John Scofield, Sonny Rollins, Horace Silver, Wes Montgomery, Freddie Hubbard, Cal Tjader, Cannonball Adderly, and more! Both volumes feature instructional material tailored for each tune. Perfect for jazz combos!
Available in C, Bb, Eb and Bass Clef.

The Real Easy Book Vol. 3
A SHORT HISTORY OF JAZZ

Published by Sher Music Co. in conjunction with the Stanford Jazz Workshop. Over 200 pages. $25.

History text and tunes from all eras and styles of jazz. Perfect for classroom use. Available in C, Bb, Eb and Bass Clef versions.

The Best of Sher Music Co. Real Books
100+ TUNES YOU NEED TO KNOW

A collection of the best-known songs from the world leader in jazz fake books – Sher Music Co.!

Includes songs by: Miles Davis, John Coltrane, Bill Evans, Duke Ellington, Antonio Carlos Jobim, Charlie Parker, John Scofield, Michael Brecker, Weather Report, Horace Silver, Freddie Hubbard, Thelonious Monk, Cannonball Adderley, and many more!

$26. Available in C, Bb, Eb and Bass Clef.

The Serious Jazz Book II
THE HARMONIC APPROACH

By Barry Finnerty, Endorsed by: Joe Lovano, Jamey Aebersold, Hubert Laws, Mark Levine, etc.

- A 200 page, exhaustive study of how to master the harmonic content of songs.
- Contains explanations of every possible type of chord that is used in jazz.
- Clear musical examples to help achieve real harmonic control over melodic improvisation.
- For any instrument. $32. Money back gurantee!

The Serious Jazz Practice Book By Barry Finnerty

A unique and comprehensive plan for mastering the basic building blocks of the jazz language. It takes the most widely-used scales and chords and gives you step-by-step exercises that dissect them into hundreds of cool, useable patterns.
Includes CD - $30 list price.

"The book I've been waiting for!" – Randy Brecker.

"The best book of intervallic studies I've ever seen."
– Mark Levine

The Jazz Theory Book

By Mark Levine, the most comprehensive Jazz Theory book ever published! $38 list price.

- Over 500 pages of text and over 750 musical examples.
- Written in the language of the working jazz musician, this book is easy to read and user-friendly. At the same time, it is the most comprehensive study of jazz harmony and theory ever published.
- Mark Levine has worked with Bobby Hutcherson, Cal Tjader, Joe Henderson, Woody Shaw, and many other jazz greats.

Jazz Piano Masterclass With Mark Levine
"THE DROP 2 BOOK"

The long-awaited book from the author of "The Jazz Piano Book!" A complete study on how to use "drop 2" chord voicings to create jazz piano magic! 68 pages, plus CD of Mark demonstrating each exercise. $19 list.

"Will make you sound like a real jazz piano player in no time." – Jamey Aebersold

Metaphors For The Musician
By Randy Halberstadt

This practical and enlightening book will help any jazz player or vocalist look at music with "new eyes." Designed for any level of player, on any instrument, "Metaphors For The Musician" provides numerous exercises throughout to help the reader turn these concepts into musical reality.

Guaranteed to help you improve your musicianship. 330 pages – $29 list price. Satisfaction guaranteed!

The Jazz Musicians Guide To Creative Practicing
By David Berkman

Finally a book to help musicians use their practice time wisely! Covers tune analysis, breaking hard tunes into easy components, how to swing better, tricks to playing fast bebop lines, and much more! 150+pages, plus CD. $29 list.

"Fun to read and bursting with things to do and ponder." – Bob Mintzer

The 'Real Easy' Ear Training Book
By Roberta Radley

For all musicians, regardless of instrument or experience, this is the most comprehensive book on "hearing the changes" ever published!

- Covers both beginning and intermediate ear training exercises.
- Music Teachers: You will find this book invaluable in teaching ear training to your students.

Book includes 168 pages of instructional text and musical examples, plus two CDs! $29 list price.

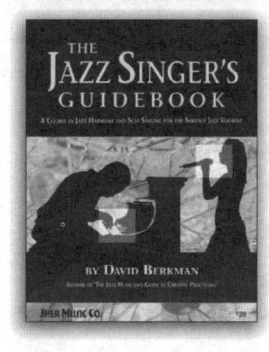

The Jazz Singer's Guidebook By David Berkman
A COURSE IN JAZZ HARMONY AND SCAT SINGING FOR THE SERIOUS JAZZ VOCALIST

A clear, step-by-step approach for serious singers who want to improve their grasp of jazz harmony and gain a deeper understanding of music fundamentals.

This book will change how you hear music and make you a better singer, as well as give you the tools to develop your singing in directions you may not have thought possible.

$26 – includes audio CD demonstrating many exercises.

LATIN MUSIC BOOKS, CDs, DVD

The Latin Real Book (C, Bb or Eb)
The only professional-level Latin fake book ever published!

Ray Barretto	Arsenio Rodriguez	Manny Oquendo	Ivan Lins
Eddie Palmieri	Tito Rodriguez	Puerto Rico All-Stars	Djavan
Fania All-Stars	Orquesta Aragon	Issac Delgaldo	Tom Jobim
Tito Puente	Beny Moré	Ft. Apache Band	Toninho Horta
Ruben Blades	Cal Tjader	Dave Valentin	Joao Bosco
Los Van Van	Andy Narell	Paquito D'Rivera	Milton Nascimento
NG La Banda	Mario Bauza	Clare Fischer	Leila Pinheiro
Irakere	Dizzy Gillespie	Chick Corea	Gal Costa
Celia Cruz	Mongo Santamaria	Sergio Mendes	And Many More!

The Latin Real Book Sampler CD
12 of the greatest Latin Real Book tunes as played by the original artists: Tito Puente, Ray Barretto, Andy Narell, Puerto Rico Allstars, Bacacoto, etc.

$16 list price. Available in U.S.A. only.

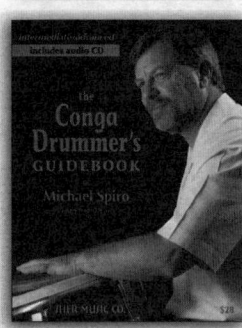

The Conga Drummer's Guidebook
By Michael Spiro

Includes CD - $28 list price. The only method book specifically designed for the intermediate to advanced conga drummer. It goes behind the superficial licks and explains how to approach any Afro-Latin rhythm with the right feel, so you can create a groove like the pros!.

"This book is awesome. Michael is completely knowledgable about his subject."
– Dave Garibaldi

"A breakthrough book for all students of the conga drum."
– Karl Perazzo

Introduction to the Conga Drum - DVD
By Michael Spiro

For beginners, or anyone needing a solid foundation in conga drum technique.

Jorge Alabe – "Mike Spiro is a great conga teacher. People can learn real conga technique from this DVD."

John Santos – "A great musician/teacher who's earned his stripes"

1 hour, 55 minutes running time. $25.

Muy Caliente!
Afro-Cuban Play-Along CD and Book
Rebeca Mauleón - Keyboard
Oscar Stagnaro - Bass
Orestes Vilató - Timbales
Carlos Caro - Bongos
Edgardo Cambon - Congas

Over 70 min. of smokin' Latin grooves!
Stereo separation so you can eliminate the bass or piano. Play-along with a rhythm section featuring some of the top Afro-Cuban musicians in the world! $18.

The True Cuban Bass
By Carlos Del Puerto, (bassist with Irakere) and **Silvio Vergara**, $22.

For acoustic or electric bass; English and Spanish text; Includes CDs of either historic Cuban recordings or Carlos playing each exercise; Many transcriptions of complete bass parts for tunes in different Cuban styles – the roots of Salsa.

101 Montunos
By Rebeca Mauleón

The only comprehensive study of Latin piano playing ever published.

- Bi-lingual text (English/Spanish)
- 2 CDs of the author demonstrating each montuno
- Covers over 100 years of Afro-Cuban styles, including the danzón, guaracha, mambo, merengue and songo—from Peruchin to Eddie Palmieri. $28

The Salsa Guide Book
By Rebeca Mauleón

The only complete method book on salsa ever published! 260 pages. $25.

Carlos Santana – "A true treasure of knowledge and information about Afro-Cuban music."
Mark Levine, author of The Jazz Piano Book. – "This is the book on salsa."
Sonny Bravo, pianist with Tito Puente – "This will be the salsa 'bible' for years to come."
Oscar Hernández, pianist with Rubén Blades – "An excellent and much needed resource."

The Brazilian Guitar Book
By Nelson Faria, one of Brazil's best new guitarists.

- Over 140 pages of comping patterns, transcriptions and chord melodies for samba, bossa, baião, etc.
- Complete chord voicings written out for each example.
- Comes with a CD of Nelson playing each example.
- The most complete Brazilian guitar method ever published! $28.

Joe Diorio – "Nelson Faria's book is a welcome addition to the guitar literature. I'm sure those who work with this volume wiill benefit greatly"

Inside The Brazilian Rhythm Section
By Nelson Faria and Cliff Korman

This is the first book/CD package ever published that provides an opportunity for bassists, guitarists, pianists and drummers to interact and play-along with a master Brazilian rhythm section. Perfect for practicing both accompanying and soloing.

$28 list price for book and 2 CDs - including the charts for the CD tracks and sample parts for each instrument, transcribed from the recording.

The Latin Bass Book
A PRACTICAL GUIDE
By Oscar Stagnaro

The only comprehensive book ever published on how to play bass in authentic Afro-Cuban, Brazilian, Caribbean, Latin Jazz & South American styles. $34.

Over 250 pages of transcriptions of Oscar Stagnaro playing each exercise. Learn from the best!

Includes: 3 Play-Along CDs to accompany each exercise, featuring world-class rhythm sections.

Afro-Caribbean Grooves for Drumset
By Jean-Philippe Fanfant, drummer with Andy narell's band, Sakesho.

Covers grooves from 10 Caribbean nations, arranged for drumset.

Endorsed by Peter Erskine, Horacio Hernandez, etc.

CD includes both audio and video files. $25.

Standards Supplement - U.S.A. Only

All Or Nothing At All

Music by Arthur Altman
Lyric by Jack Lawrence

Med. Swing

Alternate changes for first 4 bars of letter C: | B♭ B♭+ | B♭6 B♭+ | 2/4 |

Do Nothing 'Til You Hear From Me

Music by Duke Ellington
Lyric by Bob Russell

Don't Get Around Much Anymore

Music by Duke Ellington
Lyric by Bob Russell

Med. Swing

©1942, 1973 Harrison Music & Robbins Music. All Rights Reserved. International Copyright Secured. Used By Permission.

Bars 3 & 11 of letter **A** and bar 3 of letter **C** may also be played.

Good Morning Heartache

Dan Fisher
Irene Higginbotham
Ervin Drake

Med. Ballad

Misty

Music by Erroll Garner
Lyric by Johnny Burke

Med. Ballad

*can also be played as Ami7

©1939, renewed 1983 Warner Bros. Inc., Marke Music Publishing Co., Limerick Music Corp., Timo-Co Music & Reganesque Music.
All Rights Reserved. Used By Permission.

Speak Low

Music by Kurt Weil
Lyric by Ogden Nash

Med. Swing*

*may be played as a medium Latin tune, with a swing feel at letter C.

TRO - ©1943, renewed 1971 Hampshire House Publishing Corp. and Chappell & Co., Inc.. New York, NY. International Copyright Secured. Made In U.S.A. All Rights Reserved Including Public Performance For Profit. Used By Permission.

C
GMI7
E♭9
(C#MI7(♭5) F#7
B7
E7
)
FMA7
E♭7
D7
D
AMI9
D13
AMI9
D13
AMI9
D9
AMI9
D9
G6
E7
CMI9
F13
G6
E7
A9
D9(#5)
G6
(BMI7
E7
)

Stormy Weather

Music by Harold Arlen
Lyric by Ted Koehler

Med. Ballad

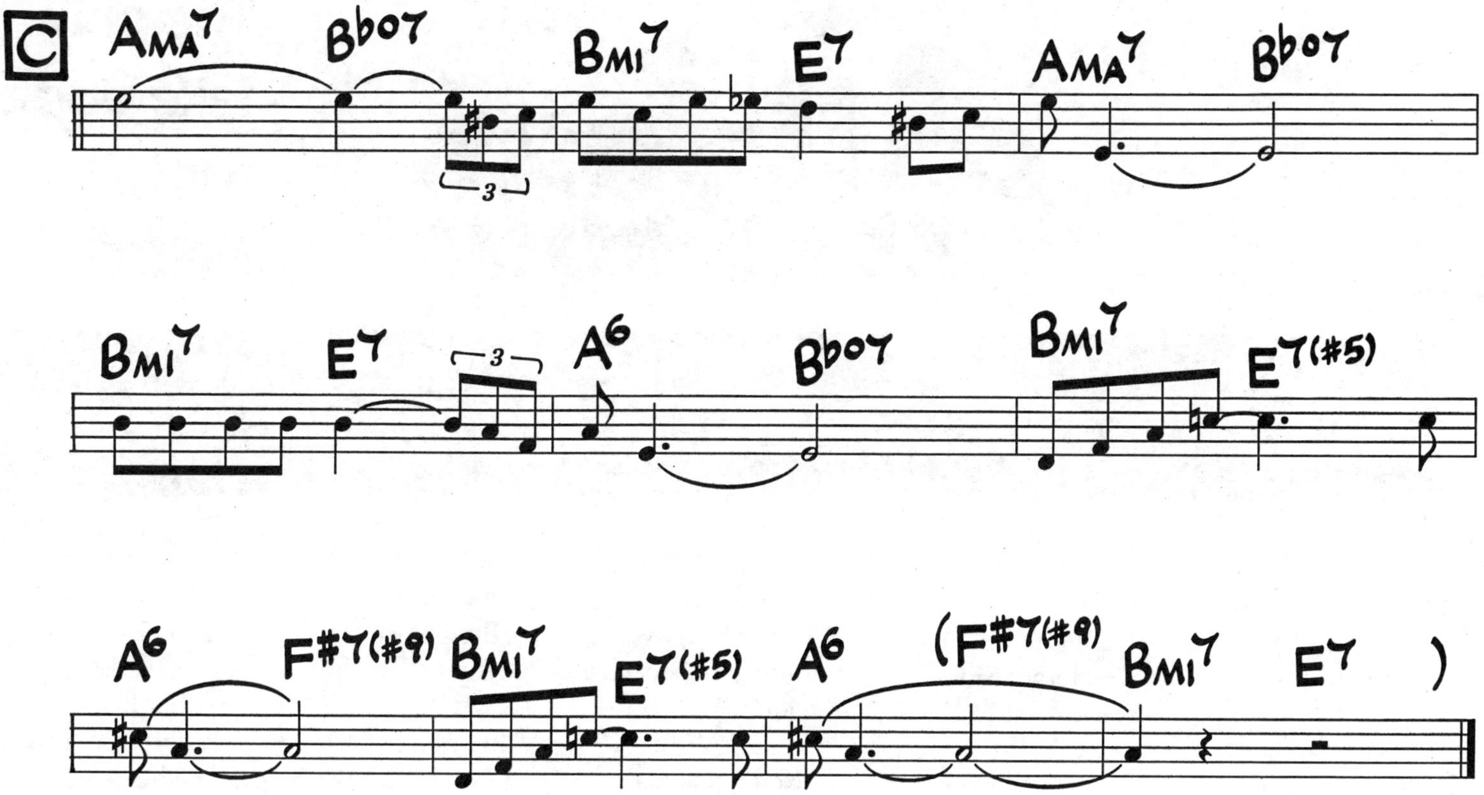
C
AMA7 Bbo7 BMI7 E7 AMA7 Bbo7
3
BMI7 E7 A6 Bbo7 BMI7 E7(#5)
3
A6 F#7(#9) BMI7 E7(#5) A6 (F#7(#9) BMI7 E7)

The All-Jazz Real Book

The only fake book with a FREE CD!

CD INCLUDES 37 OF THE MELODIES PLAYED BY:

Bob Sheppard—saxes and flute • Steve Houghton—drums • Dave Carpenter—acoustic bass
Paul van Wageningen—drums • Marc van Wageningen—electric bass • Larry Dunlap—piano & synthesizer

Miles Davis	Herbie Hancock	Sonny Rollins	Joey Calderazzo	Maria Schneider
Charlie Parker	McCoy Tyner	Cal Tjader	Cedar Walton	Steely Dan
Bill Evans	Ornette Coleman	Eric Dolphy	Brad Mehldau	Scott Henderson
John Coltrane	Horace Silver	Cannonball Adderley	Vincent Herring	Hal Galper
John Scofield	Michael Brecker	John Patitucci	Mark Levine	Ray Barretto
Jerry Bergonzi	Russ Ferrante	Gary Willis	Christian McBride	Paquito D'Rivera
Michel Petrucciani	Bob Mintzer	Kenny Garrett	George Mraz	Eddie Palmieri
Kenny Werner	Stanley Clarke	Billy Childs	New York Voices	The Fania All-Stars
Tom Harrell	Ralph Towner	John Abercrombie	Don Grolnick	Issac Delgado
Fred Hersch	Kurt Elling	Richie Beirach	Andy Narell	Celia Cruz
Mulgrew Miller	Alan Broadbent	Jimmy Smith	Rebeca Mauleón	Eddie Gomez
Denny Zeitlin	Ivan Lins	Antonio Carlos Jobim	Djavan	Toninho Horta

C Version, 550 pages. $44 list price
For a complete list of tunes and sample mp3 files of the free CD, see www.shermusic.com

Also New! from Sher Music Co., the world's finest jazz publisher

Metaphors For The Musician
by Randy Halberstadt

This practical and enlightening book will help any jazz player or vocalist look at music with "new eyes". Music theory with a human touch. We guarantee it will help you improve your musicianship or your money back! Over 350 pages. $36 list price.

"Randy knows how to break things down so a student can actually understand it. This book is chock full of great gems that both students and professional players could really benefit from." **JERRY BERGONZI, jazz saxophonist**

"Randy talks about the experience, the real-time event, the nuts-and-bolts reality of making music from the heart. I recommend this book to anyone who is serious about music."
JESSICA WILLIAMS, jazz pianist

"Never pedantic, this book moves in a logical, step-by-step, "hands-on" and easy to understand manner. It helped solidify and codify many things I 'knew' but had never been able to articulate. I highly recommend 'Metaphors For The Musician'."
BILL MAYS, jazz pianist

"Metaphors For The Musician" is an excellent tool for students and teachers alike."
GEORGE CABLES, jazz pianist

Inside The Brazilian Rhythm Section
by Nelson Faria & Cliff Korman

This is the first book/CD package ever published that allows you to play along and interact with a master Brazilian rhythm section. Includes 8 different Brazilian grooves as played by: Nelson Faria—guitar, Cliff Korman—piano, Café—percussion, David Fink—bass, Paulo Braga—drums
$28 list price for book and 2 CDs. Satisfaction guaranteed!

"This book makes me want to pick up my bass and play! It's a great method to learn and practice Brazilian rhythms and an outstanding contribution to music instruction. We've needed this for a long time." **JOHN PATITUCCI, bassist**

"This book is a marvel that shows you what it takes to achieve those wonderful grooves on the samba, bossa nova and other Brazilian rhythms. It is a must for any serious student of Brazilian music." **KENNY BARRON, pianist**

"I love the way this book is organized. It gives me the information I need and gets right to the music."
LINCOLN GOINES, bassist

"This book will put a stop to our searching for authentic Brazilian rhythms. And the play-along CDs are pure serendipity." **MANNY ALBAM, arranger**

Sher Music Co. • P.O. Box 445, Petaluma, CA 94953 • www.shermusic.com • Tel: 800/444-7437 • fax: 707/763-2038